ROUTLEDGE LIBRARY EDITIONS: LINGUISTICS

Volume 37

MORPHOLOGY AND MIND

MORPHOLOGY AND MIND
A unified approach to explanation in linguistics

CHRISTOPHER J. HALL

LONDON AND NEW YORK

First published in 1992

This edition first published in 2014
by Routledge
2 Park Square, Milton Park, Abingdon, Oxfordshire OX14 4RN

Simultaneously published in the USA and Canada
by Routledge
711 Third Avenue, New York, NY 10017, USA

First issued in paperback 2016

Routledge is an imprint of the Taylor & Francis Group, an informa business

© 1992 Christopher J. Hall

All rights reserved. No part of this book may be reprinted or reproduced or utilised in any form or by any electronic, mechanical, or other means, now known or hereafter invented, including photocopying and recording, or in any information storage or retrieval system, without permission in writing from the publishers.

Trademark notice: Product or corporate names may be trademarks or registered trademarks, and are used only for identification and explanation without intent to infringe.

British Library Cataloguing in Publication Data
A catalogue record for this book is available from the British Library

ISBN: 978-0-415-64438-9 (Set)
ISBN 13: 978-1-138-97635-1 (pbk)
ISBN 13: 978-0-7007-1598-5 (hbk)

Publisher's Note
The publisher has gone to great lengths to ensure the quality of this reprint but points out that some imperfections in the original copies may be apparent.

Disclaimer
The publisher has made every effort to trace copyright holders and would welcome correspondence from those they have been unable to trace.

Morphology and Mind

The central concern of this book is the explanation of linguistic form. It examines in detail certain cross-linguistic patterns in morphological systems, providing unified explanations of the observation that suffixes predominate over prefixes and the correlation between affix position and syntactic head position. The explanation of the suffixing preference is one which appeals to principles of language processing, tempered by cognitive constraints underlying language change. These factors, coupled with generative morphological analysis, also provide an explanation for the head/affix correlation.

The extended case-study illustrates a unified, integrative approach to explanation in linguistics which stresses two major features: the search for cognitive or other functional principles that could potentially underlie formally specified regularities; and the need for a micro-analysis of the mechanisms of 'linkage' between regularity and explanation. The natural methodological consequence of such an approach is a move towards greater co-operation between the various subdisciplines of linguistics, as well as a greatly needed expansion of cross-disciplinary research. The author's broad training in theoretical morphology, formal and typological universals, and language processing, allows him to cross traditional boundaries and view the complex interactions between theoretical linguistic principles and cognitive mechanisms with considerable clarity of vision.

Morphology and Mind
A unified approach to explanation in linguistics

Christopher J. Hall

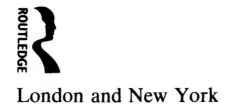

London and New York

First published 1992
by Routledge
11 New Fetter Lane, London EC4P 4EE

Simultaneously published in the USA and Canada
by Routledge
a division of Routledge, Chapman and Hall, Inc.
29 West 35th Street, New York, NY 10001

© 1992 Christopher J. Hall

Typeset in 10/12pt Times by
J&L Composition Ltd, North Yorkshire
Printed in Great Britain by
Biddles Ltd, Guildford, Surrey

All rights reserved. No part of this book may be reprinted or
reproduced or utilized in any form or by any electronic,
mechanical, or other means, now known or hereafter
invented, including photocopying and recording, or in any
information storage or retrieval system, without permission in
writing from the publishers.

British Library Cataloguing in Publication Data
Hall, Christopher J.
  Morphology and mind: a unified approach to explanation in linguistics.
  1. Language
  I. Title
  401.4

Library of Congress Cataloging in Publication Data
Hall, Christopher J.
  Morphology and mind: a unified approach to explanation in linguistics /
Christopher J. Hall.
  p. cm. —(Theoretical linguistics)
  Includes bibliographical references and index.
  1. Explanation (Linguistics) 2. Grammar, Comparative and general-
Morphology. 3. Psycholinguistics. 4. Linguistic change.
  I. Title. II. Series: Theoretical linguistics (Routledge (Firm))
  P128.E95H35 1992
  415—dc20   91–10049

  ISBN 0–415–04142–2

for
Juan Gustavo Galindo González

Contents

Preface	xiii
Abbreviations	xviii
1 Explanation in linguistics	1
1.1 The formal approach to explanation	2
1.2 Problems with the formal approach	6
1.2.1 The fundamental problem	6
1.2.2 Alternative sources of explanation	8
1.2.3 Empirical evidence for innateness	15
1.2.4 Typological universals	22
1.2.5 Explanation of historical change	24
1.2.6 The achievement of explanatory adequacy	26
1.3 The functional approach to explanation	27
1.4 Problems with the functional approach	32
1.5 A unified approach to explanation	36
1.5.1 Defining the unified approach	36
1.5.2 Applying the unified approach	37
2 Morphological regularity	39
2.1 The data and universals	40
2.1.1 Greenberg (1966)	40
2.1.2 Hawkins and Gilligan (1988)	41
2.2 Problems with the data and universals	44
3 Affixes and heads	49
3.1 The notion 'head of a word'	50
3.1.1 Syntactic approaches	51
3.1.1.1 X' syntax and percolation	51
3.1.1.2 The positional criterion	55
3.1.1.3 A revised definition of headship	63
3.1.1.4 Assessment	65

x   *Morphology and mind*

3.1.2 Semantic approaches	66
3.2 Cross-linguistic factors	70
3.2.1 Head serialisation	70
3.2.2 A diachronic perspective	74
3.3 Psycholinguistic factors	78
3.3.1 Serialisation in the syntax	78
3.3.2 Serialisation in the morphology	80
3.4 Conclusion	82
4 The diachronic link	84
4.1 The historical account	85
4.1.1 'Today's morphology': the origin of affixes	85
4.1.2 'Yesterday's syntax': SOV as universal word order	91
4.1.3 Problems with the SOV account	93
4.1.4 Assessment of the historical account	96
4.2 Phonological decay and semantic redundancy	97
4.2.1 Phonological decay	97
4.2.2 Semantic redundancy	103
4.3 A revised historical account	107
5 Understanding affixes	112
5.1 Modelling the mental lexicon	112
5.1.1 Three models of lexical access	113
5.1.1.1 The Cohort Model	114
5.1.1.2 The Logogen Model	123
5.1.1.3 The Search Model	125
5.1.1.4 Assessment	127
5.1.2 The global organisation of the lexicon	128
5.1.3 Morphologically complex words	130
5.1.3.1 Representation	130
5.1.3.2 Access	135
5.2 Morphologically complex words in a Cohort-based model	143
5.2.1 Representation	143
5.2.2 Access	149
5.2.3 Opacity	152
5.2.4 Some conclusions	155
5.3 A processing explanation for the suffixing preference	156
5.3.1 The Cutler et al. processing account	156
5.3.2 Problems with the Cutler et al. account	159
5.4. Conclusion	162

Contents xi

6 A micro-analysis of historical change   164
6.1 Refining the hypothesis   165
   6.1.1 The flirting process   165
   6.1.2 Objections and exceptions   171
   6.1.3 Simplicity of representation   175
   6.1.4 Lexical reanalysis and borrowing   178
6.2 Testing the hypothesis   183
   6.2.1 Novel forms   184
   6.2.2 Experimental evidence   186
     6.2.2.1 Rationale   186
     6.2.2.2 The experiment   188
     6.2.2.3 Results and analysis   190
   6.2.3 Discussion   191
6.3 Conclusion: a unified explanation of morphological
   regularity   192

Appendices   195
   1 Pretest materials   195
   2 Test items with pretest familiarity scores   197
Notes   198
Bibliography   210
Index   221

I showed my masterpiece to the grown-ups, and asked them whether the drawing frightened them.

But they answered: 'Frighten? Why should anyone be frightened by a hat?'

My drawing was not a picture of a hat. It was a picture of a boa constrictor digesting an elephant. But since the grown-ups were not able to understand it, I made another drawing: I drew the inside of the boa constrictor, so that the grown-ups could see it clearly. They always need to have things explained.

Antoine de Saint-Exupery, *The Little Prince*

Preface

This book is about the explanation of regularities in language. It examines in detail a single such regularity: the cross-linguistic distribution of affixes, and particularly the observation that suffixes predominate over prefixes. The extended case-study is intended to illustrate a unified, integrative approach to explanation in linguistics which stresses two major features: firstly, the need to search for cognitive or other functional principles that could potentially underlie formally specified regularities (e.g, cross-linguistic structural patterns or universal grammatical principles), and secondly, the need for an explicit description (a 'micro-analysis') of the mechanism(s) of 'linkage' between regularity and explanation, i.e., an account of how languages come to incorporate such properties. The natural methodological consequence of such an approach is a move towards greater co-operation between the various subdisciplines of linguistics as well as a greatly needed expansion of cross-disciplinary research. In the case-study documented in this book, I take advantage of the results of research in almost all the major areas of linguistics, and integrate them with work in cognitive experimental psychology in order to come up with a unified explanation of one important regularity in morphological systems.

Since the 'Chomskyan Revolution' got underway in the late 1950s, the notion of explanation in linguistics has been given special attention by scholars within linguistics and in related disciplines (particularly in cognitive psychology and philosophy). Chomsky, following Lenneberg and others, proposed that the proper way to view language was as a faculty of mind, a 'mental organ' subject to the same logic of investigation as physical organs in the body (e.g., Chomsky 1972). His characterisation of the language faculty as a highly complex and constrained innate system of principles (Universal Grammar), to which he imputed biological reality, provided him with

xiv *Morphology and mind*

an effectively linguistic-internal mode of explanation, which did not seem to require reference to the environment, other than through appeals to grammaticality judgements. After an initial period of excitement for psycholinguists and others, a reaction began to develop amongst those who felt that Chomsky's framework was too narrow, and too abstract for the purposes of explanation in linguistics. (Many objected too that the theory was inadequate as a *descriptive* model, and was misguided in its fundamental assumptions and methodology, although much of this criticism was, and still is, based on misunderstandings of Chomsky's work.)

As a consequence of this reaction, scholars, notably at first in phonology, began to search for more 'natural', less abstract, characterisations of linguistic knowledge. Appeals were made to 'functional' factors, and increasing numbers of students found themselves attracted to natural and functional schools in the fields of syntax (e.g. Halliday 1976; also Haiman 1980, Givón 1979), phonology (e.g. Stampe 1979; Hooper 1976), and morphology (e.g. Bybee 1985; Dressler 1986). But at the same time the flow of studies and the growth of sophistication within the generative school did not diminish, and Chomsky began to place a great deal more stress on the biological/cognitive basis of the theory. In addition, a number of empirical studies appeared which have attempted to validate this new conceptualisation through psycholinguistic modelling and, to a lesser extent, experimental data (e.g. Berwick and Weinberg 1984; Roeper and Williams 1987). Philosophers, traditional functionalists in linguistics and psychology, as well as universalists in the Greenbergian school, were thus prompted to readdress their concerns with explanation and to advocate more forcefully their position in the literature. Finally, the growth of interest in the role of linguistics in cognitive science (again thanks mainly to Chomsky) has, ironically, heightened people's awareness of how linguistic knowledge interacts with other cognitive faculties, and so has led to a re-appraisal of Chomsky's narrowly autonomous conception of the explanatory options for language regularities.

This book, then, is an attempt to contribute to what is patently a lively ongoing debate, and it tries to move this debate forward in two ways: (i) by analysing in great detail a single problem of explanation, the well-documented cross-linguistic asymmetry in the distribution of affix positions (and, crucially, by specifying in equal detail the mechanisms which link data to explanation (cf. Clark and Malt 1984; Bybee 1988); and (ii) by showing a complementarity between formal and functional approaches to explanation in linguistics through the

Preface xv

integration of superficially unrelated or incompatible methodologies and goals from the highly schismatic world of linguistics, whilst still arguing for a consistent, well-defined, ultimately functionally-oriented model of explanation within the overall purview of an interdisciplinary cognitive science.

The central importance of the theme of morphology and mind in this study arose as part of another important trend in current linguistics: the re-emergence of the word and its cognitive repository, the lexicon, as a principal object of study. Since the development of the Lexicalist Hypothesis (Chomsky 1970), focus has been placed more and more on the lexicon and away from the transformational component in grammatical theory (cf. e.g. Hoekstra *et al.* 1981). Similar developments are seen in competing generative models (e.g. Bresnan 1982). Likewise, in superficially unrelated work in psycho-linguistics and artificial intelligence, a substantial body of research on processing at the word level is being accumulated (cf. e.g. Cole and Jakimik 1980; Marslen-Wilson 1987; McClelland and Elman 1986; Frauenfelder and Tyler 1987; Cutler *et al.* 1985), and relatively less attention is being paid to sentence-level parsing (although, of course, this continues to be a very important area). Again, then, this book seeks to unify parallel currents and integrate them with the traditional morphological concerns of historical linguists, to suggest ways in which current developments in areas often seen as non-interactive may be placed in methodological and theoretical harmony under a broader interactive research perspective.

In short, then, three factors led me to the theme of this book: firstly, the recognition that explanation, in linguistics as in any science, is a key goal which unites all areas of investigation and is currently under new scrutiny since Chomsky's challenge; secondly, the re-emergence of the word as the object of much important study in many areas of linguistics, and its promise to be the source of many new important advances in these disparate areas; and thirdly, the observation that too much of the research conducted in linguistics departments is, at best, too narrow in its concerns and, at worst, too divisive in the theoretical tenets underlying it.

The book is organised as follows. Chapter 1 constitutes a general discussion of the two dominant approaches to explanation in linguistics, the formal and the functional, giving prominence to psycholinguistic factors. Chapter 2 introduces the data and universals relating to the cross-linguistic distribution of affixes, and chapter 3 discusses the attested correlation between affixes and dominant head position in the syntax, drawing heavily on the resources of generative

xvi *Morphology and mind*

morphology. Discussion of the 'suffixing preference' begins in chapter 4 with an analysis of its historical origins and a preliminary outline of the linkage between the distributional data and their proposed explanation. In chapter 5 the processing account of Cutler *et al.* (1985) is subjected to detailed analysis from the point of view of a model of affix representation and access inspired by the Cohort Model (e.g. Marslen-Wilson and Tyler 1980). Preceding this a survey of some of the relevant psycholinguistic literature is provided. The historical dimension to the explanation is developed in tandem with psycholinguistic experimentation and modelling in the final chapter, chapter 6, to demonstrate how the various distinct but indispensable elements of explanation in linguistics can function in harmony to yield a fully plausible explanatory account of regularity in language.

This book is intended primarily for students and teachers of linguistics and psycholinguistics, and so presupposes a basic familiarity with the various areas of research which contribute to these fields. I have tried to avoid the over-usage of unfamiliar terms and the inclusion of technical detail not necessary for following the argument, but this has not always been possible given the breadth and depth of analysis called for in the approach adopted. The extent to which confusion remains is in part a comment on the lack of communication prevalent within research on language, which this book seeks, in part, to redress.

This book is a much modified (I believe much improved) version of a doctoral dissertation submitted to the University of Southern California, Los Angeles, in May 1987, entitled *Language Structure and Explanation: A Case from Morphology* (Hall 1987). Much of the material in chapter 4 appeared as a chapter in *Explaining Language Universals*, edited by John A. Hawkins and published by Basil Blackwell (Hall 1988). The research for the dissertation was carried out mainly in the Linguistics Department at USC, but all the experimental work was prepared for at the Max Planck Institute for Psycholinguistics in Nijmegen, The Netherlands, and in the Department of Experimental Psychology at the University of Cambridge, where the experiments were actually run. After submission of the dissertation, the lengthy process of collecting more material for the historical sections, extending the introductory chapter, and revising and extending much of the psycholinguistic model took place while I was a Visiting Scholar in the Centro de Estudios Lingüísticos y Literarios at El Colegio de México in Mexico City, and, latterly, again, in Cambridge. A Routledge reviewer provided helpful comments on the preliminary draft (for which I am most grateful),

Preface xvii

and following this, I gave the manuscript its final shape during the summer and autumn of 1990 in the Departamento de Lenguas at the Universidad de las Américas in Puebla, Mexico. My respectful thanks go to the relevant authorities of all these institutions and especially to Rebeca Barriga at El Colegio.

I owe a great debt of gratitude to friends, mentors and colleagues in Los Angeles, Cambridge, Nijmegen, Mexico City, and Puebla, principally: my PhD Committee members Pat Clancy, Jack Hawkins, Doug Pulleyblank, and especially Elaine Andersen, my chair; my hosts and teachers in Cambridge and Nijmegen, Lolly Tyler and William Marslen-Wilson; and my valued colleagues and close friends in Mexico City, Juan Galindo González and Marianna Pool. In addition I record thankfully the debt I owe to the following who at various times have provided valued comment and criticism (and in many cases also friendship and moral support): Cindy Allen, Julio Alves, Mary Alvin, Joan Bybee, Howard Cobb, Anne Cutler, Violeta Demonte, Ed Finegan, Gary Gilligan, Heather Holmback, Larry Hyman, Marie Jefsoutine, Linda Lippand, Mary McGinniss, Anna Miecznikowski, Mohammad Mohammad, Lori Powell, Ian Roberts, Bonnie Schwartz, Debbie Schlindwein, Shelley Smith, Thomas Smith Stark, Nigel Vincent, and Paul Warren.

Finally, I thank my parents, John and Joan Hall, whose encouragement and support have never faltered over the years, and who are always a source of great inspiration and contentment.

C. J. H.
Cholula, November 1990

Postscript: Two important papers have come to my attention too late to be discussed here. The first, an article by Frederick Newmeyer, followed by extensive peer commentary, argues for a position on explanation which corresponds to my Unified Approach, and stresses, as I do, the importance of the evolutionary perspective (Newmeyer, F.J. (1991) 'Functional explanation in linguistics and the origins of language', *Language and Communication* 11, 1/2, 3–28). The second, a paper by Joan Bybee, William Pagliuca and Revere Perkins, unveils a lot of new cross-linguistic data on affixal asymmetries, which permits the authors to evaluate explanations for the suffixing preference from a much more adequate typological base (Bybee, J.L., W. Pagliuca and R.D. Perkins (1990) 'On the asymmetries in the affixation of grammatical material' in W. Croft, K. Denning and S. Kemmer (eds) *Studies in Typology and Diachrony for Joseph H. Greenberg*, Amsterdam/Philadelphia: John Benjamins).

Abbreviations

A	adjective
ADJ	adjective
ADJP	adjective phrase
ADP	adpositional phrase
AdpP	adpositional phrase
ADV	adverb
af	affix
AFF	affix
ANOVA	analysis of variance
Aux	auxiliary
C	consonant
CCH	(Principle of) Cross-Category Harmony
CNP	common NP
Comp	complement
DNP	determined NP
DP	Dissimilation Principle
Eng	English
fem	feminine
FI	Full Interpretation
Fr	French
G	genitive
Gen	genitive
HFP	Head First Preference
HOP	Head Ordering Principle
H&G	Hawkins and Gilligan (1988)
IE	Indo-European
inf	infinitive
IP	isolation point
IPP	IP as percentage of stem length
It	Italian

Abbreviations xix

L	Language
Lg	language
LHR	Left-hand Head Rule
LF	Logical Form
Lt	Latin
mod	modifier
msec	milliseconds
N	noun
NP	noun phrase
O	object
OE	Old English
OP	Operating Principle
OV	object-verb (ordering)
P	preposition/postposition
perf	perfect
pers	person
PF	Phonetic Form
PIE	Proto-Indo-European
pl	plural
Po	postposition
pos	possessed noun
PossPh	possessive phrase
Postp	postposition(al ordering)
PP	prepositional/postpositional phrase
Pr	preposition
PREF	prefix
Prep	preposition(al ordering)
pres	present
PRES	present
PROG	progressive
PrPr	Projection Principle
PS	phrase structure
Rel	relative clause
RHR	Right-hand Head Rule
RP	recognition point
RPP	RP as percentage of stem length
RT	reaction time
S	sentence
SFP	Stem First Preference
sing	singular
SOED	*Shorter Oxford English Dictionary*
SOV	subject-object-verb (ordering)

xx *Morphology and Mind*

Sp	Spanish
SP	Serialisation Principle
Spec	specifier
SSC	Specified Subject Condition
Subj	subject
SVO	subject-verb-object (ordering)
t	time
T	tense
TOT	'tip of the tongue'
u	unmarked
UG	Universal Grammar
unacc	unaccusative
UP	uniqueness point
V	verb/vowel
VO	verb-object (ordering)
VOS	verb-object-subject (ordering)
VP	verb phrase
VSO	verb-subject-object (ordering)
WFR	word formation rule
W-syntax	word syntax
X'	X-bar

1 Explanation in linguistics

One of the fundamental goals of research in linguistics is the explanation of structural regularities which are apparently exhibited by all languages or a significant number or them. Workers in the field adopt various approaches in their pursuit of this goal, depending on a number of factors, including the academic discipline with which they identify, their speciality within that discipline, and their view of the nature of the linguistic beast. One approach, often called *formal* (or *autonomous*, *linguistic–internal*) explanation, is particularly associated with theorists working on generative grammar, and has become very influential especially since the publication of Chomsky's *Aspects of the Theory of Syntax* (Chomsky 1965). The major alternative approach, generally termed *functional* (or *interactive*, *external*) explanation, is favoured by a disparate group of general linguists, cognitive psychologists and philosophers working before Chomsky's impact was felt and, also, reacting to it once it became established. The neat label *functional* as foil to the *formal* approach is, in fact, an over-simplifying abbreviation for a broad range of perspectives on explanation covering numerous schools and paradigms; the umbrella term is justified in that it unites work exhibiting at least two factors in common: (i) an emphasis on the subordination of form to function, and hence, (ii) a rejection of Chomsky's perspective. In this chapter I introduce the basic characteristics of the two approaches (sections 1.1 and 1.3) and consider examples of the types of explanation offered, before examining some drawbacks and deficiencies of each (sections 1.2 and 1.4). I ultimately propose a unified approach which emphasises the role of function, but also incorporates fundamental features of the formal approach. This unified approach is introduced in section 1.5.

In our discussion, Chomsky's own work is concentrated on at the expense of that of other researchers. I think this is justified and, in

2 Morphology and mind

any case, inevitable, since he is the 'father' of the formal approach and is responsible for most of the theoretical developments made since its inception; also, it is he who wields the greatest influence, not only in his own area, but over many other areas of linguistics and in related fields. Much, perhaps most, recent work within the functional approach either explicitly or implicitly uses the Chomskyan paradigm as a point of departure or a point of contrast. His work is, therefore, the pivot around which I discuss the problem of linguistic explanation in this chapter.

1.1 THE FORMAL APPROACH TO EXPLANATION

In 'formal', generative models of language such as Chomsky's (1965, 1981, 1986a), the principal object of explanation (the explanandum) is the human cognitive capacity for, or knowledge of, language ('linguistic competence'). This basic knowledge is shared by all humans; it is innate and so universal. A characterisation of Universal Grammar (UG) is the ultimate explanatory goal of the generativist enterprise, although particular language grammars contribute to and benefit from the developing theory of UG, and are what most generativists work on in practice.

For Chomsky, a (particular) grammar attaining 'explanatory adequacy' is one which constitutes

> a principled descriptively adequate system, in that the linguistic theory with which it is associated selects this grammar over others, given primary linguistic data with which all are compatible. In this sense, the grammar is justified on *internal* grounds, on grounds of its relation to a linguistic theory that constitutes an explanatory hypothesis about the form of language as such.
>
> (Chomsky 1965: 27)

> A theory of U[niversal] G[rammar] that meets [the condition of explanatory adequacy] will ... permit relevant facts about linguistic expressions to be derived from the grammars it selects, thus providing an explanation for the facts.
>
> (Chomsky 1986a: 53)

Approaches which appeal to external factors in the explanation of grammatical form (or phonological form, etc.) are perceived as, at most, marginal or peripheral endeavours, not a part of linguistics proper: in Chomsky's view of the field, the generative approach 'is, in fact, the model of explanation generally used in linguistics, insofar

Explanation in linguistics 3

as one or another approach is concerned with explanation at all' (1986a: 53).

Within this framework, regularities are said to be explained when it is demonstrated that they follow from formal universal constraints and conditions on grammar proposed as part of the general theory of UG. According to Chomsky, these abstract universal aspects of grammar determine 'the innate schemata that is rich, detailed and specific enough to account for the fact of language acquisition'. Hence, through a formulation of UG, he is claiming to offer an ultimately *biological* explanation for the universality of the fundamental properties of language structure. The basic properties of the particular language to which the child is exposed are acquired by the setting of parameters of UG, on the basis of exposure to adult input. The empirical evidence for what is and is not a property of UG rests almost entirely on assumptions made about the nature of the evidence available in the language input received by children – the 'poverty of the stimulus' or the 'lack of negative evidence'. According to Hoekstra and Kooij (1988):

> It is the task of general linguists to determine which properties [of language] belong to UG. Whether or not a particular property of a particular language can be assumed to derive from UG is an empirical matter, that is, claims made in this respect are falsifiable in principle. A sufficient criterion to establish any such claim would be that the property in question is underdetermined [i.e. by the available evidence]. (p. 38)

As a typical example of the Chomskyan approach to explanation, let us consider how, in an earlier version of the theory (Chomsky 1977a: 71–5), he accounted for the inadmissibility of the strings given in (1)–(3). Although parts of the analysis have been superseded by more recent developments in the theory, the philosophy underlying the analysis has not undergone any substantial change and the trace theory aspects, in which we are particularly interested, remain in current practice.

(1) *The candidates wanted [John to vote for each other]
(2) *Who did you hear [John's stories about]
(3) *John seemed to the men [to like each other]

Construing the reciprocal 'each other' with 'the candidates' as antecedent in (1), moving the *wh*-form 'who' from object of the preposition in (2), and construing the reciprocal with 'the men' in (3) are all disallowed. The structures may appear on a shallow analysis

4 *Morphology and mind*

to be unrelated, but Chomsky showed that in fact they are all inadmissible because they violate the same universal grammatical principle. The principle involved in each case was the 'Specified Subject Condition' (SSC) (Chomsky 1977b; cf. also Aoun 1985), assumed to be a principle of UG, which disallowed any relation by rule of terms with an intervening 'specified subject' between them: in (1) and (2), the specified subject is *John*, and so the SSC blocks the rules of reciprocal interpretation and *wh*-movement from applying. Chomsky claimed that a further sub-component of UG, the 'trace theory of movement rules', can explain the susceptibility of (3), too, to the SSC, despite the apparent lack of a specified subject in the subordinate clause:

> The facts reflect a biologically given precondition for learning. The child learning English simply imposes the requirement that mentally present subjects function as though they were physically present. He does this even in the absence of relevant evidence, so it appears. A theory of universal grammar – that is, a theory of the language faculty – must seek an explanation as to why this is so. The answer, I think, lies in the 'trace theory of movement rules,' which requires that when a phrase is moved by transformation it leaves behind a phonetically null but syntactically real element 'trace' that functions semantically as a kind of bound variable. Other rules of syntax and morphology have no way of knowing that this element will (ultimately) be phonetically null. Hence it operates as a specified subject, and in other ways in the system of rules, while playing an essential role in semantic interpretation. (1977a: 74–5)

So, the structure of (3) may be represented as follows:

(3′) *John seemed to the men [t to like each other]

in which the t (= trace) represents a physically unrealised but mentally present specified subject which blocks the reciprocal interpretation rule, by virtue of the SSC and trace theory. The recurrence across languages of phenomena such as those exhibited in (1)–(3) is therefore explained by the innate, specifically linguistic principles of SSC and trace theory represented in the language component of the mind.

An example of a parametrically interpreted component of UG is the X-bar theory of phrase structure (to be treated in greater detail in chapter 3). This theory constrains the patterning of syntactic categories in grammar by imposing requirements of headship and

Explanation in linguistics 5

head ordering according to a single schema which generalises over the lexical (head) categories N, V, ADJ, and P:

> For a particular (core) language L, the X-bar system is determined by fixing the values of the parameters of X-bar theory (head-first, etc.) in accordance with whatever dependencies among them are determined by UG: a particular set of choices constitutes the X-bar component of the grammar of L.
>
> (Chomsky 1986b: note 3 p. 91)

Parameters are, then, a form of 'cognitive switch', the setting of which is determined during the acquisition phase on the basis of the input to which the child is exposed. For instance, if the child's learning mechanisms establish that heads of phrases occur initially, then the X-bar parameter will be switched to the head-first setting, and thus the X-bar component of the core will be fully determined, and will constrain inferences made on future input (see Jackendoff (1977) and Lightfoot (1979); also cf. Chomsky 198eb (pp. 2–4 and note 3, p. 91) for more recent comment). The universal phrase structure regularities observed in language would then be explained in Chomsky's approach by the postulation of X-bar theory in UG. Particular language variation from the general X-bar schema is explained by the parametrical status of this component in the language faculty.

Thus, Chomsky's 'biological' explanatory paradigm for language does not appeal directly to principles of biology (or, more specifically, to evidence from evolutionary studies or the neurosciences); rather, it appeals primarily to inferences drawn from the apparent existence of universal properties of language stated in the abstract vocabulary of a highly constrained descriptive theory, and justified by the speed and apparent ease of language acquisition given the 'poverty of the stimulus' to which the child is exposed. The descriptive theory determines UG, which is proposed as a characterisation of the innate cognitive system for language. General properties of language identified within the Chomskyan descriptive paradigm are attributed to some 'module' of UG, such as D(eep)-structure, Logical Form, or the Lexicon, on the basis of considerations such as generality of data coverage, economy of theoretical structures, and elegance of representation and process *within the theory*. UG is a specialised cognitive component of the human mind just as the visual system is; as the properties of vision are innate, so are the universal properties of language.

6 *Morphology and mind*

1.2 PROBLEMS WITH THE FORMAL APPROACH

Chomsky's position on explanation has provoked a massive debate in the literature[1] but, needless to say, a good proportion of the criticism is based on misunderstandings and a reluctance to give ground to what is still perceived by many on both sides as a competing rather than complementary field; however, much of it is important and has not been satisfactorily addressed by Chomsky and his colleagues.

In what follows I briefly discuss what I see to be the major problems with the formal approach to explanation, concentrating on showing, above all, not that Chomsky's programme is fundamentally ill-conceived, but that it places too many limits on the overall endeavour of explanation in linguistics.

1.2.1 The fundamental problem

In Chomsky's approach, one of the key tasks in explaining universal properties of language structure is to establish which module of the linguistic component they derive from or may be assimilated into. This follows from Chomsky's conceptualisation of syntax and other areas of grammatical knowledge as autonomous domains (or theories), consisting, in turn, of autonomous sub-domains (or sub-theories). This autonomy/modularity is one of the most controversial features of Chomsky's programme and has provoked much debate (cf. Kac 1980; Prideaux 1980, and references cited there). Itkonen (1983) argues that the autonomous treatment of syntax is essential for purposes of description, but that this cannot on its own be seen as resulting in a *causal*, i.e. *explanatory*, theory in any sense. For reasons discussed in the following pages, I find this general stance a reasonable one both methodologically and theoretically, and it seems to me in no way incompatible with the main thrust of the generative position on grammar as a description of cognitive knowledge, and one which does not preclude the position that areas of linguistic knowledge are *functionally* (psychologically or biologically) autonomous (which can be ascertained on the basis of non-linguistic data).

Such a position is not acceptable to strict formalists, who believe that doing syntax is doing cognitive psychology 'directly', and that providing a description which meets Chomsky's (1965) notion of explanatory adequacy is providing an explanation which is psychological in the sense that it accounts for cognitively stored knowledge, and biological in that it characterises innate, ultimately neurally-encoded information. If we take a less restricted view of explanation,

Explanation in linguistics 7

however, which encompasses UG but seeks also (i) to explain UG itself, and (ii) to explain universal phenomena which are unrelated to UG, then the narrow generative enterprise no longer provides a full and satisfactory account.

In this more general conceptualisation of the linguist's task, generative linguistics should be seen as one research programme within a collective cognitive science, having as its specific goal the identification of principles and parameters which determine grammatical knowledge in its final state, rather than, as it is wont to be conceived by many in the cognitive science community, as virtually the only viable approach to the study of all matters linguistic from a cognitive-scientific perspective (cf. Pylyshyn 1984; Jackendoff 1983; Fodor 1984; cf. also the discussion in Gardner 1987, chapter 7). Given this narrower interpretation of the role of generative grammar in linguistics, the cognitive-scientific study of language will be conducted in at least four major areas: (i) the formulation of generative theories of grammar, specifying the form of cognitive knowledge of language and what parts of it are biologically given; (ii) the formulation of psycholinguistic models of linguistic processes and representation, including comprehension, production and acquisition, and their relationship with (and potential causal influences on) the system of grammatical knowledge and its evolution; (iii) artificial intelligence projects, testing the computational viability of both grammatical and process models, and providing a source of conceptual analogies for them; and (iv) neurolinguistic studies, investigating the neural realisation of linguistic representation and process, and identifying the neurologically-real or 'brain-style' computational resources appropriate for AI modelling.[2] No one area can afford to conceive of itself as self-sufficient in the overall cognitive-scientific study of the language faculty.

The narrow UG approach *can* be part of the explanation for some – perhaps *many* – aspects of linguistic regularity, but as currently practised by many in the Chomskyan school it tends to displace rather than complement other approaches to the explanation of genetically and non-genetically determined universals, and therefore, though worthy and important as a source of accurate description and as an indicator of the locus of ultimate explanation, the notion of explanation via postulation of UG is too often abused by providing a convenient though unjustified termination point for enquiry and by excluding competing or complementary lines of enquiry by fiat. The following sections illustrate this shortcoming in some depth, and attempt to place the autonomous study of syntax (and other areas of

8 *Morphology and mind*

formal linguistic knowledge) in their proper methodological and theoretical context within a collective cognitive science.

1.2.2 Alternative sources of explanation

Chomsky's autonomous, internal view of explanation is, then, a particularly narrow one; it is over-restrictive, I feel, in three main areas, which I outline in this and the following subsections. The first problem, though not necessarily the most important one, is that it takes no account of the wealth of alternative or complementary explanatory sources from other domains, such as other aspects of the cognitive system or factors external to the individual, e.g. from pragmatics (which contribute to Itkonen's notion of 'causal linguistics' – see section 1.3 for examples). Let us take language processing as an example here. A rich interpretation of the Chomskyan research programme might permit the processing mechanisms, for example, to contribute principles to a rather less monolithic UG than is assumed in practice (which would, however, still exclude the contribution of other, specifically non-grammatical factors, such as discourse pragmatics). Although such a rich interpretation does not enjoy much currency in the generative school, Chomsky himself has expressed a willingness, amounting almost to a future obligation in some writings, to utilise non-grammatical data (Chomsky 1980: 202 ff; 1986a: 34–6, 264). However, there is a general dismissiveness of such data, even when its relevance *is* recognised. For example, in a discussion of the relationship between perceptual strategies and syntactic rules, Chomsky and Lasnik (1977) concluded the following:

> While there may indeed be links between rules of grammar . . . and perceptual strategies, and even functional explanations for these rules, the matter does not seem to bear on explanatory adequacy in the sense relevant for linguistics or psychological theory. That is not to dismiss the issue as uninteresting – quite the contrary – but merely to place it in what seems to be its proper place.

J. D. Fodor, a psycholinguist working within the generativist framework, did find it worthwhile to examine the possible influence of the parser on the shaping of UG, but concluded that:

> there are no practical reasons behind the limitations on possible grammars [i.e. UG] other than reasons having to do, for example, with the availability and adaptability of certain preexisting neurophysiological structures when the grammar-representation system was evolving. (1984: 10)

Explanation in linguistics 9

What is puzzling about such statements is that although they exclude functional factors from the search for explanation in linguistics, they *do* acknowledge the possible force of the parser in determining structural properties in language, albeit at the level of determination of UG in the process of human evolution, rather than as sources of explanation *in competition* with the UG hypothesis.[3] Both Chomsky and Lasnik, and J. D. Fodor recognise, but dismiss, the possibility of explanation for UG itself; having gone thus far beyond their rubric, it is not clear to me why they do not believe that it is permissible for them to go further and acknowledge that UG is only one possible component in the explanatory process, or at least that the investigation of functional motivations by linguists, psycholinguists and others can yield strong evidence for the innate status of some of the descriptive principles attributed to UG, and render others questionable or perhaps open to other types of explanation. Furthermore, their half-hearted recognition of functional pressure represents only a limited and apparently temporary departure from the prevailing sentiment within the generativist school, which sees the specification of UG, i.e. the satisfaction of Chomsky's grammatical evaluation level of 'explanatory adequacy', as the unique and final explanans (although see the following section for important exceptions). Indeed, in a recent article Chomsky (1991) has made perhaps his strongest statements yet about the marginality or irrelevance of potential functional explanations of UG principles, claiming, in effect, that least effort 'guidelines' for language design, which 'legislate against "superfluous elements" in representations and derivations', actually have nothing to do with 'effort' in the sense of computational or motor resources as it is usually understood:

> language design as such appears in many respects 'dysfunctional', yielding properties that are not well adapted to the functions language is called upon to perform. There is no real paradox here; there is no reason to suppose, *a priori*, that the general design of language is conducive to efficient use. (p. 448)

This conclusion is in direct opposition to the essential rationale of the functional approach to explanation in linguistics, a basic tenet of which is that many aspects of linguistic form are determined by pressures for economy ('least effort') from various cognitive and motor mechanisms such as the processing system, memory, and the articulatory system.

His surprising conclusion that 'least effort' guidelines lead to dysfunctional language design appears to result from a rather

10 Morphology and mind

unorthodox conception of what happens during the process of sentence parsing in natural language. Let us try to clarify his position on this issue. In his attempt to elevate 'least effort' guidelines to the status of principles of UG, he identifies prohibitions on superfluous rule application and superfluous symbols in representations. These prohibitions are pan-modular, holding at the levels of D-structure, PF (Phonetic Form) and LF (Logical Form), and at their interface, S-structure. The prohibition on superfluous elements in representations is enforced through the requirement of FI (Full Interpretation) of symbols, which are legitimate if 'licensed'. Superfluous rule applications are prohibited through a general principle of 'minimality' in derivations, governed by their length (shorter being preferred over longer) and the *type* of rules involved (UG principles being 'less costly' than language-specific rules). Such principles are, according to Chomsky, incorporable into UG and, given the context of 'language design' in which they are presented, they are presumably intended to account for the non-occurrence of certain grammar types in natural language; it would seem, then, highly unlikely that they would be invoked in the day-to-day recovery of meaning from sound in the parsing process. But this is exactly what Chomsky seems to have in mind when he dismisses functional explanations for 'least effort' effects:

> From the point of view of parsing, suppose that we have a process recovering an S-structure *s* from the PF representation *p*. Then to determine the status of *s*, we have to carry out a number of operations. We have to determine whether *s* is derived from a properly formed D–structure *d* licensed by the lexicon, and whether the derivation from *d* through *s* to the LF representation *l* is minimal in the required sense, less costly than any other derivation from *d*. Furthermore, we have to determine whether *l* satisfies the conditions of external licensing, FI, and other properties of LF. In general, these computations may be non-trivial. In these respects, language design appears to be problematic from a parsing-theoretic perspective, though elegant regarded in isolation from considerations of use.

(1991: 447–8)

Does Chomsky intend to mean here that the parser, on receiving an input string, must, for example, calculate all alternative derivations $d \rightarrow s \rightarrow l$ in order to determine whether the input matches the most minimal of these? What would it mean for the processor to be dealing with a sentence which did *not* follow the most minimal derivation? The derivational history of an input sentence to the parser is not

Explanation in linguistics 11

given in the surface string, and people do not speak in ungrammatical sentences (in the sense of flagrantly violating UG principles at the syntactic planning stage); it would appear, then, that the types of procedure Chomsky envisages as part of the parsing process are mostly completely redundant, serving only the theoretical linguist or parsing theorist in their efforts to identify UG principles and implement them in effective procedures. Nothing that Chomsky proposes here has any bearing on the evolution of the grammar which encodes our knowledge of language and the parsing mechanisms which decode the acoustic signal into a representation consistent with this knowledge. His reading of the concept of 'least effort', stripped of any significance for usage, seems to me a vacuous concept, with no role in the explanation of the form of grammar.

What I am advocating in place of this commitment to uncompromising, uninformative formalism is a less restricted view of explanation in linguistics, which seeks to identify factors from any source, linguistic or otherwise, which may suggest a causal mechanism for universal language regularities, whether these are part of UG or are universal in the typological sense. Consider the following example. Chomsky and Lasnik (1977) discuss a particular constraint, namely the grammatical filter in (4), below, which accounts for the unacceptibility in many varieties of English of phrases like (5), and the difficulties associated with those like (6):

(4) *[$_{NP}$ NP tense VP]
(5) *The man met you is my friend
(6) The horse raced past the barn fell

The authors consider the argument that (4) might be explainable at the level of the evolution of the species by pressure from a perceptual strategy such as the following:

(7) In analysing a construction C, given a structure that can stand as an independent clause, take it to be the main clause of C.

However, they claim that such a contention is untenable, since sentences like (5) are attestable, for example in Black English, and so the rule cannot hold at the level of UG. Neither can it be a feature of specific languages or varieties, since then learning *ex nihilo* would be necessary, and it is very unlikely that sufficient negative evidence (corrections of violations of (4)) or positive evidence (exposure to further input) would be available for this to take place. They conclude that, in fact, (4) must be included in UG as the unmarked setting of a parameter, and that the parsing strategy in (7) makes no

12   *Morphology and mind*

contribution to the 'explanatory adequacy of linguistic or psychological theory'.

It seems to me that no new explanation has been offered in this case; certainly they provide no evidence against the influence of the parsing strategy, and no explanation for the correlation between it and the filter (4). What in fact Chomsky and Lasnik achieve is a more accurate characterisation of the explanandum, which still remains to be explained: once (4) is hypothesised as the unmarked setting of a parameter in UG, we must attempt to explain why this might be so. It seems very plausible to me that at this level the parsing strategy *may* have had an influence, and may very well explain the unmarked status of (4) as a parameter setting in UG. The parsing strategy is, then, precisely the sort of evidence which linguists should welcome as support for the inclusion of principles in UG, and, in fact, as a defence for the postulation of UG at all.

As I have indicated, Chomsky sometimes appears to be on the point of recognising the inevitability of such an extension to his research programme, e.g. when, in a rare moment, he appears to admit that UG is not necessarily the end of the story in terms of explanation. Of the ungrammaticality of movements from *wh*-clauses he writes:

> If, say, we find extensive evidence that the principles that underlie the *wh*-island constraint belong to universal grammar and are available to the language learner without relevant experience, then it would only be rational to suppose that these mechanisms are genetically determined and *to search for a further account in terms of biological development*.
>
> (1980: 209; my emphasis)

Of course, it may be that Chomsky is using 'biological' here in the quasi-metaphorical sense he uses when talking of UG as a biological theory, or of the language capacity as an 'organ' – i.e. he may have in mind a more general but still *linguistic* explanation. If, however, we interpret 'biological' here in its less esoteric sense, i.e. the sense in which practising biologists understand it, which I feel must be how it was intended, we glimpse a potential concession on his part of the fact that generative explanatory adequacy is only a special, very restricted aspect of a larger explanatory endeavour which may include biological and (phylo)genetic considerations.

If we are willing to recognise that the mode of development of UG in biological terms is part of an ultimate explanation of its formulation, we should be ready to go a step further and admit that the biological formation of UG, in the evolution of the species, may have involved the satisfaction of functional factors in the environment, through *natural selection*, by exploiting the choices offered by the exigencies of the existing neuro-physiological apparatus in the organism in accordance with environmental advantages (such as processibility in real time, optimality of information flow, etc.: 'least effort' guidelines in their traditional sense). This position is held by few linguists today, although perhaps the climate will change in the light of the impressive array of arguments offered by Pinker and Bloom in a recent paper (Pinker and Bloom 1990) and references cited there, which make a neo-Darwinian account of the evolution of natural language look most attractive. It follows quite naturally from such an approach that the explanation for the unmarked status of (4) may lie in the satisfaction of the claims of the parsing strategy in (7) during the emergence of UG at the evolutionary stage.

Chomsky does not, however, explicitly endorse this extension of his notion of explanatory adequacy, partly, as far as I can see, because it is not specifically linguistic in nature – i.e. it lies outside the linguistic component proper, and so apparently violates the autonomy/modularity thesis which is the cornerstone of his approach. As Pinker and Bloom (1990) comment:

> One gets the sense that the autonomy of grammar is so fundamental to Chomsky's views that he is not only unwilling to grant its utility any role in language development or use but is also unhappy at the prospect of it being the driving force in evolution, the process that created human language.

It seems that, for Chomsky, the inclusion of functional factors in satisfying explanatory adequacy would serve little purpose because he sees the structure of UG as largely arbitrary and fortuitous or as the result of neural architecture unrelated to language processes (cf. Pinker and Bloom 1990: 24 for a critique of this position). Possible evidence of a functional nature which may be adduced to support the fixing of certain principles in the evolution of UG are thus effectively excluded from consideration by the serious linguist (or are – recall – put 'in what seems to be [their] proper place'):

> The processes by which the human mind achieved its present state of complexity and its particular form of innate organization are a total mystery. ... It is perfectly safe to attribute this development to 'natural selection', so long as we realize that there is no substance to this assertion, that it amounts to nothing more than

14 *Morphology and mind*

a belief that there is some naturalistic explanation for these phenomena.

(Chomsky 1972: 97)

And, again:

What the evolutionary origins of these principles [of UG] might be is unknown, although some vague analogies have been considered in terms of hierarchical properties, locality principles, and the like, and there are some suggestions about possible functional properties of efficient processing.

(Chomsky 1986a: 264)

There is little reason to take for granted that properties of the language faculty have been specifically selected ... certainly evolutionary biology is not committed to such a view in general.

(Chomsky 1986a: note, p. 274)

As we have seen, J. D. Fodor (1984), on the other hand, entertains more seriously, but nevertheless somewhat reluctantly, the possibility of functional pressures in the evolution of grammar. She begins by arguing that once UG was established as part of the human genetic code, parsing pressures could operate only minimally, and without the capacity of altering UG in any way. This is perhaps what Chomsky and Lasnik were getting at in their article, and it seems to be fair enough, although – and this is important – it does not mean that other, learned aspects of the grammar shared by a wide number of languages (or common to all), may not be affected by parsing preferences that did not win out at the evolutionary stage of UG (I shall be returning to this theme repeatedly, since it is crucial to my critique and general approach). Fodor's subsequent conclusion, that parsing therefore was probably too weak an influence to have affected UG in its development, is arrived at rather tentatively. She admits that

it is possible that the unresolved parsing problems that we now observe represent just those cases in which the parser happened to be the loser in long-past evolutionary battles – perhaps the parsing problems would be far worse were it not that the parser also won some of those battles. (p. 16)

She supplies only the following motivation, though, for dismissing this uncertainty from her final conclusions: 'Universal properties of grammar could in principle have been very different from what they are, in a way that would have guaranteed that the parser would never

Explanation in linguistics 15

have to struggle with ambiguity' (p. 16). In other words, if the parser could win some of the battles, then why didn't it win all of them? Since it did not, then it must not have been a very significant influence on the development of UG, and hence, Fodor concludes, its evolution seems more likely to be due to neurophysiological chance.

This seems to me to be an extraordinarily dismissive approach to the available data on parsing and to a large part of the set of logically possible hypotheses that follow from them, not to mention the vast array of evidence for natural selection in other biological domains (as Pinker and Bloom (1990) demonstrate). In arriving at this conclusion Fodor also dismisses the very competitiveness amongst functional pressures on language which she previously acknowledged. This view of language as a monolithic, autonomous, discrete phenomenon, common amongst generativists, is at odds with the wealth of evidence amassed by others from distinct perspectives (cf. Greenberg 1966; Hawkins 1983; Givón 1984; Marslen-Wilson 1983, 1987; McClelland 1988, *inter alia*) which suggests the highly contingent, probabilistic, interactive nature of many language-related phenomena. We might expect, following such a line, that explanations for language regularities would be equally complex and multi-faceted: throughout this book evidence will be presented which strongly supports this view for important areas of linguistic knowledge.

1.2.3 Empirical evidence for innateness

The second major shortcoming of the generative approach, following naturally from the first, is the lack of a solid empirical base for the type of explanation it *does* entertain, namely the so-called 'innateness explanation'. Setting aside for the moment the question of whether innateness *can* on its own count as a satisfactory explanation, let us briefly examine the basis upon which claims for innateness are made. Nothing *in the theory* specifies unambiguously on what grounds some property is designated innate, other than that it may be derived from some other more general principle within the same theory, which is itself assumed to be innate in order to explain 'the fact of language acquisition'. But, as we have seen in the discussion of the data in (1)–(3), no appeal is made by Chomsky himself to the facts of the language acquisition process as far as they are now known, except for the very general observation that the task is successfully accomplished at a rapid rate and without negative evidence: the 'logical problem' of language acquisition. Most linguists inspired by Chomsky adopt this position, and do not generally refer to specific functional

16 *Morphology and mind*

factors emerging from work on acquisition in order to justify their theoretical proposals.

There does exist, however, a growing pool of research on acquisition and parsing (sentence processing) based on the UG-parametrical approach, in which the explanatory potential of functional factors such as learnability constraints and processing efficiency *are* acknowledged. Berwick and Weinberg (1984), for example, discussing the functional significance of locality constraints on rule application, conclude that

> apparently . . . the exigencies of language processing are intimately connected to the abstract constraints advanced by current theories of grammar; many of the same constraints that ease parsing, forcing decisions to be made locally, also aid the cause of acquisition. (p. 240)

They claim that their parsing model 'shows how the constraints of current transformational theory conspire with natural restrictions on computational power to explain why certain universal constraints on linguistic systems take the form that they do' (p. xiii). This seems exactly the sort of research that can truly have a chance of *explaining* principles proposed by Chomsky and his associates for inclusion in a theory of UG which claims to characterise the innately encoded language faculty; however, such an approach is rare in generative psycholinguistics, and is even more rarely cited or taken into account in the purely grammatical literature, which is more than a trifle odd given Chomsky's recognition of linguistics as a branch of theoretical cognitive psychology. In any case, it is more usual in generative psycholinguistics for researchers to use the theory of UG to 'explain' the psycholinguistic processes themselves, rather than the other way round. Flynn (1987) and the papers in Roeper and Williams (1987) are examples of this tendency, and even Berwick and Weinberg's central concern seems to fall into this category: in the preface to their book (entitled, significantly, *The Grammatical Basis of Linguistic Performance*), they state that one of their goals is to show that 'in many respects transformational grammar offers the best explanations we have of language processing and acquisition' (p. xi).

Berwick and Weinberg also display considerable confusion about exactly what is explaining what in their model. Consider again the passage cited earlier, from p. xiii of the Preface; part of their explanans for 'constraints on linguistic systems' are the hypothesised 'constraints of current transformational theory' themselves, conspiring with parsing factors. In what way the constraints as formalised by the

Explanation in linguistics 17

theory can actually *explain* the constraints so formalised is not at all clear; and surely what is involved is not a relationship of *conspiracy* between grammar and parser, but rather one of *causality*? The constraints cannot serve both as explanans *and* explanandum. Consider, too, the following passage, in which the second sentence, presumably offered as an expansion on the first, actually expresses an entirely different research goal, inasmuch as, in the two, explanans and explanandum are reversed:

> Our strategy ... is to show how rules and representations of transformational grammar can be independently justified by the theory of language use. By assuming that mental computations are 'projections' of a transformational grammar, we can actually explain part of what we observe to be true about sentence processing and language development. (p. xv)

There seems to be a chicken and egg problem here. The locality constraints on grammar expressed through subjacency, binding and the like, *can* be explained by locality constraints on parsing and development, i.e. function can determine (or influence) form, as expressed by Berwick and Weinberg in the first part of the passage cited, and elsewhere (see quotations above); it is true, too, that a theory of grammar like the Principles and Parameters model can provide useful tools for characterising the knowledge stores accessed by the parser and can make predictions for the course of acquisition (cf. Roeper and Williams 1987 and Flynn 1987, with reference to parametrical theory). However, I would argue that the (theory of) grammar can *explain* neither the functional processes which exploit it, nor the phenomena which it encodes, as Berwick and Weinberg claim, given the *causal* sense of explanation adopted here. The problem, I think, is that Berwick and Weinberg are using the term *explanation* in two ways: (i) in the causal sense, i.e. where the function involved *causes* (in some sense) the grammar to take the form it does, and (ii) in the 'expository' or analytical sense, i.e. where the form of the (theory of) grammar sheds light on the functions which operate on it, thereby facilitating the formulation of concrete predictions in the functional domain. It is with the latter sense in mind that most empirical work in the Chomskyan framework is currently conducted.

What is needed to bolster generative claims of explanatory adequacy for theoretical postulates in UG is clearer discussion of the linkage between them and the functional pressures acknowledged by generative psycholinguists like Berwick and Weinberg. As these

18 *Morphology and mind*

authors discuss it, the relationship between form and function may as well be completely fortuitous: the issue of explanation is not placed in the biological context of grammar provided by Chomsky (1981), or more clearly by Lightfoot (1982) – i.e. the locus of the grammatical principles in the innately specified human language faculty is not invoked to entertain the notion of functional pressures at the evolutionary stage, as one would naturally expect from this biological context (J. D. Fodor (1984), as we have seen, is a reluctant exception). Rather, the recognition of 'correlations' between functional and formal factors (e.g. the significance of the concept of locality in both domains), itself is seen as fulfilling the explanatory goal. A discussion of linkage which dares to be explicit about the locus of functional determination of principles of UG may therefore clarify empirical evidence for innateness collected by generative psycholinguists, and serve to contribute to complete explanations of the phenomena in question (cf. 1.4 for similar criticisms of the functionalist approach).

Exactly how clear the existing evidence is for innate, specifically linguistic principles is a matter of considerable debate. Non-generative approaches to language acquisition such as those taken by Bowerman (1982, 1988), Rumelhart and McClelland (1986) or Arbib, Conklin and Hill (1986), have constantly spawned criticisms that Chomsky's parameter-setting account is too simplistic, and is not warranted by the data, even given lack of negative evidence. In a paper dedicated to reviewing our current understanding of the 'no negative evidence' problem, Bowerman (1988) attempts to undermine the generativists' 'innate UG' solution, by showing that no satisfactory explanation of the child's tendency to formulate over-general grammars has been given by workers adopting this approach. Her fundamental criticism is this: if we have to posit innate knowledge of certain universal principles of grammaticality in order to explain the aquisition of universal features of grammar for which positive evidence does not suffice, i.e. in order to constrain the child from constructing over-general grammars, then (i) why does the child, albeit temporarily, construct grammars which *are* over-general, and (ii) how does the child recover in cases where universal constraints are not involved (i.e. in errors affecting language-particular areas of the grammar)?

As far as the problem in (i) is concerned, some proponents of UG claim that the principles only come into play *after* the phase in which errors and overgeneralisations are produced, but, according to Bowerman, a motivation for such delayed awareness of innate properties, supported by empirical evidence, has not been provided.

Explanation in linguistics 19

Borer and Wexler (1987) argue that the innate linguistic capacity matures, just like other genetically-determined properties, e.g. the emergence of secondary sexual characteristics at puberty. This means that at certain stages in the acquisition process, certain UG principles are not yet available to the child, and so at these stages over-general grammars result. Their hypothesis is very plausible, but lacks the fine-tuning necessary for concrete predictions to be made, and is essentially unfalsifiable since it involves no rationale for exactly what is subject to maturation and what is not (and why there should be this distinction), and also *when* or in what order particular properties will emerge.

Many non-generative psycholinguists who work with real data from children acquiring language or computational models criticise Chomsky and his followers for underestimating the complexity of the input received by the acquirer, and the capacity of its learning mechanisms to work actively on the problems posed by this input. They believe that because of this, the step in the chain of argument from no negative evidence to innate, specifically linguistic principles is unmotivated. According to Rumelhart and McClelland (1986), working within a connectionist model of learning (a parallel distributed processing model), grammatical rules and principles of the type proposed by generativists are not preprogrammed genetically in a specifically linguistic component of the brain; rather, an innate neural apparatus, dedicated to general cognitive operations, is allotted for linguistic purposes in the process of language acquisition. No negative evidence is required for the acquisition of correct adult linguistic behaviour, and this behaviour is not governed by a set of rules. Arbib and Hill (1988: 67) provide a succinct characterisation of Rumelhart and McClelland's connectionist modelling of over-generalisation in verb acquisition:

> The model makes no appeal to explicit representation of a general rule. Rather, the decentralized interaction of many components, representing different verbs, yields a coordination of their behavior which is *describable* by a rule, but which in no way is the *expression* of any such rule, innate or otherwise.

Thus the connectionist conceptualisation of language acquisition allows access neither to negative evidence nor to fixed constraints in the system in the form of rules, conditions on rules, filters and the like. Instead, as in connectionist models of other cognitive processes concerning language (e.g, spoken word recognition (McClelland and Elman 1986)), the input processed is encoded in a network of

20 *Morphology and mind*

connections between a large number of simple processing units. The network learns on the basis of the 'excitatory' and 'inhibitory' interactive activation of these units, with the degree and type of activation reflecting the degree of confidence attached to the hypothesis or hypotheses currently being entertained by the learner. On encountering a particular structure in the input, the weight attached to the hypothesis which the structure instantiates will be incremented. In this way, learning becomes dynamic and probabilistic, and rules become procedures executed at a certain degree of confidence – accounting for the co-occurrence of competing structures in the child's output when the weighting attached to them is roughly equal.

Rumelhart and McClelland's model succeeded in learning the idiosyncratic structure of over four hundred regular and irregular past tense forms in English. This does not, of course, in itself refute the existence of UG, since the structures learnt are very language-particular; however, in modelling the complex learning processes required for the English past tense system, through the production of overgeneralisations, co-occurrences, and subsequent corrections, the connectionist framework reveals suggestive evidence for a learning process which is much more complex than generativists credit, and its proponents see it as calling into question the indispensability of specifically linguistic principles and parameters as part of our genetic inheritence. Of course computer modelling of learning processes is still an infant discipline, and much more work in the connectionist framework needs to be carried out (Pinker and Prince 1988 point out a variety of flaws in the Rumelhart and McClelland model); the successes of connectionism so far, though, cannot be ignored by linguists who make claims about what the child can do with the data, on the basis of evidence limited almost exclusively to characterisations of a static adult grammar.

There are two central issues in this debate. One is the type of representational structures which encode the adult linguistic capacity and the other is the specificity of the neural 'functional architecture' (Pylyshyn 1984) which accounts for the speed and ease with which children attain this capacity. Chomsky (1970: 426–7), writing before the advent of connectionist models, made the following assessment of his detractors' position on these issues:

> [I]t is taken for granted without argument or evidence (or is presented as true by definition) that a language is a 'habit structure' or a network of associative connections, or that knowledge

Explanation in linguistics 21

of language is merely a matter of 'knowing how', a skill expressible as a system of dispositions to respond. Knowledge of language, accordingly, must develop slowly through repetition or training, its apparent complexity resulting from the proliferation of very simple elements rather than from deeper principles of mental organization which may be as inaccessible to introspection as the mechanisms of digestion or coordinated movement.

Although most psycholinguists have long since rejected the behaviourist position implied in the characterisation of language as 'a skill expressible as a system of dispositions to respond', and although few who have worked with child language data would concede a significant role to 'training' in the acquisition process, parts of the conceptualisation of language criticised by Chomsky in 1970 are now taken very seriously indeed by many psycho- and neurolinguists. As we have seen, connectionists in fact believe that language may be represented by 'a network of associative connections' and that 'its apparent complexity [results] from the proliferation of very simple elements rather than from deeper principles of mental organization'. Chomsky has, more recently (1986a: 43), in direct conflict with the connectionist position, characterised the language faculty as 'at its core, a computational system that is rich and narrowly constrained in structure and rigid in its essential operations, nothing at all like a complex of dispositions or a system of habits and analogies' (1986a: 43). The question of the computational (representational and functional) architecture of the language faculty is the key to a resolution of the generativist–connectionist dispute. For Chomsky, knowledge of language is represented in a narrow, rigid symbol-manipulation system, the 'core' of which is innately specified, and the 'periphery' of which is constructed on the basis of input from the processing system, mediated by innate learning procedures. For the connectionists, on the other hand, knowledge of language is represented in the functional architecture itself (through connections between the neuron-like elements of the processing system), and it evolves dynamically during the maturation process.

As Gardner (1987: 398) suggests, the reality may, however, lie in between the two positions. Parallel distributed processing may be the key to low-level dynamic aspects of the language processor, and a rigid, narrow, symbolic, linear system may be indispensable in the representation of specifically linguistic knowledge (particularly at the syntactic and morphological levels, which do not interface directly with non-linguistic faculties). A mixture of connectionist and

22 Morphology and mind

symbolic cognitive architecture may well be implicated in other aspects of the language faculty. Alternatively (and more unfortunately for proponents of strong connectionism), it might transpire that connectionist architecture is appropriate only at the neural *implementation* level, and that at the cognitive level we crucially need symbolic structures to encode higher-level functions (a position forcefully argued in Fodor and Pylyshyn (1988)).

A result of the dispute is that those looking for explanatory power from either of these approaches are unlikely to be fully convinced on the innateness/specificity issue. As I have argued in this section, the generativist position is without the sort of empirical evidence that a process-oriented extension to the research programme could provide. Connectionism, in its turn, has not yet modelled the acquisition of phenomena captured by principles of UG such as the binding theory, and existing connectionist modelling still requires a good deal of wired-in 'tinkering' to make it work effectively (cf. Lachter and Bever 1988). The challenges to each are strong ones. The generativists, who unlike the connectionists have had a few decades to develop their approach, need to get round to providing positive evidence to support the specification of some linguistic principles as innate other than that linguistically the theory works best that way. The foundation of Chomsky's notion of explanatory adequacy for UG is too restricted: it appeals only to the 'logical problem' of language acquisition, which too often translates into purely theoretical considerations of internal consistency, generality and simplicity in the adult grammar; evidence from processing and acquisition which may provide an empirical basis for many of the postulates advanced is virtually ignored.

1.2.4 Typological universals

A third major problem with the generative model is that research within this paradigm is restricted to identifying only a certain class of universal language regularity. It cannot, for example, identify implicational regularities such as those yielded by the universal–typological school (e.g. Greenberg 1966; Lehmann 1978; Hawkins 1983). Also, there is no clear-cut principle which governs the decision of which statistical universals should be handled parametrically by UG, and which relegated to theoretical insignificance on 'the periphery'. Hawkins (1982, 1983, 1985), for example, discusses some of the pitfalls associated with the strict interpretation of the determination of basic word order implied by Chomsky's X-bar

Explanation in linguistics 23

theory (cf. section 1.1.1), pointing out that the distributional data cannot be fully accounted for by the limited set of choices presented by a parametrical approach. He argues that his universal–typological approach, involving a principle of Cross-Category Harmony, based on the attested implicational/distributional regularities (Hawkins 1983) and the theoretical framework of Jackendoff's X-bar system (1977), provides a more plausible account of cross-categorial generalisation in language, in which the degree of generalisation manifested cross-linguistically lies along a continuum, from strict head-ordering (the preferred arrangement) at one pole, to random ordering (presumably) at the other. This is, though, only a descriptive principle: unlike in Chomsky's framework, description and explanation are not necessarily conflated in the universal–typological approach.[4, 5]

The cross-linguistic phenomenon discussed at length in the body of this book, namely the asymmetrical distribution of affix positions, is not something that would be theoretically interesting for most generativists; indeed, it has no place at all in such a theoretical framework. What this means is that, within the model, the only interesting properties of language structure are the innate ones, either absolute or statistical in the parametrical sense, i. e. the ones identified as part of UG by the theory. A particularly strong statement of this position is made by Hoekstra and Kooij (1988), who argue that

> what is and is not universal can be established only on the basis of a theory of UG ... and ... consequently, what is and is not relevant within the many phenomena that appear to be universal in an absolute or statistically significant sense cannot be decided on the basis of these data themselves. (p. 53)

In effect, they are claiming that generativists have a monopoly on universals: a phenomenon is only universal if it is identified as part of UG by generative linguists working on descriptions of language and so is assumed to be dictated by our genetic code; nothing else is permitted. This seems to me an extraordinarily limiting view, and although perhaps not widely shared, it does reflect, albeit at the extreme, a tendency for generativists to ignore or deny the validity of data forthcoming from other research paradigms. This practice follows in large part from the limited scope of the generative enterprise, itself surely justified on theoretical grounds; however, a corollary decreeing that everything else is unworthy of serious study is, to my mind, patently *un*justified.

24 *Morphology and mind*

1.2.5 Explanation of historical change

Criticisms similar to those expressed in the preceding sections have also been levelled over the last few decades at attempts at description and explanation in language *change*, especially in phonology, where the explanatory mechanisms usually posited involve processes of analogy (in traditional non-generative approaches, but subject to identical criticisms), and rule addition/loss (in the generative approach). Jeffers (1974), for example, criticises the descriptive nature of most such accounts of language change, suggesting that explanations can usually be discovered if the context of the rule is examined, whereas Lass (1980) reaches the conclusion that explanation in phonological change is impossible. Harris (1982) is less pessimistic, pointing to the possibility of psychological and biological explanations; he does, however, have this to say on the non-explanatory status of many principles vaunted as explanatory:

> Almost all the 'explanatory' principles so rightly attacked by Lass [1980] are in fact descriptions of how language re-establishes equilibrium, not explanations why. A modified vowel system, a re-organized tense system, the replacement of one comparative structure by another, all of these may be described in terms of structural pressure, analogical change, the principle of natural serialization or whatever and this is perfectly legitimate provided these terms are seen not as explanations in themselves but rather as labels for various processes whereby the speakers of a language reorder their material as we have seen in accordance with their own needs [i.e. coherence, economy, consistency]. . . . So long as we unequivocally understand that concepts such as analogical change, the principle of cross-category harmony [cf. chapter 3] and the like in themselves do not – cannot – tell us *why* change takes place, then the overall picture becomes clear, and their role in historical linguistics secure. (pp. 13–14)

Similarly, Andersen (1973) criticises King's early generative approach to historical linguistics (King 1969) for lacking any explanatory dimension in the characterisations of change offered. For example, consider the phenomenon observed in the Tetak dialect of Czech, where labials change to dentals in certain environments. According to Andersen (1973: 766 ff.), King would hold that

> the Tetak phenomenon could be described very succinctly as a 'rule addition', . . . a rule changing certain labials to dentals was

Explanation in linguistics 25

added to the speakers' grammar; this changed certain labials to dentals. But this concept would provide no answer to the question of where the speakers of these dialects got the rule which they supposedly added to their grammar. Judging from King's exposition (e.g. p. 85), one would have to surmise that they conceived it spontaneously. Nor would this model of change suggest an answer to the question of why the speakers would add such a rule. Indeed, this theory can do nothing with the Tetak change – or any other phonological change – except restate the diachronic correspondences to which it gave rise.

The generativist answer to this sort of criticism may be found at least in part in Chomsky's defence of the concept of 'rule' as explanatory or causal, in that it accounts for linguistic behaviour at the generative level of explanatory adequacy:

> I cannot see that anything is involved in attributing causal efficacy to rules beyond the claim that these rules are constituent elements of the states postulated in an explanatory theory of behavior and enter into our best account of this behavior. We will say that our theories of S_O [the initial state = UG] and S_L [the attained state = adult, particular language grammar] involve encoded rules that guide Jones's behavior when our best theories [i.e. using *all* the evidence] attribute these rules to Jones and resort to them in accounting for his behavior. (1986a: 253)

Of course, this statement has no direct relevance to the question of explanation for language change; rather, it responds to those who have criticised generative grammar for lacking 'psychological reality'. However, Chomsky's conceptualisation of grammar does go part of the way towards accounting for diachronic change by establishing the locus of change as the mind, and, therefore, rightly in my view, giving historical linguistics an ultimately psychological interpretation (see chapter 6). But, of course, accepting that language change is instantiated through rule loss, addition, etc. in a great number of individual stores of linguistic knowledge in the minds of a speech community, although satisfying the claims of 'expository' explanation, does not answer Andersen's and Harris's major charge, which is that the causal question has not been addressed.

If, improbably, Jones happens to be a native speaker of Tetak and he employs dental articulation where the linguist might expect labials (because Jones's grandfather's generation is known to have used labials in this environment, or, alternatively, because the system

26 *Morphology and mind*

would be less marked, more consistent, this way), then, yes, we can say that part of his mental state may be described by a rule which changes labials to dentals, and we can even say, perhaps, that we have explained his behaviour by reference to his mental state. But we cannot claim to have explained this mental state, nor why it differs from his grandfather's when they supposedly both speak the same dialect of Czech. The diachronic dimension of explanation is similar to that of the phylogenetic and the ontogenetic, in that it deals with mechanisms of change in a linguistic system, which can serve as *linkage* between explanans and explanandum, or as explananda themselves, but not *per se* as explanans. The mechanism of change (be it growth or whatever) is essential in explanation because it indicates the locus of the causal element (it may even be thought of as causal itself in an explanatory chain of explanans – mechanism of linkage – explanandum), but it really does not tell us *why* the change took place and *why* the phenomenon to be explained resulted. This theme is taken up in more detail in subsequent chapters, particularly the final two.

1.2.6 The achievement of explanatory adequacy

The main achievement of the generative requirement of 'explanatory adequacy' is, I would argue, a deeper, more general and insightful level of descriptive analysis and abstraction which can *facilitate* the identification of ultimately explanatory principles; which of these principles turn out to be biologically given is a moot point, and should be pursued by linguists, psycholinguists, and neurolinguists (and perhaps biologists and geneticists when the time comes); however, we owe much to Chomsky for opening up the possibility and so casting linguistics in a new cognitively-oriented mould.

The deep generalisations yielded by the Chomskyan approach, such as trace theory and the binding principles, are necessary in any approach to explanation in linguistics in that they can define more precisely for us the nature of some explananda, and thus, allow us to identify the correct and more general underlying explanans. I quite agree with Lightfoot (1979: 71) when, in defence of the generative model, he asserts that:

> The crucial factor in science is depth of explanation, not data-coverage. Any non-trivial scientific theory is apparently falsified for much of the time, but one persists with it if it is providing explanations within some domains and offers a useful and productive research programme.

Explanation in linguistics 27

My major misgiving, though, is that the principles yielded by this research programme (in the narrow sense in which it is commonly practised) are insufficient *in themselves* to provide explanations for the complex computational structures they describe. To this extent, then, as I have argued in this section, I find Chomsky's theoretical stance explanatorily *in*adequate.

I contend that a truly adequate explanatory model for linguistics must take into account a much broader range of factors, including at least the following: (i) the potential role of functional pressure (particularly from the processing and learning mechanisms, but also perhaps from non-linguistic sources) in the evolution of innately-specified grammatical principles; (ii) the requirement for non-linguistic empirical evidence to justify the postulation of a descriptive grammatical principle as biologically wired-in; (iii) the importance of linguistic regularities not directly derivable from principles of UG, e.g. many statistical or implicational universals identified within the universal–typological paradigm; and (iv) the necessary elaboration of models of developmental linkage between explanans and explanandum and the specification of the locus of explanation.

Note that points (iii) and (iv) bring historical linguistics and universal–typological linguistics clearly into the purview of a cognitive–scientific study of the language faculty, thus increasing to six the number of basic component areas outlined earlier for a cognitive science of language (the others were formal linguistics, psycholinguistics, artificial intelligence and neurolinguistics): this would constitute a threat to the autonomy of syntax which would doubtless be intolerable to Chomsky. Although *some* strands of opinion within the formal approach recognise the importance of *some* of the expansions on the Chomskyan notion of explanatory adequacy listed in (i) to (iv) above, no formalists go so far as endorsing co-operative work on *all* these fronts, and the formal approach as a whole continues to discard or ignore work outside of formal grammatical description.

We now turn to the functional approach to explanation in linguistics, seeking to clarify the goals espoused by the loose federation of scholars associated with it and the conceptualisation of the language capacity which underlies work in this area.

1.3 THE FUNCTIONAL APPROACH TO EXPLANATION

Givón (1979), exemplifying the functional approach, rejects the unitary, theory-dependent conceptualisation of explanation held by

28 *Morphology and mind*

the formalists, and, instead, suggests that explanations for language regularities lie along a number of general parameters of which at least the major ones are essentially either psychological or otherwise functional in nature. These are: *propositional contents* (referring to clause-level notions such as subject and object and their thematic correlates); *discourse pragmatics* (topic-comment, presupposition, etc.); *world-view pragmatics* (the importance of 'a constructed view of the universe'); *the processor* (production and comprehension constraints); *ontogenetic development* (acquisition constraints); and *cognitive structure* (more general, non-linguistic cognitive and perceptual apparatus). Others, for example Keenan (1978: 1979) and Bybee (1985), have appealed, in addition, to the nature of *semantic* dependencies/properties as determinants of syntactic and morphological structure. Much of this particular explanatory source can be seen as deriving, in turn, from the more general coding principle of *iconicity* (Haiman 1980, 1983; Givón 1984: 40), whose explanatory potential will be exploited in any domain where features of the non-linguistic world are encoded in a non-arbitrary manner. From a functionalist perspective, then, linguists have a far broader range of options to choose from than the formalists in supplying explanations for regularities in language.

Let us look briefly at a few examples from this pool of potential sources of explanation. Starting with semantics, Keenan (1978, 1979), for example, has appealed to semantic iconicity in an attempt to explain why it is that adjectives agree morphologically with nouns, subjects with verbs etc., but not vice versa. He proposes a 'Meaning–Form Dependency Principle' which states that the structural phenomenon of agreement reflects the direction of semantic dependency between the agreeing elements. So, for example, adjectives can agree morphologically with nouns (but not vice versa) because adjectives often vary their semantic interpretation with the choice of noun (but not vice versa). The semantic variability is seen in the contrast between English *strong* (referring to power exerted) in *strong man* and (referring to power resisted) in *strong box*. The word for 'strong' may, in some languages, agree morphologically with the noun it modifies, but the word for 'box' may never agree morphologically with the adjective that modifies it – i.e. dependencies of meaning are reflected in dependencies of form. A similar proposal of semantic iconicity is made by Bybee (1985) for the ordering of affixes relative to the verb: the more 'relevant' the meaning of the affix is to the verb, the *closer* it will be to the stem in a multi-affixal word. As Lee (1988) has pointed out, these are, strictly speaking,

Explanation in linguistics 29

instances of *automorphism*, where the structure is an icon of some other part of the grammar, or, more broadly, some other part of our cognitive capacities, rather than of the world which they are involved in perceiving and representing.

General, shared cognitive architecture is also often invoked to provide explanations for language regularities, especially in latter years from a neo-Piagetian perspective (e.g. Arbib *et al.* 1986). As an example from the preceding discussion, notice from Chomsky's exposition of trace theory (discussed in section 1.1) that the 'explanation' for the mental reality of physically unrealised elements is given in terms of a descriptive theory of their behaviour: children treat physically absent elements as present in this way because the trace theory, constructed to account for the distribution of such elements, demands this. The trace theory predicts a number of other phenomena in grammar, and is therefore assumed to be an innate component of UG. Some generativists, however, notably Lightfoot (1982), are open to the possibility of the sharing of linguistic principles with other components of 'mind'. Those who adopt a functionalist approach would applaud this view, suggesting that, in this case, the trace theory of movement, whilst (perhaps) optimally describing the phenomenon in language, is probably derived from higher level mental processes shared with other cognitive domains (such as visual processing, for example), which involve the representation of (physical or mental) 'location' of objects in working memory, despite their lack of physical representation in the input signal.

Note, though, that evidence which supports the functionalist view that trace theory is one reflex of a broader cognitive principle, does not in any way weaken the validity of trace theory as it is conceived of in generative grammar, as some functionalists would undoubtedly claim. Rather, I would argue, in the conceptualisation of the role of Chomskyan theory I advanced in 1.2.6, such evidence should be construed as contributing to the quest for validations of and, consequently, explanations of the principles attributed to UG. We know that trace theory applies, very probably universally, in language, but evidence of the sort envisaged here forces us to address the question of whether the general principle encoded in the theory is instantiated separately in different cognitive components, for example the visual and the linguistic, as assumed in a narrow generative approach, or whether some master cognitive knowledge pool is accessed by different components. I have no idea of the answer to this question, or how to go about finding out; the point I am making is that linguists working from the two approaches are

30   *Morphology and mind*

often working towards complementary rather than mutually exclusive goals.

Functionalists also often appeal to psycholinguistic mechanisms and processes as an important source of potential constraints on language structure. We discussed the involvement of processing principles in the previous section, showing how some of the principles of UG may have become fixed at the evolutionary phase because they conformed with processing requirements imposed by the temporal nature of comprehension and production. It also seems clear, however, that processing principles may continue to affect the structure of grammars of particular languages in ways which do not involve UG, a possibility ignored, and sometimes apparently denied, by those working within the formal approach to explanation. Consider the following passage by Lightfoot (1982: 32), on the perceived error of functionalists in offering explanations which hold at the ontogenetic rather than phylogenetic level:

> the heart serves the function of pumping blood and one might say that its structure is determined by that function. But a heart does not just happen to develop in each individual because it would be useful to pump blood: a group of cells do not 'decide' to become a heart. A heart develops because the genetic program determines that it will develop as it does. Functional explanations do not account for how organs develop in an individual embryo; they do not hold at the ontogenetic level, although they may cast some light on evolutionary change at the phylogenetic level. Similarly with cognitive capacities: *if it were proposed that some aspect of a grammar is determined by communicative needs, the proposal would hold of the evolutionary development of the species, not of an individual child attaining a particular language.* Functional considerations may complement claims about genetic structure, but they do not usually offer an alternative to genetically prescribed principles.
>
> > [My emphasis]

Lightfoot is perfectly right in pointing out that functional explanations for UG will hold at the phylogenetic level rather than the ontogenetic; but when he claims that aspects of a grammar cannot be determined at the ontogenetic level by functional pressure, he is on much shakier ground. If by 'some aspects of a grammar' he means aspects determined by UG, then all well and good: but if he is referring to features of the periphery, or even parameter settings within the core, i.e. aspects of the grammars of individual languages

Explanation in linguistics 31

not determined exclusively by the genetic programme, then such a view would be subject to a powerful challenge from a wealth of evidence, especially from psycholinguistics, which suggests the contrary. Kuno, for example, has provided quite a compelling argument to the effect that the parsing dispreference for centre-embedding has, in SOV languages, led to the introduction of a therapeutic rule of extraposition (Kuno 1974). Similarly, Antinucci *et al.* (1979) explain the cross-linguistic observation that prenominal relatives serialise to the right more readily than other structures on the basis of a parsing preference for heads to occur early, and Hawkins (1983) has argued that this explanation may be extended to many serialisation phenomena (cf. his 'Heaviness' and 'Mobility' principles). On the lexical level, Cutler *et al.* (1985), and the research reported in subsequent chapters of this book, show how psycholinguistic principles of lexical access and organisation seem to determine the preponderance of suffixes over prefixes in the languages of the world. None of these phenomena appear to have been determined exclusively by principles of UG: all seem to have resulted *after* the human capacity for language was fixed in its genetically determined aspects.

The difference between the heart and the grammar of an individual is that whereas the defining structure of the former is fixed entirely by the genetic programme, the structure of the latter is in very large part fixed by the individual's interaction with the environment, and the varied functions which that environment may impose: one cannot speak in UG alone. Consequently, in constructing the grammar at the ontogenetic stage, the child's learning mechanisms may be called upon to respond to a variety of pressures from various sources, some particular to the language being acquired, but some stemming from the exigencies of speaking and understanding common to all humans (cf. Slobin 1977).

Some communicative needs will very likely, then, influence aspects of grammar at the ontogenetic level, where diachronic changes observed in the language variety of the community as a whole are played out within the changing grammars of individual children. This set of demands placed upon the learner, only a few of which will be responded to, accounts not only for much of the variation amongst grammars, across both time and space, but also for much of the commonality between them, as expressed through universal statements of the typological variety. These demands, unlike those imposed by the fixed principles of UG, must 'fight for re-election' every time the language is learnt anew, and they constitute a

32 *Morphology and mind*

potentially very significant element in the explanation of language regularities at two levels: (i) the phylogenetic, by influencing the emergence of portions of mental architecture as linguistically specific (principles of UG); and (ii) the ontogenetic, by constraining choices made by individuals as they develop through exposure to input a fully communicative system around the abstract principles already *in situ*.

We conclude this section by addressing the status of two other areas in Givón's (1979) list of parameters of explanation for linguistics, namely *phylogenetic evolution* and *diachronic change*. It will have become clear by now that these are not explanatory parameters in the same sense as the others. I propose that they should rather be viewed as mediating mechanisms between explanandum and explanans. Chomsky's biological 'explanation' of the human language capacity is, then, of this order, and functional/psychological principles may then be seen as complementing Chomsky's approach by providing explanations for the non-arbitrary portions both of UG and of non-genetically determined regularities observed cross-linguistically. Phylogenetic and diachronic principles determine the causal mechanism or linkage between functional principles on the one hand and the descriptive principles which encode the form of grammars on the other.

1.4 PROBLEMS WITH THE FUNCTIONAL APPROACH

As I see it, the main problems with the functional approach result from its immaturity and lack of cohesion as an academic endeavour, and the methodological difficulties inherent in collecting reliable and revealing data in the psychological and social sciences. The former problem can be surmounted as more evidence is amassed and recognition of a common goal emerges, thus encouraging greater interdisciplinary co-operation and the consequent development of a consistent approach. The resolution of the latter problem, however, will depend partly on technological developments outside the field (i.e. advances in methodology), and partly on the growing recognition by many modern linguists who are used to the unambiguous, 'sanitised' results of the formal approach, that universal linguistic phenomena are often the product of complex interactions between linguistic and non-linguistic principles, and so do not *necessarily* follow exceptionless universal laws. This should lead to a more realistic appreciation of the sort of evidence likely to be forthcoming and its necessarily incomplete role in the entire jigsaw puzzle of explanation.

Explanation in linguistics 33

The problem of vagueness, of absence of detail, is one reflex of the immaturity of the approach. As Levinson has noted (1983: 40 ff), the degree of complexity achieved in theories of language use, whether in processing, pragmatics or any other area, often is simply not yet adequate enough to allow them to be exploited in explaining the intricate regularities expressed in the abstract vocabulary of a well-defined theory of grammar such as the Principles and Parameters model. Two of the most persistent areas in which vagueness hinders the achievement of convincing results are in the characterisation of *linkage* and the definition of *locus* of explanation. A typical functional explanation states that regularity R is shared by a majority (or all) of the languages of the world because it affords a functional advantage A in that, for example, it results in more efficient discourse processing. However, as Bybee (1988: 357 ff) points out, what is seldom given is an account of plausible processes which could be involved in achieving the cross-linguistic dominance of R over some alternative R', that is, how is the pragmatic preference translated into change in the grammar, perhaps at the expense of R'? This is the problem of *linkage*. However, before investigating historical motivations and mechanisms we have to be clear about the hypothesised *locus* of the explanation: we have to ask whether R was conceivably fixed at the level of evolution of the species, thus avoiding diachronic competition with R' in subsequent historical development.

As a well-known example of work in the functional school, consider Hopper and Thompson's (1980) explanation of the cross-linguistic phenomenon of transitivity marking. They define transitivity in terms of the clustering of a number of morphosyntactic clause features such as number of participants, agency, and individuation of the object. Each feature has a value which reflects either high or low transitivity – for instance, two participants indicate high transitivity, one participant indicates low; a highly individuated object is high in transitivity, a non-individuated object is low; etc. What Hopper and Thompson seek to explain is why such features regularly co-occur in language, i.e. why transitivity is encoded in this systematic way. They seek the answer in discourse pragmatics, and, on the basis of cross-linguistic textual analysis, discover a strong correlation between transitivity and *grounding*. Grounding is the encoding in language of information as either *foregrounded*, i.e. crucial to the basic structure of a sequenced text, or *backgrounded*, i.e. incidental, unsequenced comment on, or amplification of the main text. They found that foregrounded clauses tend to be high in transitivity, and backgrounded clauses low. So, they surmise,

34 *Morphology and mind*

> [f]rom the performer's viewpoint, the decision to foreground a clause will be reflected in the decision to encode more (rather than fewer) Transitivity features in the clause. ... This hypothesis is borne out by the numerical correlations between grounding and degree of Transitivity. (Hopper and Thompson 1980: 284)

The features, are not, of course, arbitrary encoders of grounding: the authors point to a semantic–pragmatic relationship between each feature value and the relevant grounding type, e.g. backgrounded clauses are often likely to be scenic in nature, and so may be expressed using stative verbs, typically involving one participant, rather than two.

The explanation seems appealing: the numerical correlation is strong, and the semantic–pragmatic relationship transparent in most cases. But can we be sure that the discourse function actually determined the encoding of transitivity in languages in this way? I.e. is there a causal mechanism which provides the crucial linkage between explanans and explanandum? Bybee (1988) suggests that discourse explanations usually do provide causal mechanisms in the form of grammaticisation of frequently occurring patterns. According to her, the paradigmatic discourse explanation goes as follows:

> A certain configuration of syntagmatic, grammatical or semantic elements is shown to be frequently occurring in discourse, due to the way that information flow is typically structured. These frequently chosen patterns, it is argued, become rigidified or frozen into syntactic rules in some languages. Thus what is optimal discourse structure in one language is grammatical rule in another.
> (Bybee 1988: 261)

What is missing in Hopper and Thompson's account is any discussion of the possible processes by which independently occurring semantic–pragmatic features become associated with discourse structuring, and subsequently get grammaticised *because* of this association.

The historical scenario is one in which, presumably, grounding *is* a vital aspect of discourse structure. It happens that the values of certain semantic–pragmatic features present in clauses co-vary with the grounding distinction, although they are not in themselves directly related to grounding. What one would need to argue in order to make the explanation complete is that such features co-occur with each other and one or other of the grounding types consistently and frequently enough for them to become grammaticised, i.e. encoded

Explanation in linguistics 35

explicitly in the morphosyntax, *in order to convey grounding information to the listener*. It is this last step that seems particularly unjustified, whatever the intuitive appeal of the explanation, because the correlation between feature values and grounding type has not been shown to be *causal* in any way: it is not shown that the features occur frequently *because* of the structuring of the information flow rather than because of the inherent semantic–pragmatic nature of the clauses involved, which is not exhaustively captured by the grounding distinction. It is also not shown *how* these semantic–pragmatic features came to signal grounding, other than that they co-vary in the way observed, and follow naturally from the semantic–pragmatic nature of the grounding distinction. Hopper and Thompson summarise their main conclusion as follows:

> The fact that semantic characteristics of high Transitivity such as perfective Aspect, individuated O[bject], and agentive subject tend strongly to be grammaticized in the morphosyntax of natural languages points to the importance of the foregrounding/backgrounding distinction, and suggests that this distinction is valuable in explaining certain universals or near-universals of morphosyntax. (p. 294)

Although the correlation is very suggestive, and probably *is* very valuable in an explanation of the cross-linguistic regularity of transitivity marking, it remains, in Hopper and Thompson's account, a correlation only, and not a full explanation.

This problem of *linkage* in functional explanations is taken up in much greater detail in subsequent chapters, especially the final two, where it is shown that a psycholinguistic account of the suffixing preference such as the one offered by Cutler, Hawkins and Gilligan (1985), cannot be considered a complete explanation without a specification of the kinds of processes by which the preference could operate (*linkage*) and at what stage in the development of language these processes take place (*locus*).

A final observation and comment: many in the functional school criticise the formalists for not taking into account functional factors, for being 'unempirical' and too limiting in their scientific stance, and so they reject the value of generative analyses *in toto* (for examples, cf. much of the literature cited in note 1). What they fail to recognise, however, is that the extraordinarily rich theory elaborated by the formal school contains a vast pool of descriptive principles crying out for empirical, *functional* investigation. The majority of functionalists resist the conclusion that the methodology which yielded this wealth

36 *Morphology and mind*

of regularities results in deep, theoretically coherent analyses of language phenomena, and consequently this resource is seldom exploited by those seeking functional explanations. Moreover, if functionalists were to apply where appropriate the rigour of generative methodology to the phenomena they wish to explain, they would have a much surer footing upon which to base their explanatory hypotheses.

1.5 A UNIFIED APPROACH TO EXPLANATION

1.5.1 Defining the unified approach

The foregoing discussion strongly suggests to me that linguistics needs a unified approach to explanation, compatible with the study of language as a cognitive phenomenon *and* its extension as a socially shared communicative system. Such an approach will have as its goal the explanation of regularities across all or significant numbers of languages, in the hope of revealing important aspects of the fundamental nature of the human language faculty, in the context both of our genetic endowment and of its actual manipulation by speakers, hearers and learners in a communicative setting. Thus, data from both generative and universal–typological descriptive paradigms must be addressed, but explanations will necessarily demand the consideration of extra-paradigmatic factors, since specifically linguistic accounts can do no more than specify the variation space of human language through parametrical or statistical *description* (whether this is seen as a characterisation of our internal mentally-represented *knowledge* of language, or its external manifestation in the social context of discourse and texts). Explanation will therefore be necessarily *causal*, rather than 'expository', and so *external* to the descriptive theory within which the regularity is identified, specifically in contradistinction to the generative tradition which claims to be explanatory *within* the terms of the descriptive theory employed. However, it is important that the *object* of explanation in this unified approach, regardless of the descriptive framework which yields it, should be construed in terms° of Chomsky's biological view of language, i.e. as ultimately a cognitive phenomenon, even if it is governed by strong pragmatic, social, anthropological or other external factors.

An important feature of the approach is that it will involve multi-disciplinary investigation of linguistic phenomena, a course of research unfortunately rare this century (for obvious logistical reasons as well

Explanation in linguistics 37

as others related to the theoretical viewpoint and perceived scope of the field adopted by different schools of research – as documented in the preceding sections). In attempting to explain language, no data from any source should be rejected *a priori*, although, of course, some areas of research may have more to offer than others, and certain types of phenomenon may be more amenable to one source of explanation than another. One area of research that is an indispensable element in all attempts at explanation is psycholinguistics (broadly construed to include all theories or models of the relationship between linguistic representations and processes involving mind or brain), whether it supplies the immediate explanans, or is used to specify the processes of linkage, i.e. the way in which our linguistic knowledge or behaviour was formed or subsequently changed so as to embrace the phenomenon under investigation. In turn, it will be immediately apparent that this latter goal cannot be achieved without recourse to research in diachronic, ontogenetic, and/or (ultimately) phylogenetic processes.

In fully explaining consistent regularities of structure across languages, therefore, the scholar (or, more realistically, interdisciplinary *team* of scholars) working within this unified approach must (i) rigorously describe the data in the most complete, consistent and cognitively-insightful manner (as in the enormously successful analyses of the generativists), but also (ii) examine all levels (or 'parameters') of analysis and function to determine potential underlying principles and pressures, probably of a psychological or otherwise functional nature, rather than perceiving the descriptive principles themselves as satisfying explanatory requirements. In addition, they must (iii) attempt to establish the causal mechanism(s) by which the underlying pressure or pressures actually instantiate in language the regularity under investigation. This latter requirement will involve the investigation of diachronic change, ontogenetic development, or phylogenetic evolution – or some combination of these. Further tests of the feasibility of explanations proceeding from this approach should, in certain cases, be conducted in the laboratories of computational linguists and neurolinguists, although this kind of completeness will be difficult to achieve until cognitive science becomes far more consolidated in academic institutions.

1.5.2 Applying the unified approach

The case-study reported in this book concerns the well-documented cross-linguistic preference for suffixing over prefixing; my major

38 *Morphology and mind*

focus of interest is, therefore, the *morphologically complex word*, and I examine it from the point of view of cognitive science – from the perspective of *mind*. To illustrate the interdisciplinary nature of the unified approach to explanation laid out here, I examine the problem from four perspectives, drawing on a number of linguistic traditions to formulate an account at a level of specificity and completeness seldom attempted in linguistic explanation.

First, I examine the cross-linguistic distributional evidence on complex words as it currently exists in the Greenbergian literature. Second, I take a close look at the internal structure of the word using the techniques of generative morphological analysis, in order to shed some light on the reported head/affix correlation. Third, I draw on work from diachronic linguistics to identify the historical origins of morphologically complex words, thus establishing the importance of the linkage mechanisms for both the head/affix correlation and the suffixing preference. Finally, I employ current methodology and theory in psycholinguistics on the processing and storage of affixed words to explore how they are accessed in comprehension and how aspects of language change have been moulded by this process.

This 'micro-analytic', multi-disciplinary examination of the units of morphology allows us to reach a deep understanding of the intricate causal network explaining the cross-linguistic pattern of affixal distribution. In taking the broader perspective permitted by this 'non-autonomous' approach, it is also possible to reveal the explanatory redundancy of apparently independent grammatical principles advanced in the autonomous linguistic literature. In this case I show how diachronic semantic and (morpho)phonological principles seem to be quite transparently derivable from processing and higher level communicative principles; but at the same time I stress the importance of identifying these surface reflexes of underlying principles so that the link between explanans and explanandum can be tracked, thus substantiating the dynamic explanation.

The suffixing preference is, then, an ideal case to investigate in order to illustrate and justify the approach to explanation in linguistics advocated here. In the next chapter we undertake the first stage of our study of morphology and mind with an examination of the distributional data on the suffixing preference and the head/affix correlation.

2 Morphological regularity

Affixal morphology is employed by nearly all the world's languages to express modifications or specifications of the role or the meaning of a stem morpheme in its sentential context.[1] A single affix may appear fixed before, internal to, or at the end of the stem form (i.e., prefixing, infixing or suffixing), although the internal affix is extremely rare compared with prefixation and suffixation.[2] When more than one morpheme at a time is fixed in prefix or suffix position, their order of proximity to the stem is highly constrained within languages. We therefore recognise two critical dimensions on which languages may vary: (i) the linear position of affixes relative to the stem (i.e. prefix or suffix), and (ii) the order of affixes relative to each other when they co-occur on the same side of the stem. Variation along the former dimension is exhibited across and within languages, but along the latter almost exclusively[3] only across languages (i.e. a language may utilise different positions but not different orders). Bybee (1985) has shown that the ordering of affixes with each other is highly constrained across languages, and argues that this ordering follows universal principles of semantic relevance. For the present work, however, we are restricting our attention to cases of single affix occurrences and their positional preference with reference to the stem.

In this chapter, section 2.1 reviews the data and descriptive universal statements proposed to characterise the patterns they exhibit, and section 2.2 discusses some reservations to be borne in mind when such data and universals are brought into the explanatory domain characterised by the unified approach.

40 *Morphology and mind*

2.1 THE DATA AND UNIVERSALS

2.1.1 Greenberg (1966)

The data in Greenberg's (1966) sample reveal a significant preference for suffixing over prefixing or infixing. Infixing is very rare, and even rarer are circumfixing and intercalation (cf. note 2). No language uses exclusively such discontinuous affixing systems:

> Universal 26. If a language has discontinuous affixes, it always has prefixing or suffixing or both.

> (Greenberg 1966: 92)

In the light of this observation, we are concentrating solely on prefixing and suffixing. The preference for suffixing is quite striking in Greenberg's data; although seventeen of the thirty languages studied allow both prefixing and suffixing, only one language in the sample is exclusively prefixing, compared with twelve which are exclusively suffixing. In addition, there is a correlation between these facts and word order:

(1) Greenberg's sample: Number of
    languages with affix position
    correlated with verb/object order

	Prefix only	Both	Suffix only
VO	1	16	2
OV	–	1	10

(2) Greenberg's sample: Number of
    languages with affix position
    correlated with adposition order

	Prefix only	Both	Suffix only
Prep	1	15	–
Postp	–	2	12

The figures in these tables suggest that VO/Prep (i.e. head-initial) languages tend to have both suffixes and prefixes, but on the other hand OV/Postp (i.e. head-final) languages (i) do not include any exclusively prefixing systems and (ii) include many more exclusively suffixing systems than suffixing *and* prefixing systems, and more than the VO/Prep group. On the basis of these figures Greenberg proposes cross-linguistic regularities such as his implicational Universal 27 which states:

Morphological regularity 41

Universal 27. If a language is exclusively suffixing, it is postpositional; if it is exclusively prefixing, it is prepositional. (p. 93)

Broadly speaking, both head-initial and head-final language groups favour suffixing but prefixing only occurs productively in head-initial languages.

2.1.2 Hawkins and Gilligan (1988)

The work of Hawkins and Gilligan (1988) has considerably improved on the quality of Greenberg's universals by putting meat on the skeletal corpus of the 1966 study. Hawkins and Gilligan's sample comprises around 200 languages, drawn from three separate samples collected by Stassen, Perkins, and Gilligan.[4] On the basis of these data, some of Greenberg's claims need to be modified. For example his Universal 27 is accurate only in the second clause; of the four logical possibilities for the first implicational statement, the zero cell of the standard tetrachoric table in (3) (i.e. *[+exclusive suffixing →
−postp]) is in fact filled in both Stassen's and Gilligan's data.

(3) Implicational table predicting co-occurence
of affix and adposition types

	− Postp	*+ Postp*
− Exclusive suffixing	+/−	+/−
+ Exclusive suffixing	−	+

Stassen records eighteen exclusively suffixing languages in his 113 language sample which are prepositional and Gilligan finds five such examples in his sample of fifty languages. According to Hawkins and Gilligan's (henceforth H&G's) data, the second clause of Universal 27 holds cross-linguistically (but not quite absolutely: one of Stassen's four prefixing-only languages does appear in a postpositional language). The figures are as in (4) and (5) (from H&G).[5]

(4) Stassen's sample: Number of languages with
affix position correlated with adposition order

	Prefix only	*Both*	*Suffix only*	*None*
Prep	3	18	18	11
Postp	1	18	29	3

42 Morphology and mind

(5) Gilligan's sample: Number of languages with
affix position correlated with adposition order

	Prefix only	Both	Suffix only	None
Prep	2	22	5	1
Postp	–	10	10	–

The suggestion in Greenberg's data that almost all Postp languages
are exclusively suffixing and that almost all Prep languages employ
both prefixes *and* suffixes seems also to be too strong. Stassen's
sample shows twenty-nine Postp languages which are exclusively
suffixing (out of fifty-one overall); Gilligan has ten out of twenty overall.
This suggests that around 55 per cent of Postp languages are exclusively
suffixing. As for Prep languages, Stassen records eighteen languages of
fifty overall which employ both types of affix; Gilligan records twenty-
two, of thirty languages. The figures correlating verb position with
affixation position show a remarkably similar picture. Taken together
these sets of data suggest that even in head-first languages the suffixing
preference is strongly felt. The general trends in H&G's data are
summarised in (6) and (7) (adapted from tables on pp. 228ff).

(6) Affix position type correlated with word order type
(% languages)

	Exclusive prefixing	Exclusive suffixing	Both
VO	10.0	17	73.0
OV	–	62	38.0
Prep	7.0	21	72.0
Postp	0.7	65	34.3

(7) Ratio of prefixing to suffixing correlated
with word order type (% languages)

	Prefixing	Suffixing
VO	43.0	57.0
OV	17.5	82.5
Prep	38.5	61.5
Postp	19.0	81.0

All in all, H&G's extended sample yields a far more robust set of
generalisations than Greenberg's; however, the overriding tendencies,
summarised in (8), are the same:

Morphological regularity 43

(8) Morphological Regularities
    (a) i. Languages which are exclusively suffixing are considerably more frequent than those which are exclusively prefixing.
      ii. Across languages, suffixal morphology is more frequent than both prefixing and infixing, i.e. more functions are expressed by suffixes than by prefixes or infixes.
    (b) i. If a language is exclusively prefixing, it is prepositional (one exception) and verb-initial.
      ii. Around 60 per cent of postpositional and verb-final languages are exclusively suffixing; the majority of prepositional and verb-initial languages are both prefixing and suffixing.

H&G propose a set of principles to account for why, on the one hand, exclusive prefixing occurs only in head-initial languages, and on the other (contradicting this tendency), languages show an overriding preference for suffixing. They claim that the answer to the first question is part of a general organising principle for natural languages, and they characterise this regularity as the Head Ordering Principle (HOP) which states:

(9) Head Ordering Principle
    The affixal head of a word is ordered on the same side of its subcategorized modifier(s), as P is ordered relative to NP within PP, and as a V is ordered relative to a direct object NP.
    (p. 227)

Thus, in the same way that in syntax, cross-linguistically, modifiers tend to cluster across categories (cf. Hawkins 1983: 97ff), we seem to be observing a tendency word-internally for the heads of *words* to fall in with this regularity. It is assumed by H&G that, in fact, *affixes* constitute the heads of words (although this will be disputed in the next chapter, chapter 3).

According to H&G, the HOP accounts for the preference for exclusive prefixing in Prep/VO languages; however, it does not predict the skew towards suffixing in both language types. To account for this, H&G propose a collection of counterprinciples to the HOP – different from the HOP in that they refer to specific functional categories expressed typically as affixes. What these eleven counterprinciples do is simply to identify a particular affix function (e.g., plural on nouns or tense on verbs) and specify a preference for suffixing for that function: see (10). Where this preference conflicts

44 *Morphology and mind*

with the HOP (i.e. cases in which suffixing appears in VO/Prep languages) the counterprinciple wins out in eight out of eleven cases – the percentages given in (10) represent the proportion of languages adhering to the counterprinciple over the HOP (data from H&G: 234–5).

(10) Summary of counterprinciples to the HOP

Categories suffixed	Strength (%)
1 Gender on N	60
2 Case on N	100
3 Plural on N	72
4 Nominalisers on N	86
5 Definiteness on N	56
6 Indefiniteness on N	50
7 Tense on V	48
8 Mood on V	52
9 Valence on V	100
10 Causatives on V	42
11 Aspect on V	46

For any of these categories, the percentage of languages *not* accounted for by either the HOP or the relevant counterprinciple is no higher than 9 per cent, and is 3 per cent or less for seven of the eleven functions. In addition to the details in (10), it should be noted that other functions studied, namely possessives on N and negative, voice and person (subject and object) on V, may appear as either prefixes or suffixes with either word order; these facts are not accounted for, although they are acknowledged. H&G's descriptive account of the data in the sample is confined to the functions listed in (10) and their interaction with the HOP. We turn now to an evaluation of these data and principles, and sound a few cautionary notes.

2.2 PROBLEMS WITH THE DATA AND UNIVERSALS

One of the major potential problems with the data is the form in which they reach H&G, and subsequently, us. They are, in a sense, 'sanitised' in that they come without specification of either quantity, scope or sources, or the criteria used to determine canonical forms. Presumably research methods and evaluation criteria should be held constant across languages so that we know we are dealing with roughly comparable data sets, although it is difficult to see how this could be so controlled, given the divergence of methodological and

Morphological regularity   45

theoretical aproaches taken by grammar-writers. A further complication is that within languages, methods of data collection and criteria for their selection and categorisation must be flexible enough (within predetermined limits) to take into account the specific socio-cultural framework within which the language is used. These requirements hold for the affix position data and also for the word order data with which they are correlated.

It is a general problem with word order typology that the criteria which decide which word order is *basic* are not always strictly defined, neither for a single language nor cross-linguistically. Typically, general notions of markedness and complexity are invoked, and usually frequency of occurrence plays a major role. From a psychological perspective, we may also look at child language acquisition, where much is made of the canonical sentence schema, defined by Slobin and Bever (1982: 231) as 'the neutral sentence type which transmits new information ... the simple active affirmative declarative'. Under their formulation, Givón's (1979: 49) notion of 'discourse presuppositionality' plays a much more important role than frequency:

> Canonical forms are not the most frequent, since input contains a high proportion of questions, imperatives, fragments, and focused forms. And even among declaratives, canonical forms are not always in the majority – for example, although SVO sentences predominate in English, in Turkish only 48% of simple sentences are in canonical SOV order in our sample of adult speech to preschool children. What is important is that they require the least processing of implicit discourse presuppositions in addition to the basic semantic content of the sentence.

If, as Slobin and Bever suggest, we do not base canonical order on frequency (although even in the Turkish example cited, presumably SOV is more frequent than any other single word order) but instead, if we try to quantify 'implicit discourse presuppositions' and the processing thereof, we are straying even further from an objectively verifiable cross-linguistic measure. But such factors do have to be taken into consideration: whenever linguists claim that language x has word order y, they are making a claim about a particular configuration which necessarily has psycholinguistic (and possibly sociolinguistic[6]) implications. It seems *crucial* that before we start counting languages, we should be as certain as possible that the claims we are making for each language do in fact hold.

This caution seems warranted when we look at H&G's data and

46 *Morphology and mind*

descriptive principles. The patterns are formulated to account for affixing patterns in data from around 200 languages; however, the patterns given are abstracted from the raw data, such that the factors spelled out above (i.e., the quantity, scope and sources of the data, and the criteria used to determine canonical forms) are, at least, obscured, if they are recoverable at all. The *quantity* of the lexical items used to count affix positions for each language is not available: for really robust data, we should expect that a sizeable corpus of words would be required. What, though, is to be the *source* of such a corpus? If it is *written* (a dictionary or collection of texts) then can one be sure that unwelcome skews in the figures will not arise from, for example, a disproportionate number of rare or esoteric technical words (which are typically polymorphemic)? If one uses spoken data (e.g., native intuitions or discourse data), who is talking to whom (cf. note 6)? Also, which forms are being counted (i.e. what is the *scope* of our data)? If the corpus is restricted to verbs, and nouns are ignored (as in Bybee 1985), or if inflections are concentrated on and derivations ignored (because the latter are harder to identify, as both Bybee and H&G acknowledge), how can one be sure that significant counterexamples to claims for the subset examined have not been missed?

In addition, the criteria on which the data are selected, and subsequently systematised, must be made clear. In selecting inflections, for example, one must be sure that there is a sound basis for determining the distinction between inflectional and derivational morphemes. (And before this, one must be able to define what is meant by 'morpheme': for example, are *hither, whither, thither* (cf. *hence, whence, thence; here, where, there*) counted as polymorphemic or monomorphemic in English? If it is decided that they have two morphemes, do *h-*, *th-*, and *wh-* count as prefixes, or *-ither* as a suffix?) In determining whether language x is exclusively suffixing or exclusively prefixing, presumably the measure is strict: one counterexample (discounting certain cases such as unanalysed polymorphemic loan words) is enough to put it into the third class, i.e. languages which use both. But if this is true, then the mixed camp is going to fudge significant differences, because it will include, say, language x which is 99 per cent suffixing, 1 per cent prefixing; language y which is 50 per cent suffixing, 50 per cent prefixing; and language z which is 1 per cent suffixing, 99 per cent prefixing.

Regarding H&G's collection of suffixing principles, there are further reservations, arising from the fact that they refer to specific functional categories. Identifying these categories in the first place is

Morphological regularity 47

not without problems – often categories expressed by affixes are conflated (as in tense and aspect in English) or imprecise. Assuming, however, that the categories referred to in the counterprinciples to the HOP do reflect more or less discrete properties associated with discrete forms, we still need to ascertain what is the precise status of these categories compared with those that allow both suffixing *and* prefixing in either word order type (i.e. those categories listed following (10))? It is not enough simply to count the suffixing categories and the 'anything goes' categories and compare the totals; nor is it enough to look at the relative strength of the counterprinciples to the HOP across languages. What we really need to know is what these totals and strengths represent: we need to know the productivity of each affix category within (and subsequently across) languages, and also the relative frequency of each category within (and across) languages.[7] Only when answers to these questions are forthcoming can one be 100 per cent sure that the counterprinciples will predict the observed suffixing tendency.

The drawbacks inherent in the methodology employed in the universal–typological 'many languages' approach are many. It is clear, though, that the criticisms levelled above make demands on its practitioners which are logistically rather too exacting. The depth of analysis of particular languages that is called for here is usually obtainable only given a 'limited languages' approach (such as Chomsky's); it is an unfortunate methodological irony that the success of the former approach depends very much on the strength of the latter, and the strength of the latter may only be assessed empirically by appeal to the former. However, given the general success of the many languages approach in identifying significant properties of language structure, as, for example, documented by Comrie (1981), and given the care taken in the H&G sampling, we may be more than moderately confident that H&G's statistics do reflect real phenomena in human language, although it is only right to bear these caveats in mind in the evaluation of work of this type.

Returning to H&G's account for the affixing data, we can see that as they stand, the counterprinciples to the HOP seem to range over an arbitrary collection of affixal categories. H&G presumably feel that the identification of different affixal categories provides a more transparent basis for establishing the positional distribution of affixes. The categories have, then, *methodological* significance; however, they contribute little to our *understanding* of the positional distribution and do not figure in the transition from descriptive to explanatory levels (cf. Cutler *et al.* 1985). It seems to me that unless

48 *Morphology and mind*

an explanation is proposed which makes reference to the specific functional categories cited, we might as well collapse them and simply propose one descriptive counterprinciple to the HOP. This could then be stated as follows:

> (11) Suffixing Principle
> Bound morphemes are added to the ends rather than the beginnings of words, with greater than chance frequency.

This seems to capture the fundamental generalisation that 'the counterprinciples always reinforce the HOP's independent predictions for suffixing, and oppose its predictions for prefixing' (H&G: 235). The associated processing explanation for the suffixing preference (Cutler *et al.* 1985), which followed the descriptive work of H&G but preceded its publication, is equally applicable to *all* affix functions included in the H&G sample and so is not specifically linked to its explanandum, i,e. the series of counterprinciples listed in (10). Rather, it explains the more general formulation in (11). The problem is that although the principles in (10) might suffice as albeit *ad hoc descriptive* principles, they are totally unmotivated when it comes to defining the linkage between them and the explanatory hypothesis.

This problem with the Cutler *et al.* account is manifest also with respect to the HOP. This, too, is a *descriptive* principle (though not, this time, an *ad hoc* one), and in this case *no* explanation is offered which may underlie it; indeed, for Cutler *et al.* the HOP *itself* explains the basic pattern of the data. In chapter 3, I investigate the status of the HOP and in so doing attempt to delineate further the distinction between description and explanation in linguistics.

3 Affixes and heads

In their analysis of cross-linguistic patterns of affixing, H&G observe, apart from the overall skewing in favour of suffixation, a partial correlation between the predominant (or exclusive) positioning of affixes (as either prefixes or suffixes) and the dominant order of syntactic head and modifier, particularly in the VP and PP. The table in (7), chapter 2, shows the overall ratio of prefixing to suffixing in the H&G sample, correlated with verb position and adposition ordering. The ratios for *exclusively* prefixing to *exclusively* suffixing languages are very similar: cf. (6), chapter 2. Also, of all the implicational universals constructed by H&G relating basic word order to affix position for the morphological categories studied, none contradicts the observation of head/affix correlation: 'NP + Po and/or SOV always implies suffixing, never prefixing; and prefixing implies Pr + NP and/or V̈, never NP + Po and/or SOV' (p. 228).

To account for this harmony between syntactic and morphological ordering, they adopt the position that 'derivational and inflectional affixes are always the heads of their respective lexical categories' (p. 226). Since, then, the affix is 'head' of the word, it obeys a general head ordering principle, formulated by H&G as follows, which obtains in both the syntax and the morphology (repeated here from (9) in chapter 2 for convenience):

(1) Head Ordering Principle
The affixal head of a word is ordered on the same side of its subcategorized modifier(s), as P is ordered relative to NP within PP, and as a V is ordered relative to a direct object NP.

The basic tenet underlying the HOP is that the affix is the head of the word since 'the categorial status of a word containing affixes can regularly be computed from the affix, whereas non-affixes or stems will very often have their categorial status changed through the

50 *Morphology and mind*

addition of a (derivational) affix' (p. 226). In this regard, they claim, heads in the morphology are identical as a category with heads in the syntax, which determine the categorial status of the phrase. Consequently, they assume that they will also behave identically in terms of ordering typology, hence the HOP. Cutler *et al.* (1985) advance this principle as 'part of the explanatory package' for the patterns in the cross-linguistic data.

The primary purpose of this chapter is to enquire into the validity of this particular principle by examining the notion 'head of a word'; I conclude that the HOP is, in fact, invalid as a descriptive principle. Since in any case descriptive principles cannot 'explain' structural patterns, in the sense of explanation offered in the unified approach (chapter 1), I explore, briefly, a combination of diachronic and psycholinguistic factors which may explain the correlation between affix/stem and syntactic head/modifier serialisation. Section 3.1 critically evaluates syntactic definitions of the notion 'head of a word' advanced in the literature, concluding that few of the proposals are adequate and proposing an alternative definition. This definition, along with the others discussed, does not coincide with the one underlying the HOP, since it does not assume that the category AFF (affix) has inherently the property of headship, and it allows for cases where the categorial status of an affixed word is not and cannot be computed from the affix. Semantic definitions are also briefly discussed, and these too are judged inadequate and, in any case, not compatible with H&G's definition. Section 3.2 discusses cross-linguistic factors, examining the role of heads in universal/typological theories, and introduces the idea that natural diachronic change might have led to the patterning of the data, rather than some synchronic identity or isomorphism between syntactic and morphological systems, as conceived in the HOP. Next, section 3.3 examines syntactic head serialisation and its correlation with affix serialisation from a psychological perspective, showing that the HOP is unsupported on learnability grounds. Section 3.4 draws some general conclusions.

3.1 THE NOTION 'HEAD OF A WORD'

The literature which touches on the problem of heads in syntax and morphology is a sometimes confused and confusing collection of ideas from various semantic, syntactic and morphological theories or schools of thought. Traditional, non-generative linguists typically take a combined semantic/syntactic approach to heads in syntax (e.g. Jespersen 1924; Vennemann 1974) and, when they discuss it, in morphology too (Zwicky, 1985), whereas linguists working within the Chomskyan framework (e.g. Chomsky 1970; Jackendoff 1977; Selkirk 1982; Williams 1981) and other generative models (e.g. Gazdar and Pullum 1982) take into consideration strictly syntactic factors. We concentrate in our discussion on *syntactic* definitions of headship (3.1.1), since the HOP expresses a syntactic generalisation, but semantic headship will also be examined (3.1.2).

3.1.1 Syntactic approaches

In chapter 1 I stressed the deficiencies in Chomsky's generative theory of linguistics with regard to its explanatory claims, but applauded its success in providing a consistent, thorough, cognitively-informed framework for description. The almost exclusive reliance on the tools of generative syntax and morphology in this section follows naturally from the requirement that rigorous descriptive analysis of the data play a crucial part in the explanatory process as conceived in the unified approach. In line with this approach, later sections will exploit the descriptive analysis provided here in an evaluation of the *explanatory* validity of the HOP.

3.1.1.1 *X' syntax and percolation*

A basic assumption of many morphologists working in the generative tradition (e.g., Selkirk 1982; Williams 1981; Lieber 1980; Scalise 1984) is that words are essentially similar to syntactic phrases, in that their head features 'percolate' to the node which dominates them in some phrase structure-type tree. The notion of percolation of head features was one of the initial motivations for the development of the theory of X' (X-bar) syntax, which I now turn to as a brief prelude to our discussion of heads at the lexical level.

In his *Introduction to Theoretical Linguistics* (1968), Lyons pointed out a major inadequacy in phrase structure grammar:

> Phrase-stucture grammars fail to formalize the fact that NP and VP are not merely mnemonically-convenient symbols, but stand for sentence-constituents which are necessarily nominal and verbal, respectively, because they have N and V as an obligatory major constituent. ... What is required, and what was assumed in traditional grammar, is some way of relating sentence-constituents of the form XP to X (where X is any major category: N, V, etc.). (p. 331)

52 Morphology and mind

He noted, for example, that nothing in traditional phrase stucture theory excludes rules such as NP → V + VP: a nominal element in the expansion of NP should be *obligatory*. The generalisation is that within every syntactic phrase, one of its constituent members has a special status, in that it shares categorial (and other) features with the entire phrase, or, put differently, it *determines* the features of the phrase, via feature 'percolation'. In the example given in (2), the nominal features of *border* percolate from the terminal N through the N' to the entire lower N" (= NP), similarly with *handkerchief* and the preposition with.

(2)

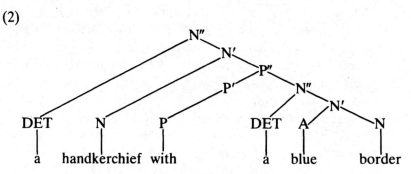

In Chomsky's formulation, the nodes of PS trees in X' Syntax represent feature bundles. The major ('lexical') categories N, V, A, P percolate the features [+N, −V], [−N, +V], [+N, +V], and [−N, −V] respectively to the phrases of which they are 'heads' (viz. N" (NP), V" (VP), A" (ADJP), P" (PP)). In addition, selectional, thematic, and subcategorial features percolate from the head; inflectional categories such as case on nouns or number on verbs also percolate to the phrasal level. Chomsky (1970) suggested that, in the base component of the syntax, head-modifier configurations can be generalised across the lexical categories according to the following rules for English:

(3) X" → SpecX − X'
    X' → X − CompX

The Spec(ifier) and Comp(lement) positions are abbreviations for material which precedes or follows the head of the Phrase (i.e. X), as in the following examples (from Scalise 1984: 186):

(4)	Spec	X	Comp	
(i)	this	professor	of chemistry	(N")
(ii)	having	read	that book	(V")
(iii)	very	useful	to smokers	(A")
(iv)	much	behind	the target	(P")

Affixes and heads 53

Chomsky 's argument for X′ Syntax is based partly on the recognition that certain verb/derived noun pairs such as *hate/hatred* share identical selectional restrictions (Chomsky 1970). Consider, for example:

(5) a. The Procurator hated the smell of attar of roses.
  b. The Procurator's hatred of the smell of attar of roses.

The set of possessive nouns selectionally appropriate for the head noun in (5b) is identical to the set of subjects of the verb in (5a); similarly, the set of objects of the prepositional phrase modifying the head noun in (5b) is identical to the set of objects of the verb in (5a). Chomsky argued that this cross-category generalisation must be realised not in the syntax by lexical transformation as had been assumed up to that point, but in the lexicon itself – this was the basis of the 'Lexicalist Hypothesis' (cf. Scalise 1984, for a detailed account of the development of the lexical component in generative grammar).

So, for Chomsky, *hate* and *hatred* share a single lexical entry, unmarked for categorial features. These features are filled in upon lexical insertion: when inserted under a V node, the phonological realisation will be *hate*; under a N node, it will he *hatred*. Alternatively, Jackendoff (1975) allots the forms separate lexical entries related by redundancy rule. The specific formulation of the lexical component of the grammar is not, however, of crucial concern here; what is important is that, for the first time in the development of the theory, major restrictions were placed on the power of the transformational component, and consequently the base (PS rules) and lexical component had to be enriched. This enrichment was effected in the development of the X′ system in the syntactic base component as well as in the recognition of an autonomous system of word formation rules in the lexicon.[1]

In her 1982 monograph, Selkirk sets out an X′ Syntax of *words* ('W-Syntax') which incorporates the X′ notion of multiple 'phrasal' levels and the percolation of features through these levels. In her formulation, the X^0 (= X) level of structure is a level shared by both the syntax and the morphology – this is the level of WORD. This contention that 'W-syntactic (i.e. morphological) categories are entities that are formally identical in character to syntactic categories' is of particular interest in the light of H&G's proposal of head identity across the morphological and syntactic components, and the definition of syntactic head implicit in X-bar syntax. We therefore pursue Selkirk's theory in some depth in the following pages (although we are not directly concerned with the ramifications of the W-syntactic

54 *Morphology and mind*

approach for other aspects of morphological theory; see Scalise 1984, for some of the problems it poses).

In Selkirk's model, words are combined to make syntactic phrases of X^n, $n>0$, and, below X^0, morphemes are combined at X^n, $n<0$, to make words.

(6)

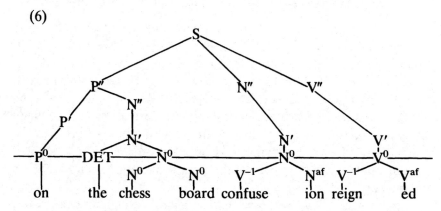

In the example given in (6), the horizontal line represents the interface between the phrase syntax (above the line) and the word syntax (below the line). Stems are of category X^{-1} and affixes are of special status X^{af}, which, for reasons that do not concern us here, does not correlate with a particular level of the X' hierarchy, but is below X^0 (note also that elements of compounds are of word level X^0 to allow for recursive expansion in such cases). In Selkirk's model each word has a head morpheme which bears the same features as the word as a whole just as in the phrasal syntax, according to the general schemata (1982: 9) given in (7):

(7) $X^n \rightarrow \Psi\ X^m\ Y^p\ \varphi$
$X^n \rightarrow \Psi\ Y^p\ X^m\ \varphi$
where X, Y are variables standing for complexes of categorial features, both syntactic and diacritic, and $0 \geqslant n \geqslant m, p$.

The bar levels of X and Y are represented by n, m, p and Ψ and φ are variables over category symbols (including 'af'). The generalisation expressed by (7) is intended to stipulate that each word (X^n) has a head (X^m) which shares the same features. The syntactic and diacritic features mentioned here are the syntactic category features discussed earlier, and other inflectional or derivational features, of which (+/− past], [+/− fem], [+/− pl] are examples of the former, and [+/− latinate], [+/− learned] of the latter. The features carried by the head of the word are percolated to the X^0 level. In Selkirk's model this is formulated as a well-formedness condition, as in (8).

(8) Percolation

If a constituent $\propto$ is the head of a constituent β, $\propto$ and β are associated with an identical set of features (syntactic and diacritic). (p. 21)

By this condition, a constituent (word or phrase) is ill-formed if its features differ from those of the head. The head could be interpreted, then, as that constituent in a word or phrase which shares its features with those of the word or phrase to which it is daughter (effectively making the percolation principle as formulated here redundant, or giving it the status of a 'checking' device to filter out ill-formed structures, given free generation in the word formation rule system (cf. case-checking in Chomskyan syntax)). Mysteriously, Selkirk does not derive such an interpretation from her percolation condition; instead, she adopts a modified version of Williams's positional criterion (Williams 1981) – a definition which I critically examine and ultimately reject in the next section.

3.1.1.2 The positional criterion

Selkirk follows Williams (1981) by defining heads of words in terms of *position* within the word structure. Williams's definition is based on the observation that most category-changing affixation in English follows the stem (i.e. suffixation), and thus he proposes that the right-hand element of a word is its head:

(9) Righthand Head Rule (RHR)

The head of a morphologically complex word [is] the right-hand member of that word. (1981: 248)

Crucially, the criterion for headship here is *position*, not percolation. Williams points out that, generally, suffixes determine category (indeed, he assigns them category status: eg. *-ish* is of category A, *-ise* of category V, and *-ion* of category N) whereas prefixes do not (e.g. *counter-* + *revolution*$_N$/*argue*$_V$/*productive*$_A$); however, he also makes the strong claim that:

[P]refixes cannot be assigned to lexical categories because *they never occupy head position*, and thus the language learner will never have any grounds for assigning them to a particular category. (p. 249; my emphasis)

In what follows I present two arguments against the positional criterion: (i) that it incorrectly predicts that inflections (for many

56 Morphology and mind

languages) will be heads; and (ii) that it does not account for all of the data, even in English, in that not all heads appear in the same position. The first point constitutes a direct argument against the HOP in that inflections are affixes, and so should follow the HOP; the second allows us to arrive ultimately at a more accurate universal definition of head which is incompatible with the HOP hypothesis.

A consequence of Williams's treatment of heads of words is that inflections will be heads in English. In fact, he argues for this independently of the issue of position, presenting as evidence the behaviour of tense and case in the syntax. He claims that tense is the head of S, because (i) it is needed as a feature of S to account for the distribution of the complementisers *that* (——S_{+T}) and *for* (——S_{-T}); and (ii) the rule of gapping, he argues, deletes only heads, and applies to tense in examples such as the pair in (10).

(10) a. *J. is reading Cicero, and B. is, Caesar.
    b. J. is reading Cicero, and B. studying Caesar.

He infers from this that the inflectional morpheme which carries tense is the head of the word of which it is part, since it must percolate its inflectional features ultimately to the S-node, and only *head* features percolate.

The evidence from percolation seems strong, given Williams's assumptions: if the S-node is to carry the feature tense, and this feature is marked by inflectional affixation, then it must percolate from the morphology through the syntactic tree to the maximal node, assuming that S is ultimately the maximal projection of V (an assumption, incidentally, that Williams fails to make explicit[2]). For example, in the sentences in (11), *that* requires a subordinate S_{+T} and *for* a subordinate S_{-T}:

(11) a. He is the man [that cited the answer$_{+T}$].
        He is the man [*for cited the answer$_{+T}$].
    b. He was rewarded [for citing the answer$_{-T}$].
        He was rewarded [*that citing the answer$_{-T}$].

However, the fact that inflectional features percolate to the word level does not necessarily entail that inflections are *heads* – it will be argued below that only the percolation of categorial (and subcategorial) features qualify the percolator for head status. The evidence from the gapping phenomenon is also insubstantial. Consider the contrast between (10) and (12), pointed out to me by Doug Pulleyblank (p.c.).

Affixes and heads 57

(12) a. John is applying to USC, just as Bill is, to UCLA.
     b. *John is applying to USC, just as Bill to UCLA.

If gapping deletes only heads, and tense is a head, then (12b) is wrongly predicted as grammatical and (12a) as ungrammatical. Furthermore, on the positional issue, languages other than English contradict Williams's stipulation that 'tense occurs strictly in head position'. Scalise (1988) points out that in the Italian verb, for example, the right-hand slot is filled by person/number, not tense, as in (13).

(13) ama **+** v **+** o **=** 'I was loving'
           [tense] [person/
                     number]

Moreover, Bybee's work on morphological universals (reported in Bybee 1985), implies that many more languages than Italian must regularly express tense in what for Williams is a non-head position. Her thesis is that when tense is expressed in an affix it is preferentially located close to the stem, with only affixes expressing aspect intervening. Since many languages employ strings of affixes on the verb expressing many other functions apart from tense and aspect, it follows that tense suffixes will not always occupy the rightmost position in the morphemic string; indeed, in morphologically rich languages they will only *rarely* occupy this position.

The evidence for positionally defined headship from case is also weak: Williams claims that (i) case is always realised on the head N of a NP; and (ii) case is always suffixed (I assume he means cross-linguistically, since he presumably cannot mean to argue that inflections are heads on the basis of only one language). With regard to (i), there is no independent evidence that case affixes explicitly carry nominal categorial features other than the circular reasoning that they are heads and therefore must have categorial features to percolate; even if case *did* carry categorial features, surely the identical features of the stem are not there only for decorative purposes, and could themselves percolate, rendering any such features on the inflection completely redundant.

With regard to (ii), firstly, this claim attempts to support the theory (that right-hand – in this case inflectional – elements are heads) by appealing to its own terms, i.e., because case is inflectional, and because it appears as a suffix, then inflections are heads, because heads appear as suffixes. Secondly, the claim is not true: although H&G find case suffixed in all the languages they sampled, it appears

58 *Morphology and mind*

that it is prefixed in at least Squamish, Shuswap, Kalispel, Chontal, Biblical Hebrew, Zhilha, Sabaic, Zapotec, Zulu, Luvale, Sakao, Cua, and Temiar (Matthew Dryer, p.c.). Even if case *were* exclusively marked by suffixes cross-linguistically, this would not constitute evidence for the headship of inflections, because many other inflectional features, such as tense, plurality, and definiteness are prefixed in a great number of languages (H&G).

Most varieties of the Lexicalist Hypothesis hold that regular inflections are affixed by rules operating after derivation. They are seen as essentially different from derivational affixes in that they do not have associated with them the features associated with lexical categories (i.e. heads) (cf. Scalise 1988). This distinction is recognised explicitly, and for the first time is motivated by independent grammatical considerations, in a paper by Borer (1984). Here she reinterprets Chomsky's (1981) Projection Principle in a way which yields external evidence for the Lexicalist Hypothesis (i.e. that words are derived in the lexical component) and for the distinction between derivation and inflection, allowing inflection to take place in the syntax. It follows from her discussion that inflections are not morphological heads. The Projection Principle (proposed as a principle of UG and presumably now subsumable under the principle of FI discussed by Chomsky 1989 (cf. 1.2.2)), given here as (14), ensures that lexical features such as those of Selkirk (above) must be represented at every syntactic level.

> (14) Projection Principle (PrPr)
> Lexical features must be represented at every syntactic level.
> (Borer 1984: 17)

So, for example, the relevant lexical features of the verb *hit*, in a sentence such as (15) are approximately those of (16) (from Borer 1984: 17).

> (15) John hit Mary
> (16) a. *hit* assigns case (accusative)
>   b. *hit* assigns 2 θ-roles (agent–patient)
>   c. *hit* is subcategorised for an adjacent NP
>   d. *hit* is a verb
>   e. *hit* means HIT

Borer argues that the PrPr is a condition on features, not on rules, and that, given this, we may distinguish rules in the grammar whose output either conforms to or violates the PrPr. For example, consider (17).

Affixes and heads 59

(17) a. [enjoy$_v$] → [enjoyable$_A$]
     category change, case → Ø
   b. [drop$_{Vunacc}$] → [drop$_{Vcause}$]
     add case, add θ-causer
   c. [inhabited] → [uninhabited]
     semantic changes

In these examples the output of some rule of affixation (in (b), zero derivation (see below)) has a different set of inherent features associated with it, i.e. one or more feature is added to or eliminated from the input set, thereby violating the PrPr. Borer concludes that such rules must operate within the lexical component.

As examples of rules which conform to the PrPr, she presents the set listed in (18).

(18) a. [hit] → [hits]
       2pers 3pers
   b. [witch] → [witches]
       sing   pl
   c. [drop] → [dropped]
       pres   past

Borer points out that this distinction identifies the familiar classes of derivational (17) and inflectional (18) morphemes. What this means is that derivational affixation tends to break the chain of percolation of stem features and to impose a new chain, whereas inflectional affixation always maintains stem percolation. This indicates that derivational rules apply in the lexicon and introduce heads, whereas inflectional rules apply in the syntactic component, and never introduce heads.[3]

Models of the lexicon which conform to the so-called *Strong* Lexicalist Hypothesis, which holds that inflection is handled entirely within the lexicon in a block of rules following the word formation rules (WFRs), are not, however, irreconcilable with Borer's proposals, if we specify that the PrPr applies to the output of the WFRs rather than of the lexicon as a whole. Wherever inflection is located in the grammar (Anderson 1982 for instance, argues that it is in the phonological component), it is clear that in English and most other languages it is a very different process from derivation in that its output does not violate the PrPr, and so inflections never fulfil the typical role of morphological heads, i.e. they never percolate categorial, subcategorial, or selectional features to the word level. As Scalise puts it, in response to Williams's proposal for headship in words:

60 Morphology and mind

we can easily see that inflectional morphemes do not 'determine[s] the properties of the whole', since the distributional properties of an inflected noun are determined by the lexical category and not by the inflectional morphemes ... inflectional morphemes are never heads ... (1988: 568)

In some languages, however, the distinction between the two morphological classes is not so clear. On the basis of evidence from such languages, morphologists such as Bybee (1985), Lieber (1980) and Jensen and Stong Jensen (1984), for example, have proposed that the distinction is one of *degree* rather than polarity. One apparent problem for our contention that inflections are not heads comes from the Slavonic group of languages, in which possessive adjective suffixes seem to combine both inflectional and derivational features (Corbett 1987). In particular, the suffix forms adjectives from nouns (a derivational process requiring categorial features on the affix, i.e. requiring them to be lexical heads), but also 'serve(s) as an antecedent for anaphors in a way that other derived adjectives do not', suggesting (along with other evidence) that it is inflectional.

The evidence from such cases does not, however, constitute a conclusive argument against the claim that inflections are not heads; the possessive adjective suffixes discussed here are not unequivocally inflectional (they have other derivational features such as partial non-productivity and irregularity in some languages in the group), and the existence of any morpheme types between the poles of exclusive inflection and derivation does not negate the robustness of the distinction for other languages, or even negate its genetically-interpreted universality if, following Scalise (1988), we view such cases as exhibiting features of defective paradigms on the *periphery*, i.e. not as core (= UG) phenomena. Furthermore, in keeping with the need for cognitive validation of principles of UG advocated in chapter 1, we may appeal to the work of Badecker and Caramazza (1989) who have found evidence from the area of language pathology for the cognitive reality of the inflection/derivation distinction.

Before returning to the theoretical discussion, let me present one more language example. The Finnish possessive suffix seems unambiguously inflectional (Kanerva 1987), however it appears on stems of various syntactic classes (nominals, postpositions, adjectives and non-finite verbs) but does not change their category. This, then, is at least one substantive piece of evidence for the claim that inflections do not carry categorial features which percolate to the word level, for if this were so we would need to posit at least *four* different possessive suffixes in Finnish, a highly marked analysis in comparison with the simplicity of the non-head characterisation.

Selkirk too contests the claim that inflections are heads. She points out that if we assume that they are heads, then, given cases of multiple inflection, we would need to be willing to entertain the notion of polycephalous words, an undesirable move without any precedent or justification. For example, consider the possibilities for Latin *amavit* 's/he loved' in (19).

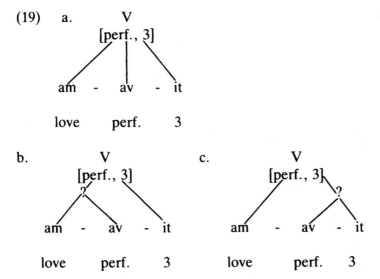

The three possibilities all involve dual headship if percolation is exclusively a feature of heads. In addition, (b) would require independent evidence to motivate the tree structure which gives prominence/scope to the last inflection: such evidence is not apparent. Further, if the inflections are heads, then in order to stipulate the category of the V^0, we would need to specify that they were all assigned categorial features, when it is vastly more simple to assume that the *stem* determines the category of the word in such cases as it does when it stands alone or occurs with non-head derivational affixes.

But, of course, if we do indeed count the stem V^{-1} *am-* as head here, how does the V^0 get its inflectional features? To answer this, Selkirk provides a revised version of percolation, given here in (20).

(20) Percolation (revised: Selkirk 1982: 76)
  a. If a head has a feature specification [$\propto F_i$], $\propto \neq$ u[nmarked], its mother node must be specified [$\propto F_i$], and vice versa.

62 *Morphology and mind*

    b. If a nonhead has the feature specification $[\propto F_j]$, and the head has the feature specification $[u\ F_j]$, then the mother node must have the feature specification $[\propto F_j]$.

This ensures that, at the word level and above, *all* features are represented (clause (b)), thereby satisfying the PrPr, but that where there is a conflict between candidate features, those of the *head* take priority (clause (a)) thereby accounting for the category-changing properties of derivational morphology, but allowing the percolation of inflectional features.

A second problem for Williams's RHR, apart from the inflectional issue, is the number of counter-examples to it (cf. Lieber 1980: 96 ff). In English there are cases in which it is not clear that the suffix is the head, e.g. the diminutive *-let* in *piglet* etc. which derives semantically modified nouns only from nouns, with no syntactic effect (cf. Marchand 1969: 228 for more examples). In Spanish the diminutive suffix *cit*+V derives nouns from nouns and adjectives from adjectives and so is clearly *not* the head (Jaeggli 1977). In English, also, there are at least eight *prefixes* which in some combinations do seem to determine the category of the word, contrary to the RHR:[4]

(21) $[\text{dis-}_V]$ + $[\text{courage}_N]$ $\rightarrow [\text{discourage}_V]$
       $[\text{dis-}_V]$ + $[\text{able}_A]$ $\rightarrow [\text{disable}_V]$
       $[\text{de-}_V]$ + $[\text{louse}_N]$ $\rightarrow [\text{delouse}_V]$
       $[\text{out-}_V]$ + $[\text{wit}_N]$ $\rightarrow [\text{outwit}_V]$
       $[\text{pro-}_A]$ + $[\text{Europe}_N]$ $\rightarrow [\text{pro-Europe}_A]$
       $[\text{be-}_V]$ + $[\text{witch}_N]$ $\rightarrow [\text{bewitch}_V]$
       $[\text{be-}_V]$ + $[\text{calm}_A]$ $\rightarrow [\text{becalm}_V]$
       $[\text{en-}_V]$ + $[\text{slave}_N]$ $\rightarrow [\text{enslave}_V]$
       $[\text{a-}_A]$ + $[\text{float}_V]$ $\rightarrow [\text{afloat}_A]$
       $[\text{non-}_A]$ + $[\text{stick}_V]$ $\rightarrow [\text{non-stick}_A]$

In compounds, which are *generally* right-headed in English, there are a few exceptions to Williams's rule which are unambiguously left-headed, although they are marked, e.g.:

(22) $[\text{court}_N]$ + $[\text{martial}_A]$ $\rightarrow [\text{court martial}_N]$
      $[\text{secretary}_N]$ + $[\text{general}_A]$ $\rightarrow [\text{secretary general}_N]$

Scalise (1984), however, points out that languages like Italian 'have a large number of compounds in which the head is the leftmost element', implying that position cannot define headship in such languages. Recall also that verb-particle forms in English such as *ring up* and *put upon* are of category V, not P. Further counter-evidence comes from the notion of 'potentiation'. Williams contends that for an affix to potentiate another affix (i.e. for the presence of one affix to be a necessary condition for the presence of another), the potentiator must be in head position. For example, *-able* and *-al* potentiate *-ity* in *affordability* and *tropicality*. Unfortunately for Williams's theory, as he himself acknowledges, there are affixes in prefix position in English which potentiate other affixes: *en-* potentiates *-ment* in *enjoyment*, and *de-* and *-ise* potentiate each other in *decasualise*. Scalise (1988: 575) points out similar examples in Italian.

3.1.1.3 A revised definition of headship

Despite the fact that percolation of categorial features seems the central criterion for Selkirk's definition of lexical headship, she still adopts Williams's RHR, but in revised form so as to exclude inflections from head position (and also to ensure that the verb–particle collocations such as *grow up* and *step out* have the *verb* as head rather than the particle):

(23) RHR (revised: Selkirk 1982)
In a word-internal configuration

where X stands for a syntactic feature complex and where Q contains no category with the feature complex X, X^m is the head of X^n.

Selkirk claims that her revised RHR accounts for left-hand heads as well as right-hand heads, because the prefix in these cases *is* the rightmost element within the word which shares its syntactic features with the mother X^0 node, thereby satisfying the definition in (23). The P and Q variables range, then, over zero and non-head elements. For example, consider the structures in (24).

With Selkirk's revisions of the RHR (23) and the percolation principle (20), the positional criterion clearly becomes redundant: there is now no reason to refer to the position of the head. Indeed, if we alter the configuration in (23) so that the labels Q and P are exchanged, i.e., so that the definition following the configuration refers to the *left*-hand element, it becomes a *LHR* (Left-hand Head

64 *Morphology and mind*

(24)

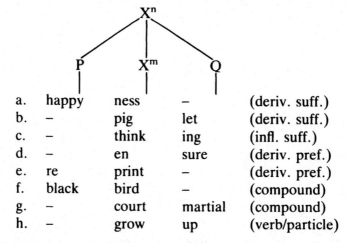

	P	X^m	Q	
a.	happy	ness	–	(deriv. suff.)
b.	–	pig	let	(deriv. suff.)
c.	–	think	ing	(infl. suff.)
d.	–	en	sure	(deriv. pref.)
e.	re	print	–	(deriv. pref.)
f.	black	bird	–	(compound)
g.	–	court	martial	(compound)
h.	–	grow	up	(verb/particle)

Rule) and yet covers exactly the same data because of the prohibition on identity of Q with the features of X, as stipulated in the definition. If, as the RHR, the definition explains the stem headship of inflected forms in English *and* the verb headship of verb–particle collocations, then a LHR must do the same. The only motivation for giving special status to Q is that in *English* heads tend to occur at the right edge of the word. As we shall see confirmed in section 3.2, a universal definition of lexical head cannot refer to position. In a reckless mix of metaphors, one might say that with regard to their heads, languages can be ambidextrous.

Let us, then, dispense with the positional criterion and specify instead that the head of the word is, simply, the element which percolates its categorial features according to (20) to the X^0 level. A cross-component element 'head' may be characterised, then, as in (25).

(25) A cross-component definition of head[5]
In the configuration

(P) X^{n-1} (Q)

where X, P, Q are category symbols,
X^{n-1} is the head of X^n.

In the syntax, X will always range over the set of lexical categories N, V, A, and P; however, the presence of one of these lexical categories in a phrase will not necessarily guarantee that *it* is the head of that phrase. For example, in the NP 'a ghastly business' the adjective *ghastly* is not the head of the phrase, even though it is a lexical category and is head in the phrase 'perfectly ghastly' – the actual head is, of course, the noun *business* since the base rule NP → (DET) (A) N stipulates, in accordance with the X′ expansion condition, that N is the head of NP. In the morphology, however, although X will range over the categories STEM and AFF as it does over the lexical categories in the syntax, the headship of each individual stem or affix will be determined not by general rule referring to the categorial formatives of the component (e.g. the w-syntactic rules of Selkirk), as they are by the base rules in the syntax, but by the particular word formation rule which introduces it. If an affix has categorial features associated with it, then these will percolate and so the affix will be deemed a head; if the affix has no categorial features, then those of the stem will percolate, and the stem will be construed as the head of the word. This is similar to the proposal made by Lieber (1980), although there are no WFRs in her formulation; instead, elements from the lexicon are inserted into unlabelled binary tree structures generated by a single rewrite rule. Information in separate lexical entries for affixes *and* stems specifies the categorial and, for affixes, subcategorial features. However, in her formulation as in this, the notion of headship is derived from a series of feature percolation conventions.

Between (20) and (25), then, we have a definition of headship: (25) states that the head is the obligatory constituent which determines category in the expansion of a non-terminal node (word or phrase) in a tree, and (20) characterises the mechanism by which this is ensured (also allowing for the percolation of features from non-heads, specifically inflections). Which element in an actual phrase or word constitutes the head is determined ultimately, however, by the rule by which it is introduced, or possibly, for words, the specifications within its lexical entry. At the word level, an affix will always be head *if* it has categorial features associated with it; in contrast it is not possible to determine the headship of individual stems or of the syntactic categories to which they belong outside of the structures in which they are situated.

3.1.1.4 Assessment

In this section I examined the major proposals in the literature relating to the notion 'head of a word', starting out with a discussion of the notion of head in syntax, in the X′ system of Chomsky's generative model, and how Selkirk extended this system into the

66 *Morphology and mind*

morphological domain. The notion of percolation in both syntax and the lexicon was examined, and it was proposed that this mechanism was more valid as a defining feature of headhood than the positional criterion proposed by Williams and at least nominally adopted by Selkirk. As part of the case against the positional criterion, it was argued, contra Williams, that inflections are never heads, a position supported by Selkirk and Scalise amongst others; Borer's reinterpretation of the Projection Principle was also offered as independent evidence for this.

H&G's Head Ordering Principle assumes that all affixes are heads and that the affix as 'head of the word' will therefore be subject to the universal serialisation tendency that had been previously advanced only for syntactic heads. The discussion so far reveals that although the notion of head in both components seems based on a common percolation condition (see (20)), the head in the morphology is not identical with the category AFF, as H&G claim, since: (i) many times the stem is the head, rather than the affix, in that the categorial status of the word may not be computed from the affix; and (ii) inflections are *never* heads, and yet inflectional categories constitute the greater part of the pool of data on which the HOP is based. The only way we could maintain the H&G position that the head of a morphologically complex word is always the affix is if we dispense with the assumption that heads determine category. If we do this, however, we readmit Lyons's criticism (cited in 3.1.1.1 above), and lose the fundamental generalisation over the syntactic and morphological components, rendering the HOP invalid, since *it* assumes that heads are the same in both components of the grammar. A principle like the HOP which lines up affixes with syntactic heads is therefore untenable, since headship in the morphology is not inherent in the particular category of AFF as it is in the lexical categories of the syntax, but is, instead, a feature of a subset of derivational affix types and stems, as recognised in the discussion of (25) above.

3.1.2 Semantic approaches

So far we have examined the notion of head from a purely syntactic perspective; we now consider semantic approaches to headship, to see if they may inform the discussion, starting with the issue of the semantic headedness of compounds. Selkirk notes that there are classes of exocentric compounds which are generable by her w-syntactic rules, some of which have clear semantic interpretations based on the transparent modification of the head by the non-head;

Affixes and heads 67

others, however, are subject to special rules of semantic interpretation and seem semantically non-headed. Consider, for example, the VN and AN compounds in (26) and (27).

(26) a. [ski$_V$] + [centre$_N$] → [skicentre$_N$]
('centre for skiing')

[scrub$_V$] + [woman$_N$] → [scrubwoman$_N$]
('woman who scrubs')

[punch$_V$] + [bag$_N$] → [punchbag$_N$]
('bag for punching')

b. [pick$_V$] + [pocket$_N$] → [pickpocket$_N$]
('person who picks pockets')

[cut$_V$] + [throat$_N$] → [cutthroat$_N$]
('person who cuts throats')

[scare$_V$] + [crow$_N$] → [scarecrow$_N$]
('dummy for scaring crows')

(27) a. [atomic$_A$] + [science$_N$] → [atomic science$_N$]
('science of atoms')

[electric$_A$] + [guitar$_N$] → [electric guitar$_N$]
('guitar using electricity')

[high$_A$] + [lands$_N$] → [highlands$_N$]
('lands at high altitude')

b. [hard$_A$] + [back$_N$] → [hardback$_N$]
('book with hard covers')

[heavy$_A$] + [weight$_N$] → [heavyweight$_N$]
('boxer of heavy weight')

[brown$_A$] + [shirt$_N$] → [brownshirt$_N$]
('supporter of Hitler with characteristic uniform of brown shirt')

In the (a) examples of (26) and (27), note that the syntactic head (as opposed to *semantic* head; cf. the definition in (25)) indicates a set of referents of which the entire compound picks out a subset, so, for example, a *punchbag* is a kind of bag, not a way of punching, and *atomic science* is a kind of science, not a degree of atomicity (cf. Hall 1985). We might therefore say that, as in the morphosyntax, the word category (X^0) is of the same 'type' as one of its constituents, and therefore that this constituent is the 'semantic head'. In Jespersen's *The Philosophy of Grammar* (1924: 96), we find a similar definition for heads:

In any composite denomination of a thing or person . . . we always find that there is one word of supreme importance to which the

68 Morphology and mind

others are joined as subordinates. This chief word is defined (qualified, modified) by another word, which in turn may be defined (qualified, modified) by a third word, etc. We are thus led to establish different 'ranks' of words according to their mutual relations as defined or defining. In the combination *extremely hot weather* the last word *weather*, which is evidently the chief idea, may be called primary; *hot*, which defines *weather*, secondary, and *extremely*, which defines *hot*, tertiary.

Observe, however, that in the examples given in (26b) and (27b), neither element of the compound identifies the 'primary' rank, or 'defines' the set of referents: a *pickpocket* is neither a kind of pocket nor a way of picking, and a *brownshirt* is neither a kind of shirt nor a shade of brown. So, although such forms seem to satisfy the obligatoriness principle on syntactic heads, they lack a semantic head, and therefore require special rules of semantic interpretation.

It seems that, as in morphology, special rules of semantic interpretation are sometimes called for in the syntax because, amongst other idiosyncrasies,[6] the phrase is not semantically headed, e.g.:

> (28) V + NP: kick the bucket ('die')
> P   + NP: in the soup ('in trouble')
> NP + VP: the penny dropped ('realisation came')

All of these structures are open to the normal rules of semantic interpretation of course ('he kicked the bucket around the yard'; 'there was a fly in the soup'; 'the penny dropped into the well'), but they have also become frozen as idioms; it is reasonable to assume that, similarly, the compounds in (26b) and (27b) are simply lexicalised idioms from earlier syntactic phrases ('he cuts throats', 'it scares crows', 'they wear brown shirts', 'it has a hard back').

Zwicky (1985: 4–5), in a very wide-ranging discussion of the notion 'head' in both syntax and morphology, notes that in syntax the semantic head is the argument; so, for example, 'in V + NP, P + NP, and NP + VP, NP is the semantic head, since the semantic interpretation of all three constructs involves a functor (represented by V, P, or VP) on an argument represented by NP'. It seems that the argument definition of semantic head in syntax is much less transparent than in non-idiomatic compound morphology. Indeed, in a footnote (p. 4), Zwicky sounds 'a serious note of caution', acknowledging that it is not always clear which element is function and which argument:

Affixes and heads 69

The mechanisms of a system of logic rich enough to provide the basis for a description of natural language semantics will not themselves force a decision as to what is functor and what is argument.... The intuitively correct assignment ... can be guaranteed only if substantive assumptions about the relationship of semantics and syntax are made.

It is difficult to reconcile Zwicky's specification of the NP as semantic head of VP with Jespersen's observations about the head of NP. For example, hitting a baby could be construed as a kind of hitting, composing a symphony as a kind of composing, explaining a universal of language as a kind of explaining, making V the semantic head of VP. If the notion of semantic head in the syntax cannot be adequately formalised, then there seems little point in attempting to specify a semantically defined formulation of headship generalisable over both syntactic and lexical levels of representation.

So much for semantic heads in compound morphology and the syntax, but what of affixes? Zwicky claims that:

The semantic argument in derivation is always the base rather than the affix, since the affix represents a functor applying to the argument represented by the base. This is as true of derivation that doesn't change the category of the base (as in *blue-ish*) as of derivation that does (as in *blue-ness*). (1985: 16)

This seems to ignore the fact that there is a qualitative difference between the role of functor in these examples: the *-ish* of *blueish* picks out a subset of the set of colours associated with 'blue', but the *-ness* of *blueness* is far more abstract, specifying 'the state of being blue'. It could be argued that the *-ness* has no semantic role at all and is, in fact, a purely *syntactic* marker. Compare this, however, with the distinction *ride* and *rider* where the affix adds an agent thematic role, as well as changing syntactic category. In Zwicky's framework the stem *ride* is semantic head, and yet it could be argued that *ride* picks out a subset of the set of people (agents) who engage in the activity of riding, thus suggesting that *-er* is the semantic head, as is *he* in 'he rides'. As in the case of syntactic phrases, we see that it is not always clear which element is the best candidate for semantic headship. If, as Zwicky argues, it is always the case that derivational affixes are functors and therefore, non-heads, we have lack of isomorphism between semantic and syntactic heads of words. One important point is, though, that in non-idiomatic compounds, the semantic head as defined by Jespersen in terms of set/subset relations

70 *Morphology and mind*

does coincide with the *syntactic* head. This is not true for semantic heads in syntactic phrases as Zwicky defines them: e.g., in V + NP, V is syntactic head, NP is semantic head; in P + NP, P is syntactic head, NP is semantic head. We shall see in section 3.2 that this constitutes a problem too for semantic accounts of head-modifier serialisation.

What emerges from this brief discussion of semantic headship is that: (i) semantic notions of head in both syntax and morphology defy clear definition and are not universally applicable, whether they are derived from the argument/function distinction, which seems based on very unclear criteria, or from set theory, which can only account for a small part of the data; (ii) the semantic head is not obligatory in syntactic phrases or in words; (iii) the semantic head when it can be identified does not necessarily coincide with the syntactic head either in words or in phrases.

Semantic definitions of the notion 'head of a word' are therefore incomplete and inadequate, and consequently we will assume our syntactic definition in (25) as the only plausible one for characterising what the notion 'head' can mean if it is used in a theoretically consistent and meaningful manner across both the syntactic and morphological components.

3.2 CROSS-LINGUISTIC FACTORS

3.2.1 Head serialisation

It has been demonstrated that the RHR is inadequate as a universal syntactic definition of the head of a word. Even given a reasonably regular positional system like that of English derivational morphology (the basis of the RHR), the number of exceptions (especially from prefixing) militates against such a definition, and, also, it wrongly predicts that inflections are heads.

In syntax, linear position plays no part in defining heads of phrases, as we saw in the discussion of X' syntax earlier in the chapter; however, cross-linguistically and within languages, there is a tendency towards harmony in the positioning of heads and their respective modifers (in X' terms, the X' and its specifiers and the X and its complements). So, for example, in some language we might expect all verb complement types to appear on one side of the V, say the right, and further, in such a language, we would expect noun modifiers after the noun, and prepositions rather than postpositions. Such harmonic ordering is well-documented in the literature on universals and typology (e.g, Greenberg 1966; Hawkins 1983). In

Affixes and heads 71

Greenberg's original cross-linguistic survey, he used word order combinations as a typological indicator and found the best represented types in his sample to be:

(29) Type 1 : VSO/Pr/NG/NA
Type 9 : SVO/Pr/NG/NA
Type 23: SOV/Po/GN/AN
Type 24: SOV/Po/GN/NA

Observe that in these language types the heads *serialise* (with only one exception): in types 1 and 9, V comes *before* NP in VP; P comes *before* NP in ADP (adpositional phrase); N comes *before* genitives in NP; and N comes *before* adjectives in NP. In types 23 and 24, V comes *after* NP in VP; P comes *after* NP in ADP; N comes *after* genitives in NP; and in type 23 only, N comes *after* adjectives in NP. The single exception (involving adjective position) occurs in type 24.

Since Greenberg's work, a number of scholars have elaborated on his principles and expanded his data base. Notable is the work of Vennemann (1974), who attempted to formalise these harmonic ordering patterns in terms of the distinction operator/operand, according to a 'Natural Serialisation Principle', offered in terms of an absolute universal:

(30) Natural Serialisation Principle

$$\{\text{Operator } (\{\text{Operand}\})\} \rightarrow \begin{cases} \text{[operator [operand]] in XV Lgs} \\ \text{[[operand] operator] in VX Lgs} \end{cases}$$

Note that Vennemann's principle takes the verb as determiner of serialisation (X ranges over the set of complements), and makes the strong prediction that *all* operators will line up either on the left or the right, according to operand position. In his original formulation, operands are at the same time both syntactic heads ('In a constituent structure AB; A is operator and B is operand if the entire construction AB is in the same syntactic category as B' (p. 347)) *and* semantic arguments; however, later, the semantic notion of head was dropped when it was determined that function/argument did not always coincide with operator/operand.

Keenan (1979), however, pursued the semantic definition of operator/operand and formulated a new and rather convoluted theory based on a 'Serialisation Principle' (SP) combined with a 'Dissimilation Principle' (DP), which referred to the semantic distinction between determined NPs (DNPs), e.g., *a student,every student, John, he* etc., and common NPs (CNPs), e.g., *student, fat student* etc.:

72 *Morphology and mind*

The SP predicts that VPs, T[ransitive]VPs, Poss[essive]Ph[rase]s, and Adpositions (= Prepositions in English) will all occur on the same side of their DNP arguments. Similarly, APs, Relative Clauses, Articles, Determiners, and Quantifiers will tend to occur on the same side as their CNP arguments. And the DP says that these two sides are different. (1979: 26)

In SOV languages (according to Keenan 'the most widespread word order type across different geographical areas and genetic groupings'), the SP and DP predict the correct word order correlations, where all functions of DNPs occur on the right, whereas, in line with the DP, all functions of CNPs occur on the left:

(31) a. Subject + VP (e.g. John sings; John Mary kissed)
       Object + TVP
       DNP + Postposition (e.g. the garden-in)
       DNP + PossPh (e.g. John's father)
   b. Adjective + CNP (e.g. tall man)
       Relative Clause + CNP (e.g. the apple eating man)
       Article + CNP (the man; this man)
       Quantifier + CNP (every man)
       Numeral + CNP (two man)

There are exceptions to the generalisation in other word order types. Keenan claims that the 'goodness of fit' of the word order type corresponds to their relative significance across geographical areas and genetic types.

Strong criticisms have been levelled against Keenan's semantically-based theory (cf. Hawkins 1983), most importantly: (i) there is no description or explanation of harmonic serialisation outside the noun phrase (and even within the noun phrase the notions of DNP and CNP are not explicitly formulated); and (ii) a principle of *dis*similation is theoretically less desirable when a more uniform generalisation (see below) is available. Bearing in mind also the problems inherent in assigning correct function/argument status to syntactic categories as noted by Zwicky, and in view of the criticisms of Keenan's theory, it seems that, as an explanation of head serialisation, the notion of semantic head cannot yield a consistent or general account.

Hawkins (1983: 133 ff) has argued convincingly, however, for a syntactic characterisation of head-modifer serialisation which is confirmed by actual language frequencies. His principle, which he calls 'Cross-Category Harmony' (CCH), asserts

Affixes and heads 73

that there is a quantifiable preference for the ratio of preposed to postposed operators within one phrasal category (i.e., NP, VP/S, AdjP, AdpP) to generalize to the others. Whatever position the operand of one phrasal category occupies in relation to all its operators will preferably be matched by the position of the operand in each of the other phrasal categories. And the more the word order co-occurrence sets of languages depart from this 'ideal' harmonic ordering, the fewer exemplifying languages there are. (1983: 134)

Thus, by taking into account distributional data and avoiding the problems associated with a semantic approach to the head-modifier (= operand–operator) issue, Hawkins has formulated a principle which is descriptively more accurate and therefore predictively more powerful than those previously advanced by Vennemann and Keenan. The principle of CCH is also amenable to a more formal interpretation in terms of X′-syntax, as Hawkins points out (pp. 183 ff). He stresses 'the explanatory potential of X-bar theory in this universal context', appealing to the notion of grammar complexity: a simpler, more economical grammar will exhibit the ordering generalisations of the X′ schema, i.e. be more consonant with CCH, hence 'explaining' the preference for CCH attested in the cross-linguistic data. We return to this claim in section 3.3.2.

Looking at the morphological level with CCH in mind, H&G observe that exclusive prefixing is predominant in syntactically head-initial languages (using the typological indicators VO and Prep) whereas exclusive suffixing is predominant in syntactically head-final languages (i.e., OV and Postp): cf. the data in (6), chapter 2. It is this correlation that leads them to formulate the HOP, based on the assumption that affixes are heads of words. We have seen in 3.1 that: (i) the head of a morphologically complex word is not always an affix; (ii) inflections are not heads, although the data on which the HOP is based constitutes mainly inflectional affixes. However, the strong correlation between *affix* and syntactic head remains. What, then, lies behind this harmony? I believe the answer may be found in an examination of *how* these morphemes became affixes in the first place, i.e. by examining their derivational history from a diachronic perspective. In chapters 4 and 6 the diachronic facts are discussed in considerable detail; however, this discussion is anticipated in the next section in order to introduce at this stage an essential factor in a potential explanation of the head/affix correlation.

74 *Morphology and mind*

3.2.2 A diachronic perspective

In an influential paper on the origin of affixes, Givón (1971b) argues that they are derived from erstwhile free lexical items which reduce semantically and phonologically to become bound on contiguous free forms. As part of his discussion he claims that the items that reduce are usually of head status in the syntax. He offers as examples from English: (i) the English noun *kingdom* where *-dom*[7] is originally head of an NP which is modified by a sentential phrase 'the king rules NP'; and (ii) the verb *purify* where *-fy*[8] is originally head of a VP with sentential complement 'NP be pure'. His reconstruction of sentential modifiers for the examples used is non-standard. More likely would be, for *kingdom*, the noun phrase 'king's domain', and, for *purify*, the verb phrase (in Latin) 'make pure'; however, this does not affect the force of Givón's argument.

In a later publication Givón (1984) gives a wider range of examples of the process of reduction from free lexical item to bound morpheme, and shows again that, typically, the major source of the bound morpheme is of head status. I summarise his data in the table in (32). Further, in Lee (1988) it is suggested, following Berlin (1972), that noun classifiers, usually expressed as affixes, derive from generic level terms. These are, in fact, consistently heads in the syntax, which reduce and become bound on their former modifiers. Note that, given the different criteria for determining head status in the syntax and the morphology (inherent in the categories N, V, A and P in the syntax, but contingent in the categories STEM and AFF in the morphology), there is no reason why head status should carry through from the syntax to the morphology upon reduction, an observation which is consistent with our hypothesis but at odds with the HOP.

Accepting, then, that affixes are typically the diachronic legacy of earlier heads in the syntax, we are now in a position to propose an explanation for the harmony between serialisation of heads in the syntax and of affixes in the morphology. H&G claim that it is because affixes are heads and therefore fall into line with the serialisation in the syntax (i.e. the HOP); however, in the above sections I have (i) shown that affixes are not always heads and that the majority of affixes that H&G looked at (i.e. inflections) are *never* heads; and (ii) suggested, following Givón, that affixes (both inflectional and derivational) are developed typically from former free-standing heads of syntactic phrases. This, then, provides a natural explanation for the patterns evidenced in (6) and (7), chapter 2: affixes which develop

Affixes and heads 75

(32) Sources of affixation (data from Givón 1984)

Morpheme function	Typical source(s)	Alternative source(s)
case	head of serial verb head of genitive compound	(not given)
tense-aspect-modal	main verb (i.e. head of VP)	(not given)
negation	negative verb (i.e. head of VP)	negative intensifiers (i.e. non-head)
verbal derivation	main verb (i. e. head of VP)	(not given)
causatives	causative verb (i.e. head of VP)	object nominal (i.e. non-head)
detransitivizing	main verb (i.e. head of VP)	reflexive from object pronoun (i.e. non-head)
noun derivation	head noun	(not given)

from heads in head-final languages will typically be realised as suffixes, and affixes which develop from heads in head-initial languages will typically be realised as prefixes, resulting in a correlation between affix position in the word and head position in the syntax.

There are, however, affixes which derive typically from non-head sources (such as those which express definiteness, indefiniteness, gender, and plural on nouns, from *modifiers* on a head noun) as H&G point out. These authors doubt the explanatory power of the free head → bound morpheme account of the head/affix correlation for two main reasons: (i) that it cannot explain the correlation between affixes derived from non-head sources and heads in the syntax; and (ii) that 'syntactic heads and modifiers from which prefixes and suffixes derive are not positioned with sufficient consistency in relation to the future stem to guarantee the prefixing/head-initial and suffixing/head-final correlation' (p. 243). They cite the non-head sources of affixes such as definiteness, indefiniteness, and gender as particularly unstable in this regard (cf. Hawkins 1983).

It is indeed puzzling that the very categories that do reduce to affix status but are *not* heads in the syntax should line up in the morphology with the dominant head position in the syntax and yet be the most positionally unpredictable syntactic categories. This is a problem for the diachronic account of the affix/head correlation I am proposing, to which I can provide no ready solution. And yet the

76 *Morphology and mind*

counter-evidence marshalled here against the HOP account favoured by Cutler *et al.* seems to me to be overwhelmingly compelling despite the problem posed by these data. Consider the arguments. Firstly, the number of categories expressed by affixation which are not typically derived from head categories in the syntax is remarkably small – Hawkins and Cutler (1988) list only four exceptions to a total of sixteen functions studied by H&G, to which total must be added others listed in (32) above (including virtually all derivational categories) as well as Lee's classifiers. The CCH (Hawkins 1983) states that head correlation in the syntax is favoured cross-linguistically. An account of the affix/head correlation which ignores the peculiar coincidence that the vast majority of affixes derive from syntactic heads, and that syntactic heads tend to cluster in relation to their respective modifiers, seems to miss a very plausible theory of *linkage*, a factor which, as I show in other parts of this book, is an indispensable part of the explanatory process. As it stands, the HOP has no explanatory status (which I demonstrate from a new perspective in the discussion of learnability in the next section).

Secondly, we have demonstrated through a thorough formal examination of the notion of head in generative morphology that the HOP is untenable, in that affixes are not always heads of words in any sense of the notion head which can be argued to span both the syntactic and morphological components – and it is this cross-component identity which is essential to the HOP account. In particular it was shown that derived affixes are not always heads and, more importantly, that inflections are never heads. The importance of a formal in-depth analysis of principles proposed to underlie surface distributional data is recognised by Hawkins (1983) who, discussing CCH and its theoretical counterpart, X-bar theory, states that the 'distributional regularity supports a theory which can recognize the appropriate heads of phrase, and define them as such in a consistent and principled way' (1983: 180). Equally, then, any principle referring to the notion 'head of word' proposed to account for distributional facts in morphology should be favoured if it is consistent with theoretical analyses of this notion. I believe that the discussion in 3.1 shows that the notion of head adopted in the HOP is not at all consistent with a principled theory such as the one presented here. Neither, it should be added, is it consistent with cross-linguistic data, as the exceptions listed in previous sections show.

In partial response to H&G's argument (ii), above, about the positional inconsistency of heads and modifiers from which affixes

Affixes and heads 77

derive, I would suggest that, in general, such free forms must at least be positioned with sufficient consistency for affixes to be formed from them, and this is presumably the result of a long-term free association followed by a long-term drift as the two begin to coalesce. In the absence of a detailed historical analysis of morphologisation for each language in the H&G sample, it is, I would argue, too early to write off the historically-based account for the HOP advanced here.

We might, in fact, turn the whole thing on its head and argue that the fact that the explanatory account offered here is statistical, i.e. accounts for only *some* of the data, is an *advantage*, since the totality of the affix distributional data does seem to evade an exhaustively principled account. If the distribution is exhaustively accounted for by the principles proposed by H&G (the HOP and counterprinciples), then we should not expect the four cells of the implicational table to be filled; consider again the figures in (6) and (7), chapter 2, and the categories studied which do not have suffixing principles associated with them (for which no principled reason is supplied). The explanation hypothesised here, although potentially flawed in some aspects, is consonant with the probabilistic nature of the data distribution; i.e. it admits of exceptions, whereas an account based on the HOP and counterprinciples cannot accommodate these exceptions. Note that the rejection of the HOP (and RHR) in an earlier part of this chapter partly on the basis of exceptions does not contradict this possible defence of the historical account, since the exceptions there are exceptions to what can only be interpreted as parametrical universals preprogrammed as part of our genetic endowment (see 3.3.2): they must count as counter-evidence in such a situation. Exceptions to a historical accident or preference or tendency, however, are to be expected and must be tolerated, as I argue in more detail in later chapters.

A further argument against the explanatory adequacy of the HOP is presented in the next section, where it is explored from a learnability perspective, to ascertain whether it does, in fact, enjoy any explanatory status in the sense introduced in chapter 1; however, it will be obvious by now that this argument is only included for completeness's sake, since the *descriptive* validity of the HOP has already been undermined, and so *no* explanatory account based upon it can provide an acceptable explanation for the distribution of the data it purports to describe. I include the argument nevertheless, in part to demonstrate again the difference between the descriptive and the explanatory status of linguistic principles.

78 *Morphology and mind*

3.3 PSYCHOLINGUISTIC FACTORS

The fundamental question underlying all this discussion is why heads should serialise at all, i.e. how can we *explain* the regularity. In this section we tackle this problem from a psycholinguistic perspective, examining first (3.3.1) head serialisation in the syntax, and then (3.3.2) the implications for morphology.

3.3.1 Serialisation in the syntax

Greenberg in his original pioneering work on the phenomenon of serialisation in syntax suggested that there was ultimately a psychological motivation for it: '[The notion of] harmonic and disharmonic relations among distinct rules of order . . . is very obviously connected with the psychological concept of generalisation' (1966: 97). The harmonic relations involved in this case are those between head-modifier orders in the syntax within and across languages. If the notion 'head of phrase' has any psychological reality, i.e., roughly speaking, if it plays a part as such in storage, acquisition or processing, then we might expect head serialisation to be geared to the effective realisation of one or more of these functions. So, for example, for comprehension, recognition might be facilitated if the processor 'knew' that all heads occurred first, or all modifiers occurred first; and for acquisition, if head and modifier position were predictable in input strings, perhaps by fixing an innate head position parameter (in a generative view of acquisition), there would be fewer language-particular rules to be learnt, and an 'operating principle' (along the lines of those proposed by Slobin 1985) could make efficient use of this generalisation.

In language comprehension there is certainly motivation for syntactic heads to serialise initially, as Hawkins suggests for NPs (1983: 98). The reality of some sort of Head First Preference (HFP) enjoyed considerable support in early psycholinguistic work (e.g. Clark and Clark 1977; Fodor, Bever and Garrett 1974; Bever 1970; Moore 1972). It was suggested there that the early recognition of the head of a phrase in real time allows for the efficient building of higher level structure in some bottom-up parsing system. So, for example Clark and Clark (1977: 64) propose strategies such as the following:

> (33) After encountering the verb, look for the number and kind of arguments appropriate to that verb.

The general idea is that on encountering the head, the processor may consult, for example, subcategorisation frames, and, on the basis of

Affixes and heads 79

the information contained there, attempt to 'synthesise' the phrase structure of the incoming string. Note that only the lexical categories subcategorise, and only these constitute heads of phrases.

However, current distributional evidence casts considerable doubt on the HFP as *sole* determiner of word order: the current ratio of OV to VO languages is roughly fifty-fifty (of the 336 languages in Hawkins's sample, 162 have V before O, and 174 have O before V (1983: 288)), i.e. showing no preference for the head V to occupy initial position. If we claim that some languages line up heads in initial position because of the HFP, then it behoves us to identify a conflicting principle of equal power which lines up heads at the *end* of their phrases in as many other languages. It is not clear to me how such a counterprinciple could be motivated from a parsing point of view, but the possibility exists that the interaction of two such opposing principles could result in the word order serialisation patterns attested.

Perhaps a more likely explanation may be furnished by a consideration of learnability requirements and on-line acquisition strategies. The system of X' syntax, which encodes the notion of cross-category harmony, captures a significant generalisation in language, thereby enhancing the theoretical economy of the grammar. The generativist strives for theoretical economy ultimately for reasons of learnability, as Chomsky articulates in his *Lectures on Government and Binding*, taking X' theory here as an example:

> Early work in transformational grammar permitted a very wide choice of base grammars and of transformations. Subsequent work attempted to reduce the class of permissible grammars by formulating general conditions on rule type, rule application, or output that would guarantee that much simpler rule systems, lacking detailed specification to indicate how and when rules apply, would nevertheless generate required structures properly. For example, X-bar theory radically reduces the class of possible base components ...
>
> ... The objective of reducing the class of grammars compatible with primary linguistic data has served as a guiding principle in the study of generative grammar since virtually the outset, as it should, given the fundamental empirical problem to be faced – namely, accounting for *the attainment of knowledge of grammar* – and the closely related goal of enhancing explanatory power.
>
> (1981: 13; my emphasis)

In terms of on-line acquisition strategies, it is not at all clear how the child might actually exploit the notion of syntactic head serialisation

80 *Morphology and mind*

in order to acquire the adult grammar more effectively. There is reason to believe, however, that children, in their attempts to isolate linguistic units in the input, can employ a segmentation strategy based on frames and templates (Peters 1983). It will be immediately noticed that what X′ theory provides is a system of templates for the structure of phrases in the syntax. It is conceivable, therefore, that the child stores and matches successive input strings according to some innate (parametrical) X′ template, along the lines of Slobin's operating principle (OP) given in (34):

> (34) OP (Storage): Co-occurrence
> For every segmented unit within an extracted speech string, note its co-occurrence with any preceding or following unit and store sequences of co-occurring units, maintaining their serial order in the speech string. (1985: 9)

The existence of generalisable patterns in language structure, such as cross-category harmony as formalised in the X′ system, and the knowledge that children employ segmentation strategies by identifying patterns and constructing frames and templates, makes an acquisition-based account of head serialisation in the syntax most attractive, though as far as I am aware, it is, as yet, lacking in empirical substantiation.[9]

3.3.2 Serialisation in the morphology

We concluded in section 3.2.2 that the HOP does not provide an accurate account of the head/affix serialisation pattern observed in H&G's data, because (i) affixes are not, *ipso facto*, heads (and inflections *never* are); and (ii) dominant affix position in the word often corresponds with dominant head position in the phrase because affixes typically arise due to the semantic and subsequently phonological decay of erstwhile syntactic heads, rather than because affixes are heads too.

What are lining up in the morphology are, therefore *affixes*, not heads. From the point of view of the language comprehender, there is no reason to suppose that head serialisation within the word would provide facilitation for their task, as we shall see in chapters 5 and 6. On the other hand, there is very good reason to believe that more efficient lexical processing can be achieved when the affix, regardless of head status, appears word-finally (i.e. in suffix position), so that early access may be made to an entry in a stem-based mental lexicon (cf. Cutler *et al.* 1985, and subsequent chapters). It seems that such a

Affixes and heads 81

Stem First Preference (SFP) will override any morphological extension of the HFP. As will be shown in chapter 6, although access to syntactic information (including categorial features, case, and sub-categorisation) may be facilitated by having affixal heads in prefix position, the need for access to *lexical* information seems to take priority. In any case, the SFP will only coincide with the HFP when stem = head of the (suffixed or morphologically simple) word. Again we can find little foundation in processing theory for the serialisation of affixes with syntactic heads.

If optimal processing does not motivate affix/head serialisation, perhaps acquisition might again be a factor. In acquisition it is once more the distinction stem/affix rather than head/non-head that seems crucial. In order to try to analyse the bound morphology, the child attempts to segment the word by identifying recurrent patterns at word margins, using OPs such as the following (Slobin 1985, following Peters 1983):

(35) a. OP (Attention): End of unit
Pay attention to the last syllable of an extracted speech unit. Store it separately and also in relation to the unit with which it occurs.
b. OP (Attention): Beginning of unit
Pay attention to the first syllable of an extracted speech unit. Store it separately and also in relation to the unit with which it occurs.

Obviously the child's task would be simpler if it had only to employ one or the other of these OPs, or if it could apply one first, with a greater than chance likelihood that it would be successful. For example, in an *exclusively* suffixing language, (35b) could be dispensed with, and in a *predominantly* suffixing language, (35b) would only be necessary as a back-up strategy.

Note that these are theoretical arguments for affix serialisation, but have nothing to say in support of a correlation between affix serialisation and head serialisation. Let us now look specifically at the HOP which constitutes a claim that such a correlation is universally preferred, just as cross-category harmony is in the syntax. As we have seen, Hawkins (1983) motivates CCH in the syntax in terms of grammar simplicity and generality, and interprets it in terms of the X-bar account of head-modifier relations. Presumably this account should extend to the morphology as well, and so must be held to underlie the proposal of a unified notion of head as expressed by the HOP. Appeals to grammar simplicity and generality are not,

82 *Morphology and mind*

however, in themselves explanatory, as I concluded in chapter 1 in relation to Chomsky's apparently vacuous notion of 'least effort guidelines' (Chomsky 1989). On their own, they mean nothing. Only when functional factors such as learnability and processing limitations are invoked do issues of simplicity and generality make any sense: a simple and general grammar is preferred because it must be both acquired by a learning mechanism and accessed (directly or indirectly) by a processor very rapidly and in less than perfect input conditions. Thus, positing head *generalisation* across rules in the syntax in UG implies a corresponding narrowing of both the child's hypothesis space in the learning process and the adult's range of strategies in the parsing process.

Similarly, head generalisation in the morphology may serve acquisition in this way, as suggested by Selkirk's work. In syntax, head *serialisation* too may be independently motivated, and, if affixes *are* always heads, then it should be motivated in the morphology as well, as shown in the previous section.[10] What I cannot see motivation for, though, is the identical serialisation of heads across both components, as stipulated by the HOP. As far as I am aware, no child language studies have ever suggested that children learn syntax and morphology by exploiting one single cross-component positional template for modifier-head relationships, nor would we expect them to. The identification of the category of head by one set of principles obtaining in both components (as suggested in section 3.1.1.3 above) may serve acquisition as a substantive universal, but serialisation across components does not appear to be motivated in this way.

Hence we may conclude, on the basis of the HOP's lack of support from learnability and the arguments offered against it in the previous section, that affix serialisation is probably simply an accident of diachrony: syntactic heads, serialised perhaps for reasons of learnability, decay and, in many cases, are frozen in serial position as affixes, but do not necessarily retain headship status in their new word-internal constituency. The result is the *appearance* of independent harmony with the syntax, an appearance mistakenly interpreted as *principled* by the HOP.

3.4 CONCLUSION

This chapter began with a discussion of the notion 'head of word', drawing on the theoretical tools of generative morphology with the objective of subjecting the HOP to thorough scrutiny as a descriptively adequate account of the distributional data. It seems clear from the

Affixes and heads 83

discussion that in morphologically complex words the affix is not always the head, contrary to the assumption underlying the HOP. However, other definitions of morphological headship in the literature, both syntactic and semantic, are inadequate. In this chapter an alternative definition was proposed which maintains the obligatoriness and category percolation stipulations required by Lyons (1968), and at the same time improves on earlier definitions by (i) dispensing with the positional criterion, thereby avoiding the numerous exceptions it entails in English and other languages (especially in regard to left-hand affixal heads and right-hand inflectional non-heads); and (ii) recognising that headship is not a feature of specific categorial formatives in the syntax or lexicon (such as AFF), but rather is dependent on categorial features associated with individual affixes or stems and the (word formation and base) rules which introduce them (although for syntax the result is inherent headship in words of category N, V, A and P within the immediately dominating phrase).

Given this definition, we would not, therefore, expect affixes *per se* to line up with heads in the syntax, especially as inflections are *never* heads, yet constitute the primary empirical basis of the HOP claim. This rejection of the descriptive adequacy of the HOP leads naturally to a rejection of its explanatory adequacy. I postulate that in place of the HOP we may probably attribute the attested correlation to historical accident, in that affixes are typically derived from former syntactic heads in the syntax due to semantic, and consequently phonological reduction. Although there is some reason to believe that serialisation of heads in the syntax and, independently, of affixes in the morphology, might serve optimally efficient acquisition and/or processing, there is little empirical support, as yet, for this claim, and it is difficult to see how such psycholinguistic motivation could actually affect the morphological and syntactic patterns of languages in this way, i.e. the proposals lack any immediately apparent theories of linkage. In any case, the psycholinguistic arguments are arguments for *independent* head and affix serialisation, and so do not constitute evidence for the identity of the two notions, as assumed in the HOP.

Perhaps the most fundamental criticism of the HOP as an explanatory principle is that it does not *explain* anything. Even if H&G were correct in assuming that the affix is always the head of the word, the HOP still fails to address the question of what *underlies* the correlation between affix/stem serialisation in the morphology and head/modifier serialisation in the syntax, and so is merely recording a generalisation, rather than explaining the facts.

4 The diachronic link

A major purpose of this work is to illustrate the need for any explanation of linguistic regularity to address the problem of what causal mechanisms (phylogenetic or ontogenetic) could have been responsible for the incorporation of the regularity into actual language systems. This is required not only as an evaluative measure, i.e. to show that the explanans could viably lead to the explanandum (cf. Clark and Malt 1984; Bybee 1988), but also because it can be of vital importance in the strict characterisation of the explanandum and in the development of a precise and thorough explanans. In the first part of this chapter (4.1), I examine a potential diachronic 'explanation' for the suffixing preference documented in chapter 2. The explanation is derivable from work by Givón (1971b), and leads Cutler *et al.* (1985) to reject diachronic principles in their psycholinguistic account since such factors arise in what they perceive as part of a 'competing' explanatory model. I call into question the explanatory potential of the historical account, but accept Givón's assumptions about the diachronic affixation process (introduced in chapter 3); I then proceed (4.2) to show how the semantic and phonological processes involved are crucially relevant to our structural regularity and its explanation. In addition, I make the claim that certain semantic and phonological descriptive principles assumed in the literature to be primitive notions, are, in fact, transparently derivable from higher level phenomena.

Before embarking upon the main discussion, I should like to sound a cautionary note about the use of examples in this chapter. Because there is as yet no ample source of representative cross-linguistic data on the phonological processes of attrition and fusion between morphemes, it is difficult to provide definitive empirical evidence for some of the cross-linguistic generalisations assumed in the following pages. Consequently, much of the data supplied below is intended

The diachronic link 85

not as comprehensive cross-linguistic evidence for the universality of the phenomena which they illustrate, but rather as suggestive examples introduced to support the reality of the sorts of mechanisms and processes proposed, i.e., to demonstrate that such mechanisms and processes *are* employed by human language, and, when taken with other types of evidence (mostly psychological in our case), they can be seen as logical candidates for universality. Hopefully, such claims can be tested with a suitable data base in the not-too-distant future.

4.1 THE HISTORICAL ACCOUNT

4.1.1 'Today's morphology': the origin of affixes

A crucial question, seldom addressed in the investigation of morphology, is where affixes come from. Cutler *et al.* (1985) offer no opinion as to the origin of the structures whose cross-linguistic patterning they seek to explain. The only reference they make to the issue is in a refutation of a potential diachronic explanation of the suffixing preference (see below): the diachronic link is not thought to be a crucial element of the explanatory hypothesis. Indeed, it is as though affixes are first 'introduced' in a language as a primitive category, and the HOP, tempered by the preferences of the lexical processor, then decides where to put them (what we might call an '*affixum ex machina*' approach). This viewpoint ignores a wealth of evidence which points to a less ethereal source, namely processes of semantic generalisation and phonological attrition and fusion which result in the boundedness of previously free-standing lexical morphemes. The postulation of this source of affixes may be traced back to Bopp (1974 [1820]), who observed, in rather less prosaic fashion than most current practitioners of linguistics,

> that words entering into conjunction with others are liable to great alterations or contractions, in order that the compound might have the appearance of a simple word; languages manifest a constant effort to connect heterogeneous materials in such a manner as to offer to the ear or eye one perfect whole, like a statue executed by a skilful artist, that wears the appearance of a figure hewn out of one piece of marble. (p. 56)

In this century Meillet (1958: 130–48) has expanded on this argument, and Bybee and Pagliuca (1985) have provided a more detailed analysis of the processes involved.

86 *Morphology and mind*

A potential diachronic explanation of the suffixing preference based on the work of Givón, introduced in chapter 3, crucially refers to this process of affixation, which he has discussed in some detail, principally in Givón (1971b). There he cites evidence from Amharic and various Romance, Germanic and Bantu languages, some of it speculative, but most of it compelling. His assumptions and conclusions are strong ones, and if true, have important consequences for linguistic theory:

> If it is true that bound morphemes, derivational as well as inflectional, arise historically from erstwhile free 'lexical' morphemes, and if it is further true that the syntax of the language, at some point of the derivation, determines the order of the free 'lexical' morphemes, then the syntax of the language ultimately also determines the morphotactics of the morphology which ultimately evolves. (1971b: 409)

As illustration, consider his account of the genesis of prefixed modality markers and suffixed verb-derivational markers on Bantu verbs. According to Givón (1971a) both affixes are derived from main verbs dominating sentential complements (and so may be construed as heads – cf. 3.2.2). He maintains that their differential positioning as prefixes and suffixes is a result of the dominant syntactic word order in Bantu at the time that they fused with the verb of the sentential complement ('comp'): there was a historical change from comp:verb to verb:comp with derivational markers arising during the former stage and modal markers during the latter, as shown in (1).

(1) a.

comp:verb (syntax)   suffixation (morphology)

$$\text{VP} \qquad\qquad \text{VP}$$

(np) S [V V] → (np) [V -[suffix]$_V$]

b.

verb:comp (syntax)   prefixation (morphology)

$$\text{VP} \qquad\qquad \text{VP}$$

[V (np) S V] → [v[prefix]- (np) V]

In support of this hypothesised word order change and its morphological consequences, Givón appeals to the positioning of the object

The diachronic link 87

pronoun affix, which appears as a verbal prefix. He reasons that the current word order (verb:comp) would predict suffixes, and so the object pronoun must have become fused at an earlier stage of Bantu when the word order was comp:verb. Syntactic change affects free lexical morpheme order but leaves bound morphemes '"stranded" or frozen in [their] earlier syntactic position'. Although the Bantu object pronoun case supports Givón's hypothesis only by virtue of its consistency with the hypothesis (and therefore is no 'independent support' as he claims), his data from other languages (Amharic, Spanish) do strengthen the empirical basis of the model.

Further evidence is offered from noun affixes, e.g. in Amharic, where some locatives appear as suffixes whereas others are prepositional. The suffixed class are the supplemental forms derived from head nouns, paralleling the English and Bantu systems: see (2).

(2) Locative systems in Amharic, Bantu, and English

AMHARIC

Original System		Supplemental System	
l-	'to, for'	ba-lay-u	'at the top'
b-	'at, in, on'	ba-tac-u	'at the bottom'
k-	'from'	ba-layu lay	'at the top'

BANTU (ChiBemba)

Original System		Supplemental System	
pa-	'at, on'	pa-isamba lya	'underneath of'
ku-	'to, from, at'	ku-muulu wa	'on top of'
mu-	'in'	pa-kati ka	'in the middle of'
		pa-nnuma ya	'behind'
		mu-nse ya	'outside of'
		pa-ntanshi ya	'in front of'
		ku-nshi ya	'downward from'

ENGLISH

Original System	Supplemental System
at	on top of
on	at the bottom of
in	inside of
to	at the back of
for	in front of
from	instead of

Givón claims, convincingly in my view, that whereas all three languages underwent a reanalysis of the head-noun:possessed-noun

88 *Morphology and mind*

relation in the supplemental genitive constructions, this reanalysis took place at different stages of word order change. English and Bantu are hypothesised to have originated the supplemental system when their syntax was noun:pos, and to have been reanalysed as follows:[1]

(3) [noun [of-noun]$_{mod}$]$_{np}$ → [[noun-of]$_{prep}$ noun]$_{pp}$

On the other hand, Amharic is claimed to have had pos:noun order when the supplemental system developed, and therefore was reanalysed as in (4):

(4) [[of-noun]$_{mod}$ noun]$_{np}$ → [of-noun [noun]$_{postp}$]$_{pp}$

The original prepositional systems in all three languages also arose from head nouns at an earlier time when all three languages had noun:pos order in their noun phrases.

Although Givón's account of the genesis of affixes is based almost entirely on hypothesised reconstructions in a less than representative sample of languages, it provides a very logical account which is generally consistent with broader diachronic facts (e.g. word order reconstructions and cognate forms). There is considerable support for Givón's account from other sources, too: Anderson (1980) and Comrie (1980) dedicate papers to the word order reconstruction issue citing much evidence which supports the reduction hypothesis, while Ashby (1980) and Champion (1980), for example, provide synchronic data from current French which show how free, but semantically reduced and syntactically limited, morphemes such as determiners, pronouns and future auxiliaries are gradually drifting towards affix status. Jeffers and Zwicky (1980) demonstrate how derivational and inflectional affixes may evolve from the reduction of clitics, the latter being the legacy of earlier full lexical items, and Mithun (1985) describes the emergence of noun incorporation in languages from verb-noun strings, with affixes subsequently developing upon further reduction of the incorporated elements.

Such movements may be seen as operating along a continuum such as that provided by Bybee (1985), schematised here in (5), which places various modes of expression of combinations of meaning relative to each other according to the degree of fusion involved. Of course, in employing Bybee's continuum in this way, I do not mean to suggest that reduction will necessarily proceed through each stage in turn: certain morphemes at certain stages might reduce but *never* pass directly to an adjacent stage, and others may simply not move at all, or else be lost before reaching a later stage. For example, free

The diachronic link   89

grammatical elements will reduce to inflectional, rather than derivational affixes, if they reduce at all; inflections will never reduce to compounds, although the latter may reduce to derivations; and clitics may be lost entirely under certain types of reanalysis before achieving affix status. The continuum suggests *direction* only.

(5) Bybee's fusion continuum (adapted from Bybee 1985)

Expression	*Examples*	*Degree of fusion*
		(less)
periphrastic/ syntactic	'come to know' = inchoative + KNOW	
free grammatical	n'est pas (Fr), wind up, have gone	
inflectional	walk + ed, prowl + ing, affix + es	
incorporation,	grocery + shopping, ditch + digging	
compounds	cricket + bat, pressure + cooker	
derivational	elect + ion, post + Thatcher	
lexical	'kill' = CAUSE + DIE	
		(more)

The process of attrition from free lexical item to bound morpheme (i.e. 'cross-component' reanalysis from syntax to morphology) is a natural phonological process (see 4.2), and as far as I can see accounts for the ultimate source of nearly all affixes in language. According to Meillet (1958: 130–48) there is only one other source of affixation, what he calls *innovations analogiques*. These constitute a type of lexical (i.e. lexically-internal) reanalysis, whereby one affix replaces another in the same functional domain. This occurs where equally productive forms compete (e.g. English *unaccountableness* (1676) → *unaccountability* (1704) (Marchand 1969)) or when one form establishes dominance in its domain and squeezes out the competition. For example, consider the following contrast between Old and Modern English plural forms (Samuels 1972:56):

(6)   Old English   Modern English

      handa   hands
      cwene   queens
      scipu   ships
      word   words
      eagan   eyes
      stanas   stones

In the first five cases the original plural markers (*-a*, *-e*, *-u*, zero, and *-an* respectively) have been replaced by the *-s* marker, present on *stanas*.

90 *Morphology and mind*

Another, related type of lexical reanalysis occurs in the phenomenon of paradigm restructuring, whereby a bound morpheme, perceived as basic in a paradigm, undergoes a sound change and the new form then replaces functionally equivalent forms in the rest of the paradigm. For example, Watkins's (1962) work on Celtic showed how the pre-Celtic forms in (8), from Indo-European (7), underwent paradigm restructuring to give the Common Celtic forms in (9).

(7) Indo-European
 *bher – s – m̥   'carry' + past + 1 pers.
 *bher – s – s   'carry' + past + 2 pers.
 *bher – s – t   'carry' + past + 3 pers.

(8) Pre-Celtic
 *ber – s – ū
 *ber – s – i
 *ber – t – ø

(9) Common Celtic
 *ber – t – ū
 *ber – t – i
 *ber – t – ø

Watkins's explanation was that a phonological cluster reduction rule /rst/ → /rt/ (independently motivated in IE) applied to the third person form and the re-analysis in (10) took place.

(10) stem + tense + person
 *ber + ø   + t   →
 *ber + t   + ø

This *t* tense marker was then spread by analogy to the first and second person forms of the paradigm, as the plural *-s* was spread from form to form in the history of English. (For an extensive treatment of paradigm restructuring which is more accessible than Watkins's, see Bybee and Brewer 1980).

Back formation is a third, much rarer type of lexical reanalysis which occurs mostly in derivational forms. In back formation a monomorphemic item is analysed as containing an affix (which already exists in other combinations) because the relevant portion of the monomorpheme shares surface similarities with the affix, and the rest of the word potentially fulfils the requirements of the appropriate subcategorial frame for this affix (this frame specifies what sort of stem it may be combined with). An example is English *orator*, where the pseudo-suffixal *-or*, an undifferentiated part of the stem, is

The diachronic link 91

reanalysed as the agentive suffix, as evidenced by the appearance of the new verb *orate*. Another case, English *pedlar*, also shares surface form with the independently existing homophonous stem *pedal*, and so the reanalysis perhaps had even greater impetus in this case.

Presumably in each of these types of internal lexical reanalysis, the source affix, i.e. the affix which (i) serves as the basis of the restructing of the paradigm, (ii) is extended to other forms in the same functional domain, or (iii) is misanalysed in a possible subcategorial frame, typically has its ultimate source in the reduction of a lexical morpheme. In all these cases, no new affix is being introduced: all that is happening is that already existing affixes are being created anew in novel functional domains or novel affix + stem combinations.

A final, but contrasting, source of affixation lies in borrowing from a second language. This is usually thought to be through the extension of affixes from loan words to native forms (as in English *pre-*, from French *pré-*) although again the ultimate origin will be a full lexical item in the supplier language or an antecedent of it (French *pré-* comes from the Latin free preposition *pre*). A related kind of process occurs when a new incidence of an existing native affix emerges from a native misanalysis of a borrowed form (e.g. monomorphemic French *cerise* 'cherry' was misinterpreted as containing the English *-s* plural, giving English *cherry*). This process will be immediately recognised as back formation on a non-native stem, so should really be treated as a lexical reanalysis, rather than as part of borrowing.

Discussion of the consequences for the suffixing preference of both borrowing and lexical reanalysis processes will be put off until the historical implications of the latter are subjected to greater scrutiny in the final chapter (6.1.4). In the meantime, let us resume our central discussion: if we accept that diachronic processes of reduction account for the ultimate origin of nearly all affixes, we are still faced with the problem of the skewing observed in favour of suffixation. We should expect that, other things being equal, the proportion of prefixes to suffixes in the languages of the world should be roughly fifty-fifty. Why should it be that suffixes predominate so markedly? Givón (1979) is again the source of an apparent explanation for this anomaly, although here the arguments are less convincing.

4.1.2 'Yesterday's syntax': SOV as universal word order

Although never offered explicitly as an explanation of the suffixing preference, Givón's claim that all human languages exhibit, either

92 *Morphology and mind*

currently or at some stage in their history, SOV word order, can be construed as such (cf. Žirmunskij 1966: 86 for an explicit suggestion of support for such a theory). In the light of the assumptions presented in the previous section, we can see that for Givón the problem of the suffixing preference can be solved by identifying a skewing in earlier syntactic word order. He notes in a section of his 1979 book:

> Greenberg [1966] ... observed that many VO languages, with English being a representative sample, do not abide by this correlation [OV/suffixation and VO/prefixation] very consistently, and exhibit mostly suffixal morphology. As I pointed out (Givón, 1971b), such inconsistencies arise because of a sequence of natural diachronic changes:
> 1. A layer of morphology arises and at that time 'conforms' to the prevailing syntactic typology of the language.
> 2. Due to highly natural processes the syntax of the language changes, while the old morphology – being bound – remains as a frozen relic.

Thus, if we can identify a skewing in 'the prevailing syntactic typology' of a *group* of languages, then we can account for the consequent skewing in the morphology which arose from it. Such a skewing is postulated by Givón – a skewing of *all* languages, in one direction: SOV. He claims that *all* languages were or are SOV, summarising the facts as follows (1979: 275–6):

> 1. It seems that the majority of language families known to us exhibit SUBJECT-OBJECT-VERB (SOV) syntax, and so far as one can tell they were always SOV (Altaic, Turkic, Caucasian, Dravidian, Sino-Tibetan, all Papua-New-Guinea philums, Kushitic, Khoi-San, Athabascan, Uto-Aztecan, Hokan, and many others).
> 2. The overwhelming majority of languages and language families which do not show actual SOV syntax currently, can be nevertheless reconstructed via internal and comparative methods back to an earlier SOV stage. In other words, either their syntax or – at the very least – their bound morphology exhibit coherent relics of the earlier SOV stage (Indo-European, Semitic, Fino-Ugric, Mandarin, Niger-Congo, Nilo-Saharan, Afro-Asiatic, Iroquois, Mayan, and in fact all currently non-SOV Amerindian languages with perhaps one exception).
> 3. Only very few language families seem to show no solid evidence for an earlier SOV stage (Austronesian, Salish (?)). Even in those the evidence is by no means conclusive.

The diachronic link 93

4. The most common natural drive in word-order change seems to be SOV > VSO > SVO, with a much more restricted drift of SOV > VSO > VOS also attested in a number of cases. The drift *toward* SOV from any other typology is relatively rare.

The argument runs as follows. The elements that are reanalysed as affixes (perhaps via cliticisation) are heads (cf. Givón, 1971b: 412 and recall 3.2.2 above): in verb phrases it is a higher verb such as an auxiliary which will develop into an affixal marker of, for example, tense. In SOV languages, auxiliaries always follow the main verb (cf. Greenberg, 1966: 85) and therefore when they lose free lexical status they will become *suffixes*. It is hypothesised that affixation, if it occurred mostly during the SOV stage of most languages, would therefore result in more suffixing than prefixing on the verb cross-linguistically.

4.1.3 Problems with the SOV account

There are two major criticisms of the SOV account: (i) that the underlying descriptive premise of primitive SOV word order in all human languages is inaccurate, thereby annulling the explanatory power of any account derived from it; and (ii) that the SOV account, if accurate, is only a partial one, covering only a minimal portion of the data.

In support of the claim for a universal primitive word order of SOV, Givón produces very little hard evidence, and, indeed, evidence for such a grand claim *can* only be speculative in nature, considering the dimensions of its breadth and depth. Hawkins (1983) offers, on the other hand, a controversial though convincing rebuttal of the claim. He demonstrates that Proto-Indo-European (PIE), at least, is more likely to have been VO than OV. His demonstration is based on the assumption that reconstructions in proto-languages and all intermediate stages be consistent with universals observed in daughter languages (the 'Logic of Competing Variants'). The synchronic universals of the current and earliest daughter languages are therefore the key to the proto-language. Hawkins's universals are multi-clausal implicational statements which determine permissible and non-permissible co-occurrence restrictions, using 'typological indicators' such as adpositions (postp, prep), verb positions (OV, VO) and N-modifier positions (e.g. NGen, GenN). Hawkins shows that the earliest IE daughter languages exhibited the following N-modifier co-occurrence sets (as defined by the Prepositional Noun Modifier Hierarchy (p. 75), i.e. using Prep as the typological indicator):

94 *Morphology and mind*

(11) Subtype 1 (Prep) NAdj & NGen & NRel
Subtype 2 (Prep) AdjN & NGen & NRel
Subtype 3 (Prep) AdJN & GenN & NRel
Subtype 4 (Prep) AdjN & GenN & RelN

Although all IE daughters have *only* the N-modifier orders shown in (11) above, they do not all have prepositions; however, no early IE languages exhibit co-occurrence sets attestable in other postpositional languages (as shown in Hawkins's Postpositional Noun Modifier Hierarchy (p. 86)). For example, no postpositional IE language has the following co-occurrence sets:

(12) (Postp) NAdj & GenN & RelN
(Postp) NAdj & GenN & NRel

This, then, is very strong motivation for reconstructing Prep rather than Postp for PIE. Hawkins also offers an argument for PIE prepositions from synchronic distributional evidence (pp. 268 ff), which suggests that the likelihood of IE innovating postpositions is far greater than of it innovating prepositions. Postpositions in IE daughters are attested in only the universal word order co-occurrences where they would be expected; however, IE prepositions are found in large numbers in word orders where they are not favoured in current synchronic samples. Thus, Hawkins argues,

> The reconstruction of postpositions for Proto-Indo-European necessarily leads to the unfortunate conclusion that prepositions were innovated not only in the majority of IE daughters, but in numerous co-occurrences for which other languages of the world demonstrate an overwhelming preference for, or strong tolerance of, postpositions rather than prepositions. (p. 271)

It follows from this that PIE is far more likely to have been VSO or SVO, since prepositions and SOV is a highly marked co-occurrence. Hawkins demonstrates this by examining compatibility with other universal co-occurrence sets and with the current distributional facts (cf. pp. 271 ff).

The importance of Hawkins's conclusions about PIE is that they considerably weaken Givón's claim for 'pan-proto-language' SOV. Furthermore, many of the reconstructions Givón cites for earlier SOV stages, for example the Afro-Asiatic group (cf. 1979: 275, note 8), are based on an analysis of the bound morphology of current family members. An explanation for the suffixing preference based on the SOV hypothesis then becomes circular: there is more suffixing

The diachronic link 95

because all languages are or were SOV; we know that all languages are or were SOV in part because they exhibit more suffixing. The current distributional evidence also speaks against Givón's thesis: at present the ratio of OV to VO languages is roughly fifty-fifty (according to Hawkins's expanded sample of 336 languages, 162 have V before O, and 174 have O before V (Hawkins, 1983: 288)).

Even if we accept Givón's claim, we may only exploit it to a limited degree, namely to account for a preference for suffixing in verbs; however, in H&G's sample, there is a greater tendency for suffixes in *nominal* morphology, as the figures in (13) (calculated from data in H&G: 230) indicate.

(13) Positional distribution of verbal and nominal affixes

	Prefixing (%)	*Suffixing (%)*
Verbal	35	65
Nominal	24	76

If, then, the SOV account is to cover the data adequately, it would need to be demonstrated that morphologised nominal elements also typically appeared after rather than before the noun to which they subsequently attached. Although tendencies of head serialisation are observed across languages and through language change (cf. e.g. Vennemann's Natural Serialisation Principle (1974) and Hawkins's more tenable principle of Cross-Category Harmony (1983: 133 ff)), there is no simple guarantee that head position in the VP will correlate with head position in the NP, i.e. that, in our case, SOV in proto-languages will imply modifier-N order in the NP. Note the co-occurrences counted in Hawkins's expanded sample (1983: 166):

(14) SOV & Postp & AN & GN: 96 languages
      SOV & Postp & NA & GN: 55 languages
      SOV & Postp & NA & NG: 11 languages
      SOV & Prep & AN & GN: 3 languages
      SOV & Prep & AN & NG: 0 languages
      SOV & Prep & NA & NG: 10 languages

Although the majority of languages obey a strict serialisation principle (96 of a total of 175), it can be seen that in 76 cases SOV does *not* predict that all modifiers precede the noun.[2]

96 *Morphology and mind*

4.1.4 Assessment of the historical account

The explanation for the suffixing preference offered in Cutler *et al.*
(1985) appeals to processing principles, and is, I would argue,
fundamentally correct (see chapter 5): however, it is substantially
incomplete – it provides no mechanism which can link explanans and
explanandum (i.e. a model of processing combined with grammatical
principles on the one hand, and the attested predominance of
suffixing across languages on the other) – and so it is impossible to
conclude whether it does, in fact, constitute a viable explanation.
Hawkins himself emphasises (1985) that when we are faced with a
choice between competing motivations for some linguistic regularity,
we must be as rigorous as possible in our criteria for choosing
between them. This condition of rigour can only be met, I would
argue, if the path from structure to explanation is clearly specified.

In Cutler *et al.* (1985) it is as if the language innovates affixes as a
general structural category (the '*affixum ex machina*' approach) and
then the processor influences a choice of where to 'place' them, either
as suffixes or prefixes. A much more tenable claim is that the
processor influences the diachronic process of fusion of the morpheme with subsequent stem, according to whether the erstwhile free
lexical item stands before or after the element with which it fuses.
Hence, the explanandum is the observation that fusion takes place
most typically *after* the stem rather than before, and the postulated
explanans becomes the contention that, although fusion is freely
allowed post-stem, it is resisted in pre-stem position, because, as I
suggest in the remaining chapters, greater comprehension problems
arise in the latter case than in the former.

I submit that (i) Givón's account of the genesis of affixes must
be incorporated into any explanatory hypothesis to provide the
necessary degree of thoroughness by detailing a mechanism which
explicitly links cause with result in a linguistically plausible manner;[3]
(ii) the adoption of Givón's theory thereby changes the nature of
both explanans and explanandum (as shown above and in much
greater detail in chapter 6), giving us a clearer insight into the
nature of the problem than hitherto attained, but without jeopardis-
ing the force or correctness of the processing explanation ultimately
appealed to; but (iii) the SOV extension of Givón's historical account
must be rejected on account of its own inadequacies and the
superiority of the psycholinguistic explanatory model.

In the next section we examine natural phonological processes of
attrition and fusion and show that they reflect an asymmetry between

The diachronic link 97

word-initial and word-final positions. This constitutes a further argument against the SOV extension of the diachronic approach by providing a broader and more empirically verifiable basis for the processing explanation: I argue that the dispreference for prefixing is part of a more general array of psychological principles which lead to often opposing demands for clarity and economy in language.

4.2 PHONOLOGICAL DECAY AND SEMANTIC REDUNDANCY

4.2.1 Phonological decay

Processes of phonological weakening, attrition, and loss are very natural diachronic and synchronic processes, attestable in probably all human languages. Such decay of phonological substance has its roots in the articulations of individual speakers of a language, particularly in rapid speech, where often drastic simplification of form occurs, as a way of transmitting the same message in a shorter time and with the least physiological effort (cf. Martinet 1964: 167 ff). According to Kaisse (1985), 'fast speech rules', sensitive to rate of speech, syllabification and local phonological features, may develop into 'phonological rules of connected speech' or 'external sandhi', sensitive to the syntactic and morphological environment:

> The source of rules of connected speech, and also of many simple cliticizations, is sometimes to be found in the grammaticalization of fast speech rules. This observation finds its parallel in Kiparsky's (1982) suggestion that phonological rules are added to grammars as postlexical sound changes and work their way upward into the lexicon over time, acquiring the characteristics of cyclicity, that is, sensitivity to the morphological analysis of the string on which they are operating. The development of a connected speech rule from a fast speech rule is very similar; it is a movement upward that entrains the development of sensitivity to syntactic structure. (p. 15)

Such rules may subsequently lose their sensitivity to the linguistic environment, resulting in across-the-board application (i.e. regardless now of both rate of flow *and* morphosyntactic context) and thus causing ultimate restructuring of the underlying representation of the items upon which the rules act. In this way, then, phonological decay becomes fossilised in the lexicon via rapid and then connected speech rules.

It seems that, in general, processes of phonological attrition take

98 *Morphology and mind*

place more typically at the *end* of words rather than at their beginning. This tendency has been explicitly recognised in Natural Phonology (Stampe 1979), Natural Generative Phonology (Hooper 1976), and the approach developed in the work of Foley (e.g. 1977). Foley's is a model of phonology in which the sounds of natural language are classified according to their 'strength' or 'weakness' on certain phonological parameters (e.g. resonance, spirantisation, lenition, etc.). Rules in his model refer not to phonetic classifications but to the strength or weakness of elements, determined by their degree of susceptibility to various phonological processes. In addition to this inherent paradigmatic determination of strength, he describes syntagmatic distinctions – i.e. the 'positional potentiation' of an element according to the 'inertial development principle' (1977: 107), given here as (15).

> (15)   Inertial Development Principle
> (i) Strong elements strengthen first and most extensively and preferentially in strong environments.
> (ii) Weak elements weaken first and most extensively and preferentially in weak environments.

Of particular interest to our present concerns is his classification of word initial position as strong environment and word final as weak environment. Examples include the following (p. 109):

> Since the beginning of a word is a strong position, we expect either simple maintenance, as in Lt *dictus* → It *detto*, with retention of *d*, or strengthening, as in Lt **rete* → Sp *red* [rred], with prolongation of initial *r*. Since the end of a word is a weak position, we expect either simple maintenance, as in Lt *amica* → Sp *amiga*, with retention of *a*, or weakening, as in Lt *dictus* → It *detto*, with loss of final *s*.

The basis for deciding which elements are strong and which weak is not made explicit in Foley's theory. He states categorically that 'relative phonological strength refers not to the absolute phonetic strength of elements, but to the relation of the elements to one another in a phonological system ...' (p. 29) and that 'phonological elements are ... properly defined not in terms of their acoustic or articulatory properties, but in terms of the rules they participate in'. These rules reflect processes of strengthening and weakening familiar in other phonological frameworks: Hyman (1975: 165), for example, defines strengthening and weakening as follows:

[A] segment X is said to be weaker than a segment Y if Y goes through an X stage on its way to zero. Strengthening, on the other hand, refers to the reinforcement of a segment, as when a nongeminate [p] becomes geminate or double [pp].

The particular mechanics of Foley's theory are not important to us (and it is certainly not necessary to adopt his assumption of a nonphonetic base for phonology). What is interesting for the present discussion is his recognition of word endings as weak environments, and word beginnings as strong environments. A few more concrete examples are in order here to justify the assumed universality of this positional asymmetry. Hyman notes (1975: 168) an example from Chinese (Chen 1973) and also, a similar phenomenon in Burmese (cf. Maran 1971). The Chinese case is illustrated in (16).

(16) Neutralisation of Middle Chinese word-final elements
   Nasal endings   Stop endings

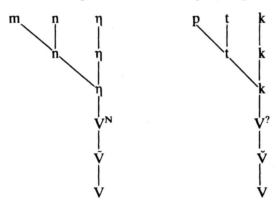

The diagram in (16) shows the set of Middle Chinese word final elements m, n, η, and p, t, k, which are currently being merged and neutralised in certain dialects.

In addition, experimental work by Cooper (e.g. Cooper and Paccia-Cooper 1980) has shown that assimilation across word boundaries in fluent speech is considerably reduced when the second of two adjacent words is of low frequency in word counts, or when it is contrastively stressed, but *not* when the first word is rare or stressed. This suggests that when assimilation between two words is possible in fluent speech, it is the phonological integrity of the word initial portion of the second word, rather than the word final portion of the first, which is maintained when one of the words requires special processing attention from the hearer.

Some particularly pertinent data are to be found in Williamson's

100 *Morphology and mind*

(n.d.) study of Ịjọ, which we therefore consider in some detail here. In Ịjọ words contain a maximum of three stem consonants C1, C2, and C3. Williamson observes that consonant types can be divided into three sets, according to their 'strength' (p. 6), as shown in (17).

(17)   The Ịjọ consonant system

Obstruents					
voiceless					
non-stop	f	s			} STRONG
stop	p	t	k	kp	
voiced					
non-implosive	b	d	g	gb	} MEDIUM
implosive	ɓ	ɗ			
Sonorants					
non-approximant	m	l	γ		} WEAK
approximant	w	r	y		

The division of the consonants into these three sets is apparently motivated by the same criterion that Hyman gives (above): stronger elements weaken to weak elements, and weak elements weaken to zero. In addition, weaker elements are subject to more phonological processes than strong ones, indicating their greater vulnerability.

In Williamson's corpus of 450 reconstructed proto-Ịjọ words, the vast majority of C2 and C3 consonants are either weaker than or of equal strength to the preceding consonant, i.e. C1 $\geq$ C2 $\geq$ C3. The figures in the table in (18) show that the majority of combinations are stronger consonant followed by weaker consonant (61.1 per cent).

Unfortunately, a breakdown of words according to syllable number is not given, so we cannot be absolutely sure that the C_{n-1} in (18) is always stem initial. In addition, there are sometimes vowel prefixes before Cl and vowel suffix enclitics after C#. I assume, however, that most words are bisyllabic (of a subset of 26 given in Williamson's paper, only three are monosyllabic and two trisyllabic). Williamson's reconstructions and synchronic studies of the various Ịjọ dialects lead her to conclude that:

> If a consonant weakens in C1 position, it will also weaken at C2 and C3: but a consonant can weaken at C2 or C3 without any corresponding change at C1. The result of this is that consonants at C2 and C3 will, over periods of time, be considerably more weakened than those at C1, as they are affected by more changes. (p. 14)

The diachronic link 101

(18) Ịjọ consonant combinations

C_{n-1}	C_n	N	%
S	S	19	7.5
S	M	15	6.0
S	W	78	30.9
M	S	7	2.8
M	M	39	15.5
M	W	61	24.2
W	S	4	1.6
W	M	9	3.6
W	W	20	7.9
Total		252	100.0

Key: n = position in word (1, 2 or 3)
N = number of combinations in corpus
S = strong; M = medium; W = weak

She speculates further that articulatory phonetics might provide us with an explanation for this tendency, in that: 'more breath force is available to articulate earlier in an utterance and that therefore a greater variety of articulations is easier to produce at an earlier stage than at a later'. This explanation is not adequate, however, since it refers to whole *utterances* rather than individual words, and so predicts in fact that the ends of words at the beginning of utterances will be articulated more fully than the beginnings of words at the ends of utterances, which patently does not inform our quest for an explanation of the data.

The answer, I contend, lies in the demand of the *hearer* for clarity of expression, at least at the *beginnings* of words. So far, we have been viewing the ends of words as particularly vulnerable to weakening processes (whether these be neutralisation or attrition or loss). It will inform our discussion more to shift emphasis and look at the *beginnings* of words as particularly *robust* and able to 'resist' such processes, maintaining (or even strengthening) their phonological integrity. In the discussion of the psycholinguistic process of word recognition in chapter 5, a crucial assumption will be that the lexical processor operates on-line (i.e. immediately on reception of the input, rather than waiting for data to accumulate), and that processing proceeds from word onset, according to some models such as the Cohort Model (e.g. Marslen-Wilson 1983, 1987). This processing model, independently of any consideration of morphological processing or structure, provides a rather transparent explanation of

102 *Morphology and mind*

the resistance of word beginnings to any processes which result in a diminishing of their phonological integrity: the processor is assumed to locate lexical entries initially on the basis of only enough acoustic information necessary to distinguish the word from all others in the mental lexicon. Hence, less redundancy word initially will result in more optimally efficient processing, by cutting down the size of the word initial cohort, i.e. the set of words which match the initial stretch of the input word (its neighbours in a phonologically organised lexicon), and which are therefore competing candidates, at that point, for recognition (cf. chapter 5, note 5). We may say, then, that although the unmarked situation is for reduction at both margins of the word, other factors (psychological ones) intervene. The apparently primitive positional principles adopted in phonological theories to explain the asymmetry between initial and final strength may therefore be seen to be straightforwardly derivable from a theory of speech processing.

The observations cited above from the phonological level about the strength of word initial position have been made independently from consideration of morpho-phonological processes leading to the reduction of lexical items and their fusion with others as affixes. When placed in the context of fusion, however, the independently attested robustness of word beginnings as opposed to endings seems to be confirmed. Consider, for example, the following pairs of stem/stem+suffix forms in English: *catholic/catholicism*, *democrat/democracy*, *cycle/cyclist*, *usher/usherette* (at least in British English), *predict/prediction*. All involve alternation at the end of the stem, whereas in the following *prefixed* forms, the *prefix* alternates, and the stem beginning remains constant: *illigitimate/inhospitable/irregular*, *compassion/condense/colloquium/correspond*, *entitle/empower*, *subdivide/suffix/suspect*. As far as I am aware, counterexamples to this trend, i.e. prefixes which provoke assimilation in the stem, are very rare (the only examples I can think of in English concern voicing of stem initial /s/, e.g. *resume* (cf. *consume*) etc., and these are only with bound stems).[4]

This maintenance of the stem initial position in prefixed words would fall out naturally from a predominance of regressive over progressive assimilation processes in language, reflecting the drive toward anticipatory economy in the articulation of spoken language. Kent (1936) makes an early claim to this effect, on the basis of a corpus of data from Indo-European languages, and Nooteboom (1981) makes a similar suggestion; Hoenigswald (1966), however, calls for caution until more languages can be studied. On the basis of

The diachronic link 103

the psychological and historical evidence presented so far, though, I would be very surprised to find a cross-linguistic study of assimilatory processes actually rebuffing Kent's supposition. Such an asymmetry between progressive and regressive assimilatory processes would find its match in a cross-linguistic asymmetry in the reduction of unstressed vowels: it is well-documented that those in initial syllables do not reduce to the extent that those in final syllables do.

So the effect on affixation of the asymmetries in these natural phonological processes should be that prefixes tend not to promote modification of the stem, whereas suffixes typically do induce stem alternations. Consequently, in the ongoing diachronic process of isolation, prefixed words should typically become lexicalised (i.e. reanalysed as monomorphemes) more slowly than suffixed words, since the integrity of the stem is maintained in the former but not in the latter. In Bybee and Brewer's (1980) terms, suffixed forms will tend towards a greater degree of 'autonomy' (i.e. representation as a single, independent unit in a speaker's lexicon) than will prefixed forms, at least on the morphophonemic opacity measure of this notion.

To sum up: this interplay between (i) the asymmetry of natural non-morphophonemic processes of phonological attrition stemming from economy of articulation in rapid speech, and (ii) the reduction and fusion processes whereby free lexical items become bound to either a prior or a subsequent neighbour in the speech string, results in a predominance of suffixes over prefixes, the whole configuration of pressures and resulting structural preferences deriving from the contingency of accessing lexical *form* in a stem-based lexicon.

In the next section we shall address the problem from the point of view of lexical *content*, and see how the process of semantic reduction or generalisation tempers the phonological processes of fusion discussed above. It will be argued, again, that psychological factors of comprehension and production underlie the types of diachronic change observed, and that all these factors again conspire in the direction of suffixation rather than prefixation.

4.2.2 Semantic redundancy

It is the differential degree of semantic content in pairs of words subject to fusion which determines which one of them reduces and becomes bound on the other. The item which reduces phonologically is the member of the pair which is communicatively the less important because (i) it is relatively 'empty' of semantic content (Greenberg

104 *Morphology and mind*

(1957) notes that the Chinese refer to affixes as 'empty words'); and (ii) what content it retains is relatively redundant and predictable in context.

That semantic reduction is accompanied by and actually is a prerequisite for morphological fusion is well attested. Žirmunskij (1966: 83) states, for instance, that:

> The grammaticalization of the word combination is connected with a greater or lesser weakening of the lexical meaning of one of its components, its consistent transformation from a lexically meaningful ... word into a semi-relational or relational word, and the transformation of a whole group of words as an entity into a grammatical form of the word.

The 'grammaticalization' referred to here is the reduction of two lexical items into a single morphologically complex item consisting of stem + inflectional/derivational affix. Žirmunskij claims that this morphophonological reduction is a consequence of the *semantic* reduction of one of the original free items. This word loses its 'lexical meaningfulness' and becomes 'relational' or 'semi-relational'. Examples of such semantic reduction from a wide variety of language families are documented in Kahr (1976) and Bybee and Pagliuca (1985). In the latter, for instance, the authors discuss the generalisation of habitual or continuous aspect markers into imperfective markers with consequently extended ranges of meaning (cf. Comrie, 1976), and show that this correlates with the degree of fusion of the morphemes with the verb stems to which they are bound. In the Perkins sample (cf. chapter 2, note 4) they found that stem changes conditioned by the imperfective marker significantly outnumbered those conditioned by habitual or continuous markers. Thus, as a general principle, according to Bybee (1985: 24), 'the greater semantic cohesion of concepts is reflected in a higher degree of fusion in their corresponding expression units'.

Perhaps one specific example will serve to illustrate more concretely the type of semantic generalisation process which renders a free lexical item susceptible to phonological reduction. One of the main sources for verbal morphology is the auxiliary verb (as noted by Givón, who, as we have seen, attempts to construct a controversial theory of word order evolution from this one observation; cf. also Benveniste 1968). The original source of these auxiliaries is typically a full lexical verb with quite restricted and specific meaning. For instance, the future auxiliaries in English, German, Old Church Slavonic, Modern Greek, Romanian, Arabic, Somali and Tagalog

The diachronic link 105

have developed from verbs of volition (Ultan 1978), and desiderative markers in Siberian and Sierra Miwok have developed future tense readings (Bybee and Pagliuca 1985, 1987). Company Company (1983, 1985) has documented the semantic shifts which resulted in the emergence of auxiliaries and subsequently tense suffixes in medieval Spanish, and Bybee and Pagliuca (1985: 71 ff) chronicle in detail the development of the English verb *have* from full lexical possessive verb to past tense auxiliary and modal of obligation and prediction. Let us review in some detail this latter study. The original meaning (*SOED*) of English *have* was 'to hold in hand'; this generalised as follows, Bybee and Pagliuca argue, by means of metaphorical extension:

(19) a. 'to hold in one's hand' →
      b. 'to have in one's immediate personal possession (physically present)' →
      c. 'to have or own as a possession (not physically present)' →
      d. 'to have as an abstract possession, such as time, an idea, an education, a debt.'

The possibility of 'having' an abstract NP object allows even further abstraction and consequent generalisation, so that the next stages of development are:

(20) a. 'to have (in a very general sense) a non-completed activity' (expressed by an infinitive verb) i.e. still having it to do (obligation, necessity).
      b. 'to have a completed activity' (expressed by a past participle) i.e. recently done.

The modal meaning in (20a) is then further extended/generalised from uniquely 'agent-oriented' modality, involving a wilful agent, to an epistemic sense of prediction: (21a) is an example of the former, and (b) of the latter:

(21) a. John has to do the dishes (because it's his turn).
      b. John has to be home by now (because he set off over an hour ago).

The possibility of phonological reduction of the auxiliary *have* can be seen in the contractions -*s*, -*ve* (used in ordinary speech), in the past tense (20b) construction:

(22) a. The children've come home for Christmas.
      b. The author's written at least twenty books.

106 *Morphology and mind*

But Bybee (1985: 42) notes that the full auxiliary forms are still used in such constructions, and in fact, children go through a long stage using them (cf. e.g. Slobin 1973), indicating that although reduced, they have not become completely fused; note, also, that in the full lexical version of *have* and in the agent-oriented and epistemic modal versions, reduction leading to fusion with the subject is impossible:

> (23) a. *The children've chickenpox.
> b. *The author's an inferiority complex.
> c. *John's (=has) to do the dishes.
> d. *John's to be home by now.

What is stopping full fusion in the cases in (22) and (23) is, in Bybee's terms, the lack of semantic *relevance* between subject and verb. In contrast, consider the cases in (24):

> (24) The children should've/would've/could've/might've gone home.

Here, as Bybee points out, the semantic relevance of the modal to *have* is much greater than that of the subject to *have*, as in the earlier cases, and so fusion is allowed. According to Bybee, such constructions are becoming reanalysed by English speakers as modal + tense marker: that the original separate verbal meaning of *have* is being lost is evidenced in the frequent spelling forms 'should of', 'would of', etc.

Hand in hand with this semantic generalisation and loss of specific lexical meaning is a certain degree of redundancy and predictability, pointed out in the work of Kiparsky (1982), who notes two semantic motivations for the diachronic reduction of phonological form in morphemes:

> (25) a. Morphological material which is predictable on the surface tends to be more susceptible to loss than morphological material which is not predictable on the surface. (p. 67)
> b. There is a tendency for semantically relevant information to be retained in surface structure. (p. 87)

This redundancy/predictability factor is important in the consideration of the numerical asymmetry between prefixation and suffixation in the world's languages. Greenberg, noting the typical modification of the stem form in suffixation as opposed to prefixation, argues that:

> this results, from the point of view of information processing, in the reduction of the amount of information given by the suffix,

The diachronic link 107

since the choice of a particular root modification narrows down the choice of possible suffixes. This is typical for many suffixing languages, with their numerous and irregular declensional and conjugational classes. As the suffixes give less information, they in turn become largely superfluous and are reduced or lost, the difference in function now being carried by alternations of the root. (1957: 93)

In prefixation, as we have seen, fusion and isolation are likely to be much delayed, although Greenberg does point out that modification of the prefix *will* reduce the number of potential candidates for the following word. However, it is clear that the closed set of bound morphemes will be far more predictable than the open set of free stems (for experimental evidence see Tyler and Marslen-Wilson (1986), summarised in chapter 5), and so the semantic generalisation and reduction of morphemes *following* the stem will lead to more predictability and redundancy, allowing, in consequence, a more forceful rationale for further phonological reduction, ultimately loss.[5]

4.3 A REVISED HISTORICAL ACCOUNT

Connecting all these strands together, we can extract the following general account of the suffixing preference and how it could come about. As semantic information in lexical items becomes more general, less specific and hence more redundant, it succumbs to phonological attrition. In terms of Slobin's 'charges to language' (1977), the charge 'to be quick and easy', a speaker-oriented principle, instantiated in language through semantic and phonological reduction, is able to exert its influence without doing so at the expense of the charge 'to be clear', which is, conversely, hearer-oriented, and requires, therefore, that reduction in content and form should not impinge too greatly on the efficacy of the hearer's comprehension mechanisms. Kiparsky suggests that the second of his two principles quoted above 'would appear to be motivated by the requirements of speech perception'; Ohlander (1976: 68) points out that the first principle 'can be regarded as the natural outcome of the clash between the two more fundamental principles of clarity and economy: the trend towards greater economy can be allowed only to an extent not threatening communicative function'. All these principles echo Martinet's discussion of the evolution of languages, in which he concludes that 'the maintenance of a certain equilibrium between the energy expanded and the information transmitted

108 *Morphology and mind*

determines to a great extent the direction and detail of this evolution' (1964: 171). ,

The principle of economy directs the reduction of semantically general free forms to affix status; however, as we have seen, prefixes and suffixes do not form a homogeneous class from all perspectives. We shall see in chapter 5 how the diachronic asymmetries are matched by psychological ones. One such is that the principle of economy will not favour prefixes as highly as suffixes, since the former entail greater representational complexity than the latter. Another is that the requirements made on language by the principle of *clarity* clearly militate against prefixation and in favour of suffixation, since in the former case access to the stem-based lexicon is disrupted by a morpheme which for a longer period than in suffixation resists complete fusion with the stem (due to the relative robustness of its initial elements) and is simultaneously 'rebuffed' by the stem (because of *its* maintenance of stem-initial position). In contrast, suffixes typically become more easily integrated phonologically with the stem, and as a consequence of this and the inherent semantic redundancy and predictability of affixes in both positions, will not constitute the same problem for the lexical processor.

One prediction of the claim that fusion is resisted in pre-stem position is that we may expect to find cross-linguistically a greater number of *free* grammatical morphemes at this site. H&G only examine bound morpheme distribution and so cannot help here: however, data from Matthew Dryer's cross-linguistic sample (p.c.) suggest that this prediction is largely confirmed; consider the example of negation, which languages typically express by a free morpheme in preverbal position, but by a bound morpheme postverbally (cf. Dahl 1979). In addition, it has been widely observed that prepositions are almost always realised as free morphemes, whereas postpositions are equally likely to be realised as free or bound (as suffixes in the latter case). Further potential support for the prediction comes from the observation that, for Indo-European at least, many prefix forms maintain for a longer period than suffixes their free counterparts, i.e. the free forms from which the affixes derive. Malkiel (1966: 321) notes:

> Many of [the prefixes of Classical Latin], e.g. *ab(s)-* 'from', *ex-* 'out', *per-* 'through', *prae-* 'in front, ahead', occur also as prepositions, and even certain contextual variants such as *ā-:ab-:abs-*, *ē-:ex-* seem to cut across the respective line of demarcation [between bound and free status]. Other elements happen to

The diachronic link 109

function as adverbs and prefixes alike: *intrō-* 'within' beside *intrōdūcō* 'I lead into', *intrōrumpō* 'I break in'; a few do yeoman's service as adverbs, prepositions, and prefixes, e.g. *super* 'above', *super templum* 'over the temple', *superfundo* 'I pour over'.

In twentieth-century English, note, it is mostly prefixes rather than suffixes which have yielded free-standing analogues: amongst prefixes we find: *ex* ('ex-lover/husband/wife'), *pro* ('in favour of', 'argument for'), *anti* ('against'), *con* ('argument against'), and *pseudo* ('not genuine'); of suffixes, however, there is only the marginal *ism* ('doctrine, theory'). The existence of free counterparts of affixes seems, therefore, to be a property associated particularly with *preposed* morphemes, in line with the argument propounded here.

As a further source of support for predictions deriving from the hypothesised prefix/suffix asymmetry, recall that in H&G's figures, reported in chapter 2, the number of languages with morphological functions expressed by means *other* than affixation was far greater in head-initial than in head-final languages (cf. chapter 2, note 5). Given the reality of the head/affix correlation (chapter 3), this distribution would be predicted by our historical interpretation of the suffixing preference.

Lastly, at some stage in the history of a language, we should also expect to find morpheme functions expressed in preposed position as free morphemes, resisting the pressure to fuse until the word order changes at a subsequent stage, or a nonbasic word order emerges, and the functions find expression postpositionally and are open to fusion as *suffixes*, resulting in the preferred morphological pattern (cf. note 5, chapter 2). What we would not predict, on the other hand, is that functions expressed in postposed position as free morphemes would at some subsequent stage, or in some alternative word order, find expression as bound morphemes in preposed position.

Evidence for such suffixing phenomena is sparse: however, there is strong indication from Mongolian languages, e.g. Buryat (Comrie 1980), that they may occur: in Buryat, person-and-number suffixes derive from postposed genitive and nominative pronouns in a nonbasic word order, i.e. in NA, rather than AN, and in VS, rather than SV. Comrie (1980:92) assumes that '... at the inception of the process of affixation, both SV and VS, both AN and NA are possible word orders, although SV and AN are by far the more usual'. He then addresses the crucial issue, for us, of *why* the nonbasic, rather than the basic, order should supply the affix position for the future

110 *Morphology and mind*

pattern of the language. The potential relevance of Comrie's problem for the suffixing preference as discussed in this chapter will be immediately apparent:

> The problem . . . is to explain why affixes should arise on the basis of the S of VS and the A of NA, rather than on the basis of the S of SV and the A of AN. Since . . . some SOV languages do develop prefixes in some instances (i.e. from SV and AN), we shall be asking primarily what pressures there may be setting up a tendency (not an absolute prohibition) against the development from the basic word order and in favour of the development from the nonbasic word order. (1980: 92)

Comrie speculates that the explanation for this tendency may lie in one or more of three features of Mongolian languages, namely that (i) the existing morphological pattern is almost exclusively suffixal, and so preference is given to maintaining that pattern; (ii) stress placement rules favour phonetic attrition after, rather than before the head; (iii) immediate adjacency between S and V, and A and N, invariably obtains in the nonbasic order but not in the basic order, and such adjacency is required for affixation to result. There is, however, a fourth possibility: (iv) that there is a universal psycholinguistic principle which causes fusion of the pronoun to be resisted when it occurs in preposed position, but to be unopposed during the nonbasic word order phase, when it appears in postposed position. (The problems of exceptions to the suffixing preference, and alternative explanations for it, both brought to light in Comrie's discussion, are addressed in 5.3.2 and 6.1.2.)

Another pre-stem/post-stem asymmetry ultimately favouring suffixation occurred in Old Norse (Samuels 1972), in which unstressed prefixes and proclitics were lost, and their functions replaced by postverbal adverbs, enclitics and suffixes, in a functionally diverse range. Here we have a case of pre-stem morphemes actually becoming bound and then being lost in favour of suffix counterparts. It is not clear, however, that this could have been the result of functional pressure from the processing component. A more transparent example is found in Greenberg's (1980) discussion of circumfixes, in which he notes their employment in Ethiopian Semitic and Iranian as a transitional stage in the change from prepositional prefixes to suffixes. As in the Old Norse case, original prefixes are lost in favour of subsequent suffixes; in addition, though, we clearly see the historical process by which this occurs, through the intermediate circumfixing stage:

The diachronic link   111

(26)   prefix + stem → prefix + stem + suffix → stem + suffix

I have come across no historical data as yet which exhibit asymmetry favouring shifts in the opposite direction, i.e. from postposed to preposed expression, where the latter exhibits a greater tendency towards affixation than the former. The prediction is therefore confirmed on the basis of the limited data presented here, but requires verification through much fuller cross-linguistic sampling.

To conclude: in this chapter we have reviewed the historical evidence relating to the creation of affixes in language, and have pointed out some positional asymmetries in phonological processes which seem derived from performance phenomena. These diachronic facts and the cross-linguistic evidence reviewed in chapter 2 converge on a position in which affixes, though a natural result of language change, are dispreferred when they occur prior to the stem. I argue that this asymmetry is ultimately psychologically motivated. Now that we have some idea of the kind of historical phenomena involved in linking the cross-linguistic facts of the suffixing preference with a potential psycholinguistic explanation for it, we are in a position to analyse this explanation much more closely than we have done up to this point, and begin to assess its empirical validity. The next chapter constitutes the first stage in this process.

5 Understanding affixes

In this chapter I start to develop a cognitive model of morphologically complex words (5.2) and examine the processing explanation for the suffixing preference first advanced by Cutler *et al.* (1985) (5.3). I spend considerable time first, however, in reviewing recent models of lexical access and representation (5.1), to enable us both to evaluate the Cutler *et al.* account and also to set a context for the experimentation and discussion in chapter 6, where I bring together the psycho-linguistic and historical facts, and propose a plausible explanation of the suffixing preference within the constraints of the unified approach.

5.1 MODELLING THE MENTAL LEXICON

This section addresses the twofold problem of the psychological status of words, namely, how they are represented in the mind, and how they are recognised in on-line comprehension (and to a lesser extent, how they are selected in production, although this is not a primary goal of the present discussion). The particular issue we are interested in here is how morphologically complex words are stored and recognised, and, more specifically, how prefixation differs from suffixation in this regard. The discussion is restricted here to affixation; compounding and other non-affixal morphological pro-cesses are not treated (although cf. note 9). We are specifically interested in the auditory domain; however, evidence from ortho-gra hic processing is also exploited (despite essential differences between the two modalities) for two reasons: (i) much of the mental processes and structures must be common across both domains, and (ii) there is considerably *more* evidence about recognition of the morphologically complex written word, though this is still embarrass-ingly scarce.

Understanding affixes 113

In what follows I review a sample of pertinent experimental results, and discuss models of the mental lexicon and lexical processor which these results have suggested. Readers unfamiliar with this area of cognitive science will soon come to appreciate the extraordinary industry of workers in the field, but will be disappointed to discover the corresponding paucity of the sort of unequivocal empirical data necessary for the development of detailed theoretical models. It should also be appreciated that no review such as this one can claim to be anywhere near exhaustive in its coverage: the numerous journals reporting a vast array of psycholinguistic experiments are packed with confusing and very often conflicting results, open to a host of different interpretations.

A major problem too is the correct level of abstraction to aim for in building models based on the results of what are, in fact, very indirect measures of processing complexity and representational structure. Processing theory lies at the interface between formal models of language competence and neurological theories of language biology. We must choose a level of abstraction which facilitates compatibility with (and, one would hope, progress towards) both of these, a balance which requires (i) answerability to the experimental data, to broader psychological and neurological theory, and to performance constraints, such as real time, with which competence models need not be directly concerned; and also (ii) a sufficient level of abstraction to be meaningful in terms of human intelligence and systems of knowledge, specifically to enable us to acknowledge and account for the richness of our language competence as described, for example, with the rigour of current generative theories of grammar.

This review is organised into separate sections and subsections, but it will soon become apparent that these are artificial divisions. The exigencies of seriality inherent in the expository process do not permit parallel discussion of the many inter-related topics involved in this domain, and it would be tedious to repeat elements of the discussion wherever they are relevant. It is particularly difficult to separate issues of access from issues of representation. Consequently, I advise the reader against adopting a strictly sequential strategy in processing the information in this chapter.

5.1.1 Three models of lexical access

The most influential models of lexical access in the past couple of decades have been Marslen-Wilson and Tyler's 'Cohort' model, Morton's 'Logogen' model, and Forster's 'Search' model. According

114 *Morphology and mind*

to Marslen-Wilson (1987), any model of lexical access must address at least the following three functions involved in the recognition process: (i) access, (ii) selection, and (iii) integration. The first, access, refers to the mode of contact between the incoming sensory information and the representations of candidate words in the mental lexicon which match that information. The second, selection, refers to the mode of discrimination between the lexical items contacted so that the best candidate is isolated. The third, integration, refers to the mode of contact between thc syntactic/semantic information in the representation of the isolated word and the higher level of analysis required to understand the whole utterance of which the word is a part.

In the majority of work in this area, it is the selection function which has received most attention. Although there is a new interest in the so-called 'front-end' of the system, i.e. the execution of the access function by some sort of acoustic–phonetic analyser (cf. e.g. Klatt 1980; Pisoni and Luce 1987; Frazier 1987a; Lahiri and Marslen-Wilson 1990), and although the integration function is not entirely ignored (cf. e.g. Tyler and Marslen-Wilson 1986; Marslen-Wilson 1987; Frazier 1987b), most models do not specify the exact realisation of these elements of the system. In this book too, detailed specification of the 'front' and 'back' end of the processor is not attempted. This, I think, is justified in so far as substantive assumptions are not being made about these functions as a consequence of the elaboration of the selection function as it is formulated here.

In the following sections and throughout, the term 'lexical access' will be used in its traditional sense, referring to the process of word recognition, i. e. the process which encompasses at least the first two functions recognised by Marslen-Wilson. The term should be distinguished from the restricted sense in which Marslen-Wilson uses it above.

5.1.1.1 The Cohort Model

The Cohort Model of lexical access, developed by Marslen-Wilson, Tyler, and their associates (Marslen-Wilson and Welsh 1978; Marslen-Wilson and Tyler 1980; Marslen-Wilson 1983, 1987) is based on the observation that language processing operates on-line in real time and is, in addition, extremely rapid. This rapidity must be central to any model when one considers the ease with which we process language: words in a typical utterance context are delivered at a rate of two to three per second in less than perfect transfer conditions, and

Understanding affixes 115

yet are usually perceived immediately, accurately, and effortlessly. In their experiments, Marslen-Wilson and Tyler have investigated the effects of real time constraints on lexical access by manipulating (i) the nature of the linguistic stimulus (i.e. the material presented to subjects), (ii) the linguistic context in which the stimulus is heard, and (iii) the task which the subject must perform (i.e. their *response* to the input material). They have shown that lexical access occurs typically *before* the whole word has been heard, and that the point of recognition is essentially a function of the extent to which the phonological form of the word measured from its onset is shared by other entries in the lexicon (i.e. which similar-sounding words compete for recognition), as well as of the degree of contextual constraint provided by linguistic cues in the utterance. In the following sections I review the major experimental techniques and findings in some detail, summarise the Cohort Model itself, and, finally, discuss some potential problems for the model. I spend considerable time here discussing the model's experimental techniques and theoretical assumptions so as to provide readers unfamiliar with the esoteric practices of psycholinguists with some background for the arguments developed later in this chapter and in chapter 6, since those arguments are constructed within the framework provided by the Cohort Model.

A great range of techniques has been employed in Marslen-Wilson and Tyler's research programme, all of which have yielded consistent results, giving the model of processing advanced a particularly strong empirical base, unparalleled by other paradigms. The first technique, speeded speech shadowing (Marslen-Wilson 1975), requires subjects to repeat back as fast as possible speech input they are hearing through headphones. 'Close shadowers' repeated back the input at delays as short as 250 msec (milliseconds) which is well before the end of most words. If we allow roughly 50 msec for execution of the response, this gives us an average word recognition time of 200 msec.

In a variant on this experiment (Marslen-Wilson and Welsh 1978), subjects heard speech input with one phoneme replaced by another (e.g. *travedy* for *tragedy*) in various syllable positions in the word. Such mispronounced words were of either high or low 'cloze' value (high cloze value words are highly predictable given appropriate context, e.g. *salt*, in 'pepper and ——': low cloze words are (relatively or totally) unpredictable, e.g. *cravat* in 'he gave me a —— '). The task was, again, to repeat back the input as rapidly as possible. In this experiment mispronounced words of high cloze were fluently restored to their correct pronunciation in 57% of cases: low cloze words were

116 *Morphology and mind*

fluently restored in 41% of cases. This suggested to Marslen-Wilson and Welsh that mispronunciations are not detected in cases of fluent restoration, and that the replaced segments are synthesised on the basis of access to the lexical entry made *before* the segment is reached. In addition, the stronger the contextual cues, or the later the mispronunciation occurs in the word, the less the acoustic signal is needed and, therefore, the more fluent the restoration (i.e. the less likely the mispronunciation will be detected).

In a second series of experiments (reported in Marslen-Wilson and Tyler (1980)) the word-monitoring technique was used. Subjects were 'primed' for a particular word to be recognised in a subsequently heard sentence. Priming involves prior presentation to subjects of a word related in some way to the target word. This has been shown to facilitate subsequent access to the target, and the degree of facilitation may be measured to provide an indication of the internal functioning of the access process. Three different types of prime were employed in the experiment: identity, rhyme, and semantic category. Priming by *identity* provided the subject with the target word itself, thereby supplying phonetic, syntactic and semantic information in advance. So, in the test sentences in (1), identity priming for the target item *lead* would be with the word *lead*:

(1) The church was broken into last night. Some thieves stole most of the *lead* off the roof.

For priming by *rhyme*, only a phonological template is provided: no semantic cues are available. Here subjects would be told, for (1), to locate a word rhyming with *red*. In semantic *category* priming, subjects are given a word in the same lexical field (e.g. *metal*, for (1)). In such cases phonological information is absent (*metal* shares no significant degree of phonological information with *lead*) but semantic information is available (*metal* is a hypernym of *lead*). In addition, the sentences in which the targets appeared were of three types, as in (2).

(2) a. normal prose: +syntactic, +semantic cues
    b. anomalous prose: +syntactic, −semantic cues
    c. scrambled prose: −syntactic, −semantic cues

Anomalous prose is grammatical but selectionally aberrant (e.g. 'No buns puzzle some in the *lead* off the text'), whereas scrambled prose is both semantically and syntactically uninterpretable (e.g. 'Some the no puzzle buns in *lead* text the off').

The results of various manipulations of the experimental procedure

Understanding affixes 117

and stimulus materials confirmed the conclusions drawn from the shadowing experiments. Prior priming was found to facilitate recognition, but the degree of facilitation thus provided was determined by the amount of relevant information contained in the priming word: cf. the table in (3).

(3) Results of word monitoring experiment
(Marslen-Wilson and Tyler 1980): mean RTs in msec

	prose type		
	normal	*anomalous*	*scrambled*
prime type			
identity	273	331	358
rhyme	419	463	492
semantic category	428	528	578

With identity priming, the mean reaction time (RT) was 273 msec in normal prose conditions (58 msec higher without semantic cues, and a further 27 msec in scrambled prose, i.e. on the basis of acoustic cues alone). For rhyme monitoring, RTs increased to a mean of 419 msec for normal prose – this was within 50 msec of the end of the word (mean length of target words was 382 msec). Allowing, again, 50 msec execution time, this suggests that access to the form representation is made *before* the end of the word. Increments from normal through anomalous to scrambled prose contexts were similar to those observed in the identity condition. For category priming the mean RT for normal prose was 428 msec – comparable to rhyme monitoring, and again indicating access to lexical entries *before* the end of the word, bearing in mind the 50 msec execution time. In the other prose contexts an extra 100 msec was needed when semantic cues were absent, and an extra 150 msec when the sentence was completely uninterpretable. Again, these results suggest that words are recognised before they are completely heard, and that prior cues to word identity (in the form of priming and sentential context) are active in shifting the recognition point towards the beginning of the word.

Using the 'gating' technique (Grosjean 1980), further evidence for the earliness of word recognition and the importance of contextual constraints was accumulated by Tyler and Wessels (1983). Here Dutch-speaking subjects were presented with the target in Dutch

118 *Morphology and mind*

sentences again of various degrees of contextuality, combining the features listed in (4).

(4) a. weak syntactic constraint: minimal subcategorisation of syntactic category of target.
   b. strong syntactic constraint: target following *te*, which requires an infinitive verb.
   c. weak semantic constraint: appropriate but low cloze context.
   d. no semantic constraint: anomalous prose.

Sentence sets used, including a neutral 'carrier' phrase to provide a control condition, are listed in (5) (in English glosses).

(5) a. neutral:
      The following word is BENEFIT/inf.
   b. weak semantic/strong syntactic:
      The appointment with the dentist goes not through. John tries to BENEFIT/inf . . .
   c. weak semantic/weak syntactic:
      The appointment with the dentist goes not through. John can BENEFIT/inf . . .
   d. no semantic/strong syntactic:
      The breath with the lie shuffles only through. The terrace tries to BENEFIT/inf . . .
   e. no semantic/weak syntactic:
      The breath with the lie shuffles only through. The terrace will BENEFIT/inf . . .

The target words were 'gated', i.e. presented to subjects in fragments, which were increased on each subsequent trial by an increment of 50 msec; words ranged in length from eleven to nineteen such segments (i.e. 550–950 msec). After each fragment, subjects wrote down the word they thought they were hearing, and indicated their degree of confidence on a scale of 1–10. Recognition points were defined as that segment at which subjects correctly identified the word at a confidence rating of 80 per cent and did not subsequently change their minds.[1] Mean recognition points were as in (6).

(6) a. neutral: 469 msec
   b. weak semantic/strong syntactic: 381 msec
   c. weak semantic/weak syntactic: 401 msec
   d. no semantic/strong syntactic: 465 msec
   e. no semantic/weak syntactic: 490 msec

Understanding affixes 119

Again we see that even with neutral context (the carrier phrase) the recognition point occurs before the end of the word. Also, the earliest recognition point again occurs when the semantic and syntactic cues are strongest, and the longest RTs (*still* before the end of the word) occur when the semantic cues are absent and the syntactic constraint is weak.

Another procedure utilised in this research programme is the lexical decision method (e.g. Marslen-Wilson 1983) in which the subjects' task is to make decisions about whether a target word is a real word or a nonword (a phonologically legal but non-occurring English word). As we shall see, the Cohort Model predicts that a nonword will be detected as such at the point measuring from word onset at which no real words are compatible with the input (the uniqueness point). So, given a nonword like **trenker* we would expect it to be detected as such at the point, approximately, when the /k/ is received, i.e. at the segment at which it diverges from all real words, if the set of real words is as in (7).

(7)	treacherous	treble	trench
	treachery	trek	trenchant
	tread	trellis	trend
	treadle	tremble	trepidation
	treadmill	tremolo	trespass
	treasure	tremor	tress
	treasury	tremulous	trestle

The results of the experiment strongly suggest that this is, in fact, the point of nonword detection, providing further evidence that hearers evaluate potential candidates before they have heard the complete signal.

On the basis of the evidence from these diverse experimental paradigms, Marslen-Wilson and Tyler have developed a model of lexical access which crucially assumes that recognition of a word depends initially on bottom-up processing alone, i.e. on the acoustic properties of the beginning of the word. On hearing this, a pool of competing candidates, a *word-initial cohort*, becomes activated. The cohort may be thought of as a list of all the words in the mental lexicon which match the acoustic onset properties of the input signal. So, for example, on reception of /trɛ/ the cohort activated might approximate the set in (7) above, depending on the hearer's own accent, access to other accents, vocabulary, etc.

The activation of a cohort results from the collective responses of 'low-level' input monitors associated with lexical entries, which

120 *Morphology and mind*

monitor the input sequentially and trigger activation of the entry, i.e. enter the word into the cohort, if there is, initially, a positive match. They continue to monitor the input, and cause the lexical entry to drop out of the cohort (become deactivated) as soon as there is a mismatch.[2] So, ignoring context for the moment, given that the input is, in fact *trespass*, on reception of the first /s/, all members will drop out except for those in (8).

(8) trespass
     trestle
     tress

On reception of the /p/, *trestle* and *tress* will drop out, leaving *trespass* the sole remaining member of the cohort. It is at this point, i.e. when a unique item is isolated in the cohort, that recognition is said to have taken place, and the information in the lexical entry can be integrated into the utterance context under construction.

In the original Cohort Model, the way in which prior context facilitated recognition was by revealing contextual mismatches in competing word candidates, after the initial cohort becomes active. Items which did not match contextual expectations dropped out of the cohort, so context, as well as continuing acoustic input, had a negative effect, removing items from consideration rather than positively enhancing the status of the target (as proposed, for example, in Morton's Logogen model: see 5.1.1.2 below). In a later reformulation of the model (Marslen-Wilson 1987), however, context is seen as facilitating recognition and compensating for variability in the speech signal (e.g. in cases of impoverished input, unfamiliar accent etc.) by actively influencing choice of candidates at the integration phase, i.e. the level at which items are integrated into the higher-level utterance representation. The 'all-or-none' view of sensory and contextual matching assumed in earlier versions of the model is thus abandoned, and in its place the notion 'degree of activation' of cohort members is entertained. In this reformulation, then, degree of activation depends on contextual suitability and 'goodness of acoustic fit' of the input with the stored prototypical specifications.

With the incorporation of the notion 'degree of activation', the Cohort Model may now account for another important aspect of word recognition that earlier versions of the model did not address, namely the influence of word frequency. It has been convincingly shown in a range of experiments that the frequency of words plays a role in their comprehension: more frequent words are recognised

Understanding affixes 121

more rapidly on-line in speech (Foss 1969); they are easier to identify when the input is degraded, e.g. in noisy conditions (Savin 1963); and they are named (i e. read aloud) faster, when presented to subjects (Forster and Chambers 1973). Marslen-Wilson's (1987) modifications of the original Cohort Model allow it to capture these frequency effects by stipulating the achievement of higher levels of activation by higher frequency words. The exact way in which this activation element is incorporated into the model remains unspecified by Marslen-Wilson, but he stresses that the basic assumptions of the model are retained, namely multiple activation of competing items, and multiple assessment of their acoustic and contextual features against the accumulating sensory information, until one item emerges and can be integrated into the utterance context.

One argument that was persistently levelled against the original Cohort Model was that it is too restrictive in its specification of the sensory input required for cohort activation (cf. e.g. Taft and Hambly 1986; Pisoni and Luce 1987). Nooteboom (1981) investigated the possibility of word recognition on the basis of highly impoverished input which lacked the crucial word onset cues given such weight in the Cohort Model. His materials were words which have both unique beginnings and endings, e.g. the word *surrogaat*, which is distinguished from all other words in the Dutch lexicon by its initial string /sœro:/ *as well as* by its final string /o:χa:t/. Nooteboom presented his subjects with either initial or final fragments with the remaining portion of the word replaced by a pure tone. The subjects' task was to recognise the word. The results indicated much better performance on word-initial fragments, but significantly for the Cohort Model, it was also possible for subjects to recognise words having heard only the final segments. These results suggest that listeners can access the lexicon by a means other than a word-initial cohort.

This is an important issue for the Cohort Model; however, it must be recognised that word fragments presented in isolation confront the listener with a task which differs greatly from the more natural presentation of whole word targets in fluent speech that is used in many of Marslen-Wilson and Tyler's experiments. It is, therefore, probable that subjects were using quite a different strategy in Nooteboom's experiments, as he acknowledges. The fact that mean RTs for both types of fragment were over 1000 msec (and reached as high as 9 sec for initial and 11 sec for final fragments) suggests that an extensive search is taking place here, rather than the rapid recognition processes reported in more natural experiments.

A potential problem still remains for the model, however, since the

122 *Morphology and mind*

obscuring of initial fragments of words presumably *does* occur in natural speech conditions, and in its most restrictive formulation, the Cohort Model cannot explain how successful access is achieved when this happens. As we have seen, however, Marslen-Wilson's (1987) revisions of the model do recognise that inclusion in the cohort does not require exact matching with the input. Given the 'degree of activation' element required in the model to account for frequency and context effects, a mechanism now exists to allow 'goodness of fit' of the acoustic signal with the stored representation to participate in the recognition process.

The original model has also been greatly strengthened by the results of an intriguing study of the seldom-considered 'front-end' of the system, i.e. Marslen-Wilson's 'access' phase during which the sensory input induces activation of lexical entries containing initially matching form representations. In a cross-linguistic experimental study of the role of nasality in access to Bengali and English lexical forms, Lahiri and Marslen-Wilson (1990) demonstrate that the traditional assumption of prelexical segmentalisation of the input signal was untenable. In Bengali, unlike in English, nasality in vowels is contrastive, e.g. [pāk] 'slime' vs. [pak] 'cooking'. In both languages, consonantal nasality spreads to a preceding vowel in a VN sequence (where N = nasal consonant), as in the English [bæ̃n] 'ban'. In a gating task, these researchers found that responses to target words with nasals overwhelmingly reflected marked features in underlying representations, as summarised in the table in (9).

(9)

	underlying form	surface form	preferred response
	CVC	CVC	*CṼC
			CVC/CVN
	CṼC	CṼC	CṼC
	CVN	CṼN	1. CṼC
			2. CVC/CVN

If the representation contacted is a *surface* representation, then we would not expect nasal vowels in the input to be matched by stored items with oral vowels; however, this is precisely what Lahiri and Marslen-Wilson's gating data showed: when presented with words like *pan* which has a *phonetically* nasal vowel, subjects responded with roughly 65 per cent CVCs when no other word in the candidate cohort had a nasal vowel. This result, along with others summarised in (9), strongly supports the hypothesis that the stored form representation in lexical items is abstract and underspecified (along the lines of the notations adopted in current generative phonological theory, e.g. Archangeli 1984).

In sum, the Cohort Model is an attempt to capture the temporally sequential nature of spoken word recognition, consequently placing much emphasis on the initial autonomy of the acoustic/phonetic processor, but giving great weight also to the subsequent strong effects of context from other domains of linguistic competence. All these sources of information are tapped in parallel and interactively after cohort creation to maximise processing efficiency by ensuring the earliest possible recognition of the input word. The model is based on an impressive array of empirical data, and with Marslen-Wilson's (1987) reformulations it can also handle frequency effects and impoverished stimuli without necessarily compromising its essential features.

5.1.1.2 The Logogen Model

The Logogen Model of lexical access, proposed by Morton (1969, 1979; Kempley and Morton 1982) is, like the Cohort Model, based on the postulation that amount of sensory and contextual input determines isolation of the target word (the word to be recognised). Every word has corresponding to it a 'logogen' (from Gk *logos* 'word' and *genus* 'birth') in the input system, which is some sort of recognition unit, defined by a unique intersection of sensory and semantic information. Each logogen 'responds' to contextual and sensory information and as it accumulates matching input its 'excitation' level nears a threshold. Once it crosses threshold value, it is available in the output system for a response, i.e. it is recognised, and the information in its corresponding lexical entry may be utilised. Other logogens affected by the input will then return to their state of rest. The stimulus may be spoken or written sensory input, so for each modality there are hypothesised to be separate acoustic and orthographic analysers for separate logogen systems. The similarity between this model and recent computational modelling of language use in a connectionist framework, briefly discussed in chapter 1, will not go unnoticed.

In order to account for effects of frequency, discussed in the last section, it is assumed in the Logogen Model that higher frequency logogens have lower thresholds, and inversely for lower frequency words, so that less input will be needed to achieve threshold value for the former than for the latter, and, hence, higher frequency words

124 *Morphology and mind*

will be recognised more rapidly. In addition, it is assumed that activated logogens return only *slowly* to their states of rest, thus accounting for priming effects: again, such logogens will require less input to achieve threshold, and therefore will be recognised earlier than they would without prior activation or partial activation. (Because logogens may receive contextual input from any source, they will respond to sensory input (tapped in Marslen-Wilson and Tyler's rhyme priming) and semantic input (category priming).)

The main problem with the model as formulated by Morton is that it does not capture the on-line temporal nature of auditory word recognition in the continuous speech flow. In order to do so the input system must be specified as receiving the sensory input on-line as it accumulates. Given this extra specification, the Logogen Model becomes a metaphorical variant on the Cohort Model: as sensory input accumulates, responding logogens increase their level of 'excitation', and the logogen still responding at the uniqueness point (i.e. the point at which all competitors diverge phonologically from the target) will be the only one to cross threshold, and therefore will be recognised. The observation in the shadowing experiments that fluent restoration was more likely in later syllables, can only be handled by the Logogen Model if, as Marslen-Wilson and Welsh (1978) suggest, the elements internal to the logogen corresponding to the beginning of the word are 'weighted' more than endings, as this weighting word initially would impinge negatively on the positive power of the increments from other parts of the word, making detection of mispronunciations early in the word more likely.

In order to identify, in a lexical decision task, whether the nonword is a mispronunciation of a real word, the hearer must be able to re-enter the logogen system to discover acoustically similar words: here another problem arises for the Logogen Model. Morton suggests that in order to access the logogen system after logogen failure (e.g. under noisy conditions, with impoverished input), it is possible to lower all thresholds until a logogen responds to the re-entered target stimulus. The problem with this account is that it predicts that deviations which are closer to the real word (e.g. deviations by one feature only) will be more quickly detected than more radical deviations. However, Cole's (1973) mispronunciation detection experiment showed that one-feature change latencies took 400 msec longer to detect than two- or three-feature changes, and Marslen-Wilson and Welsh's shadowing results yielded a fluent restoration rate of 82 per cent for one-feature changes, indicating low detection, whereas the rate for three-feature changes was only 33 per cent, indicating high detection.

Understanding affixes 125

Finally, Forster (1976) points to a significant problem which is symptomatic of a broader theoretical deficiency of the Logogen Model. He notes what he calls the 'technical difficulty' of ensuring that the various level-raising and threshold-lowering features of the model actually result in the correct word being recognised. He cites as an example the logogens *blight* and *bright* which will respond together to the target word *blight* because they differ in only one feature. *Bright* is, of course, of much higher frequency than *blight* and so will have a lower threshold (or a higher state of rest – these being equivalent). What, then, will ensure that the advantage of *bright* in terms of frequency will not be greater than the one-feature phonological advantage of *blight*? This is one aspect of a larger problem: the model is highly abstract and many of its features are not amenable to empirical verification. It might be argued that cohorts also are too theoretically removed from psychological reality; however, unlike the logogen, the cohort has no primitive status in the model – it is simply the name given to the set of activated lexical entries. The logogen, on the other hand, is an element in a set of systems separate from the mental lexicon – a real psychological mechanism, for which there is no direct experimental support (cf. the richness of the Cohort Model's empirical base). Given Marslen-Wilson's (1987) reformulation of the Cohort Model, it may be argued that Forster's *blight/bright* criticism is equally valid there, since activation levels are also assumed to be rising and falling on the basis of frequency and phonological advantage and disadvantage; however, the problem should not arise, since initial activation is still determined on the basis of acoustic/phonetic input alone.

5.1.1.3 The Search Model

To conclude this discussion of the three most influential models of lexical access, I briefly describe a model which differs from the Cohort and Logogen models in a fundamental way. Both these models posit input monitors associated with each lexical item/entry, thus assuming direct or 'content addressable' access. Forster (1976) proposes an '*approximately* content addressable' system, in which some central processor monitors the input, matching it with 'access codes' listed in 'peripheral access files' where a 'pointer' determines each word's location in the main lexicon (the 'master file'). There are a number of access files, including one organised on phonological principles for spoken word recognition, one orthographically-based for reading, and one semantically organised for production purposes.

126 *Morphology and mind*

What is involved in word recognition here is a *search* through the relevant access file for the correct access code. According to this model, the search is narrowed down in two major ways: (i) the peripheral access files are organised into 'bins' which contain *similar* access codes; (ii) the access codes are listed in each bin according to frequency (most frequent codes scanned first, least frequent last).

Forster suggests that in searching the bin, not all of the input signal is used, so perhaps the first four letters (in a written word) or the first syllable only is used. This initial portion of the input word is then checked against the access code of each entry in the bin. If the word is of high frequency, then its address in the master file will be encountered earlier, and thus it will be accessed more quickly (accounting for the frequency effects discussed earlier). Once the master file has been accessed, a check is made between the full phonological (or orthographic) specification in the lexical entry, and the input stimulus. This feature of the model accounts for the longer delay in detecting a nonword which is similar to a real word: for nonwords whose initial syllable corresponds to that of a real word, an access code *is* located in the appropriate bin but when post-access checking is performed a mismatch is detected and the bin must be searched again.

The major problem with this model is that it is very loose in its description of how the search mechanism works – exactly what happens on-line as the word is processed. If, as Forster suggests, only part of the word is used in the search of the appropriate bin, this suggests that the number and content of the bins is determined by the shape of a stretch of the word which is *less* than the first syllable. If the access codes are grouped according to a longer portion of the word, and if a code may be isolated on the basis of only the initial syllable, then each bin will contain only one word – this is obviously wrong. In order to determine which bin to search, then, the processor must process less than the first syllable of each word and on this basis select the appropriate bin, at which the full first syllable must be matched with the access code. The rest of the word is then used in the post-access check. There are therefore three stages in the recognition process: (i) bin selection, using less than the first syllable; (ii) access code isolation, using the first syllable, giving access to the master file entry; and (iii) post-access check, using the full word. Only after these stages have been completed will recognition have taken place.

It seems that Forster is assuming a temporally sequenced matching at these three stages, and consequently an access file organised according to the temporal sequencing of the input; however, the

Understanding affixes 127

motivation for this does not seem to be to explain early lexical access on the basis of the redundancy of later portions of the input signal, for this must be used in the third stage, the post-access check. Rather, it is motivated by Forster in terms of economy in the matching at the first and second stages (bin selection and access code isolation): Forster states that in locating the access code for the word *henchman*, for instance, 'it would be computationally expensive to make a large number of comparisons involving all eight letters' (p. 269).

It is not clear, then, what is gained by dividing up the word into these three portions and using the information contained there at successive stages, rather than the more efficient processes postulated in the Cohort Model and a revised Logogen Model, where the minimal required amount of input information is utilised directly and on-line to isolate the target item.

5.1.1.4 Assessment

In the foregoing I have reviewed three models of lexical access: Marslen-Wilson and Tyler's Cohort Model, Morton's Logogen Model, and Forster's Search Model. Each has deficiencies. Although the Cohort Model in its original formulation was too restrictive and found no place for frequency effects and problems with impoverished stimuli, revisions have been proposed which go some way towards satisfactorily dealing with these problems. They are, however, far from being thoroughly formulated, and open up this model to potential criticisms of non-falsifiability levelled at others. The Logogen Model, without specifying the sequential nature of the processing of the sensory input (perhaps via positional 'weighting'), fails to capture the importance of the initial portion of the word in normal speech conditions; in addition, the excitation level and threshold metaphor cannot always be guaranteed to predict the correct results, and this contributes to the theory's non-falsifiability. The Search Model is not compatible with the notion of optimal on-line efficiency as demonstrated in experimentation on lexical access, and the mechanisms implicit in the model (operating at the three matching stages) do not enjoy any empirical support.

Although the Cohort Model might be, in its original formulation, too restrictive, and, in its revised form, not yet fully articulated, it goes furthest, in my assessment, towards plausibly modelling what we know about lexical access, for three major reasons: (i) it alone of the three models reflects the very reliable observation that processing of speech is optimally efficient and is executed from word onset

128 *Morphology and mind*

extremely rapidly in real time; (ii) it alone enjoys empirical support from a wide variety of experimental paradigms; (iii) its very restrictiveness, the criticism most often levelled at it by its detractors, in fact recognises that there is much evidence yet to be collected and that the evidence accumulated so far is by no means incontrovertible. A model which makes strong predictions and lacks theoretical artifice (and is therefore more open to falsification) constitutes a much more secure theoretical base from which to advance.

5.1.2 The global organisation of the lexicon

In this section and the following I examine experimental evidence for the internal structure of the mental lexicon. There are two major issues to address in this area: (i) how the information is structured *within* each lexical entry (5.1.3) and (ii) how lexical entries are organised in relation to each other (this section). As we shall see, the questions may not be answered entirely separately, especially when we are considering the problem of morphologically complex words. First, then, let us address the problem of how the mental lexicon is organised in terms of its global structure.

Experimentation by Meyer, Schvaneveldt and Ruddy (1975) and Swinney (1979), amongst others, has suggested that there is a network of semantic cross-wiring between lexical entries, so that when one entry is accessed, entries for items in the same lexical field are temporarily 'activated' in some way. For example, prior exposure to the word *doctor* leads to facilitation of the word *nurse*. Instead, though, of cross-wiring in the lexicon, we might posit a lexicon which is *ordered* according to semantic principles, so that, for example, the entries for *doctor* and *nurse* might occupy 'neighbouring' positions, due, for example, to an overlap of semantic features. Accessing one entry might lead to the activation of the other due to whatever is the cognitive analogue of physical proximity. A semantically based lexicon would make a lot of sense for language production, for the speaker needs to locate the correct word initially on the basis of output from the central conceptual systems, and then recover from the lexical entry its phonological coding. This task would presumably be facilitated by locating a semantic address in the lexicon.

But then if this is true, what of comprehension? For comprehension purposes it is clear that a phonological address is required, as we have seen in the previous section. To satisfy both demands we could posit *two* lexicons, one for input and one for output, but this would be highly uneconomical. The postulation of separate input and output

Understanding affixes 129

'files' to a single unordered lexicon, as assumed in the Search and Logogen Models, would seem more likely. However, there is compelling evidence from speech errors (Fay and Cutler 1977) which argues against this position. The source of their evidence is the production of malapropisms – words which sound like the target, but are unrelated in meaning, e.g.:

(10) a. If these two vectors are *equivalent*, then ...
       (Intended: equivocal)
    b. We have a lovely Victorian *condom* set.
       (Intended: condiment)

Fay and Cutler argue that if, in production, speakers produce such semantically unrelated forms, then there *must* be organisation according to phonological principles, so that when, in word selection, speakers mistarget, they pull out a neighbouring word which *sounds* similar.

Why, though, should the organisation of the lexicon favour comprehension over production? Fay and Cutler suggest that it is because locating words in comprehension involves an additional complication over production: the problem of noise extraneous to the system. The hearer must typically match stored items against a degenerate input signal, thus necessitating choices between similarly sounding words, whereas the production system is entirely internal, and 'can be as precise as it desires in determining the properties of the entry it is seeking'. It makes sense, therefore, to list like-sounding words together to facilitate the more sensitive matching and choice process required in speech comprehension.

Fay and Cutler investigated their sizeable corpus of malapropisms to determine how far, measured in distinctive features, the forms differed from their targets. They found that the greater the number of feature differences, the fewer the number of examples in the corpus. They took this to indicate that the lexicon is organised on the basis of phonological distinctive features, measured from word onset, like the left to right organisation of letters in a dictionary of English. In addition, they also specify a complex system of semantic cross-wiring, hierarchical in nature, which is connected to the central conceptual systems. This cross-wiring is motivated by the need for production-directed lexical access, and is assumed to be hierarchically structured to account for semantic selection errors and for semantic priming effects (for errors it is assumed that the wrong path is taken from a higher node in the network tree, and for priming, connections at higher nodes serve to activate related items).

130 *Morphology and mind*

Another factor that would seem to argue in favour of Fay and Cutler's posited 'primacy of the hearer' is that of 'temporal control' in production, by which I mean to suggest that the speaker has greater control over the time course of an utterance than the hearer, i.e. the speaker may slow down the rate of production to facilitate lexical selection or may commit 'false starts' and backtrack to an earlier point in the utterance, whereas the hearer has fewer opportunities to choose the speed and comprehensibility of the utterance which he or she is fed, i.e. is under much greater pressure to work within time limits outside of his/her control.

5.1.3 Morphologically complex words[3]

We now turn to the central discussion of this chapter, the problem posed for the mental lexicon and lexical processing mechanism by morphologically complex, i.e. prefixed or suffixed, words. The first section (5.1.3.1) deals with problems of representation, and the second (5.1.3.2), with access, though the two are intimately linked, and consequently there is considerable thematic overspill.

5.1.3.1 Representation

There is a great variety of logically possible representational principles for morphologically complex words – 'a quite unmanageable combinatorial explosion', as Butterworth puts it (1983: 260). 'Unfortunately,' he goes on (p. 261), 'the available evidence does not address the whole range of potential combinations of answers, and in many cases leaves even the simple questions unresolved.' Amongst the contenders for representational models that are considered most frequently in the literature are those listed in (11)

(11) a. A separate entry for every word, with fully specified phonological, syntactic, and semantic information in each entry (i.e. maximal redundancy).

   b. A separate entry for every word, with syntactic and semantic information listed only in the stem entry, and referred to by redundancy rule in the entries of the related forms.

   c. A separate entry for every derived word, but with inflected forms listed under the stem entry.

   d. A single entry for all related words, with derived and inflected forms listed as sub-entries to the stem entry.

Understanding affixes 131

e. A separate entry for all stems and prefixed forms, but with redundancy rules in the latter specifying the location of syntactic and semantic information in the former (i.e. a lexicon based on the temporal accumulation of input, in the same way that a dictionary is organised on left-to-right principles, at least in English).

The problem of metaphorical abstraction is a very serious one here. Often it is very difficult to distinguish between different formulations when reviewing the experimental data, and the empirical predictions of the various formulations are not always clear. It may well be that some, or *all*, of these are, in fact, only notational variants of each other. In addition, most psycholinguists assume, following theoretical linguists, that the lexicographic notion of lexical entries as lists of information headed by the stem is what the processor makes contact with, rather than a more process-oriented representation. This leads to further vagueness in the cognitive models that have been proposed, as we shall see below.

There is, however, much evidence that the key to the organisation of the mental lexicon is the *stem*. Whether this means one entry per stem plus something corresponding to the sub-entries found in dictionaries, or different entries with cross-wiring between same stems, is not yet entirely clear. What most psycholinguists are confident of is that at some point in lexical processing, hearers can recognise the difference between stems and affixes – i.e. they can, in some way, decompose morphologically complex words (*if*, I would stress, the internal structure is part of their morphological competence). *How* this decomposition is effected, and *when* in the access process it occurs, will be explored in the next section, but first we look at some evidence for how affixes may be represented in the mental lexicon in relation to their stems.

Evidence that morphological structure is represented in the mental lexicon is abundant in the area of speech error research. For example, in a corpus of speech errors collected by Stemberger (1985), we find errors with prefixes, which may be substituted one for another (12a), deleted (12b), or added (12c):

(12)   a. She's so *exquisitive*. (Intended: *inquisitive*.)
       b. They weren't *jeal*. (Intended: *conjealing*.)
       c. ... positively or negatively *remarked* ...
          (Intended: *marked*.)

132 *Morphology and mind*

They may also be anticipated (13a), perseverated (13b), or transposed (13c):

(13) a. We have 25 *dedollars* de ductable.

b. It does not explain how an apparent case of rule *exser* – insertion may arise.

c. A self-*instruct de*- a self-destruct instruction?

For suffixes, Stemberger observes, for example, anticipation (14a), and delayed execution, when the next word is a clitic (14b), and when it is another word (14c):

(14) a. ... and see if we still see that there's *differents* amount_.

b. ... look_ atting ...

c. ... where the safe part_ of the *cities* are.

There are also the typical stranding examples, such as:

(15) a. That's cause it *soes feel* ...

(Intended: ... feels so ...)

b. You want the potatoes *slicely thin*ned?

Errors such as these constitute very convincing evidence that morphological structure is present in the mental lexicon, and that in production it can be accessed, in some sense, separately. A model of the lexicon which posited separate unanalysed entries for morphologically complex words could not account for these data.

Support for the separate (but not independent) representation of affixes within lexical entries is forthcoming from early work on the 'tip of the tongue' (TOT) phenomenon by Brown and McNeill (1966). These experimenters induced TOT states in their subjects by reading to them definitions of low frequency words. They noticed that subjects occasionally gave whole prefixes such as *ex-* (for *extort*) and *con-* (for *convene*) when asked for the initial letter of the target word. This prompted an examination of same-sounding words in an attempt to recall the target: of those produced in response to targets which terminated in a three-letter suffix, thirty out of ninety-three matched in their final three letters, compared with only five out of 130 for non-suffixed targets. Brown and McNeill conclude from this that it is possible to recall suffixes as separate elements when in a TOT state; this could only be possible if suffixes were

Understanding affixes 133

separately represented and recalled selectively from the lexical entry as *units*.

Another type of speech error which has been offered in support of single lexical entries for related words is that of word stress misplacement. Consider, for example, the following, which suggests to Cutler (1980) that it is interference from the derived form *linguistics* which causes stress to fall a syllable late:

(16)   For linGUISTS, for LINguists to judge . . .

On the basis of such evidence, Cutler concludes that related words are not stored in separate lexical entries, since for the derived form to interfere in the placement of stress implies that the forms are stored together and access to the lexical entry provides access to both of them.

Evidence from priming makes some more specific predictions in this domain. Such evidence suggests firstly that we must make a distinction between regular inflection, irregular inflection, and derivation. It seems that the latter two are less closely connected with stems in the lexicon than regular inflections. Stanners, Neiser, Hernon and Hall (1979), for example, found that inflected forms provided as primes for a future lexical decision on the stem were as effective as identity primes (i.e. priming with the stem itself). This result was taken to indicate that access to inflected forms gives direct access to the stem form, suggesting a single lexical entry for both, a finding supported for Dutch by Bergman and Eling (1984).

Irregularly inflected forms also prime the stem, but not so effectively – indeed, they facilitate stem access as well as do derived forms, which *do* have a priming effect, but not as great as regular inflections. This suggested to Stanners *et al.* that derived and irregularly inflected forms have separate but not *independent* representations: i.e. that they have some form of 'sub-entry' status. That they do not have separate full lexical entries is suggested by another finding of the study: lexical decisions on derived or irregularly inflected forms took longer than on the stem alone, suggesting to these researchers that access to such forms is made *via* access to the stem. This is supported by earlier findings by Rosenberg, Coyle and Porter (1966) who demonstrated that recall from a previously presented list of adverbs with the *-ly* suffix showed frequency effects. The frequency levels involved were, however, those of the stem rather than of the inflected word, indicating that access to related forms gives access to the stem (where its frequency level will be encoded).

All these data, however, are completely compatible with a more

134 *Morphology and mind*

general formulation of the mental lexicon in which access to a derived or irregularly inflecting form *entails* access to the main stem entry, but does not necessarily require access *via* it. Such a formulation allows prefixed forms to be accessed as such, without having to stipulate affix-stripping. The order of access for derivationally suffixed words would then be main stem entry followed by suffixed sub-entry; for prefixed and stem-alternating forms, access would be via the sub-entry with *subsequent* access to the main entry. A model of access incorporating these possibilities is elaborated in some detail in 5.3 below.

Of course the metaphor caveat should be emphasised again here: simply because access to one form entails access to another does not guarantee that they are listed in the same lexical entry – it is well known that priming is also established by words which are *semantically* related, but *cannot* share the same lexical entry. As we have seen (5.1.2) lexical entries appear to have semantically-determined cross-wiring; there is no reason to believe that morphological cross-wiring is not a possibility too.

This possibility does not, of course, undermine the finding of correlation of disparity in RTs with degree of relatedness, a finding strengthened by Kempley and Morton (1982) working within the Logogen Model. They found that identical forms primed more effectively than regularly inflected forms, but, contra Stanners *et al.*, that irregularly inflected forms, like phonetically similar but un-related forms, did not prime at all (cf. also Morton 1981). Evidence from lexical decision experiments in Italian (Caramazza, Laudanna and Romani 1988) confirm the dissociation between regular and irregular inflected forms, suggesting (in line with Kempley and Morton) that 'irregular stems constitute autonomous lexical entries in the [in this case] orthographic input lexicon' (p. 321). The Stanners *et al.* results seem to suggest the organisational system in (17a), whereas those of Kempley and Morton and of Caramazza *et al.* support the representation in (17b).

For prefixes, Stanners, Neiser and Painton (1979) found that priming with a derived form such as *discomfort* facilitated a lexical decision on the stem *comfort* as effectively as did repetition priming. In addition, double priming for the word *retrieve* with the bound stem *-trieve* and the prefix *re-* in a separate word such as *remit*, was found to be more effective than no priming at all, but less effective than repetition priming. This latter effect suggested to the investigators that there is no *separate* representation of prefix and stem in the lexicon, since if this were the case, *trieve/remit* priming should be

(17) Conflicting systems of lexical representation
(Stanners et al. 1979 vs. Kempley and Morton 1982 and Caramazza et al. 1988)

    a.   RUN{s, ing}   b.   RUN{s, ing}

        a. ran
        b. runner   RAN
        c. runaway

Key: ran = sub-entry
        RAN = main entry

similar to repetition. They suggest that a prefixed word does have a unitary representation but that this can be accessed via the stem alone. They conclude from both experiments that prefixed words are listed separately from stems, but that during processing, prefixed words are decomposed and both stem and prefix + stem representations are accessed. The pattern would, then, look something like this:

(18) Access to prefix and stem
(Stanners, Neiser, and Painton 1979)

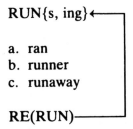

Key: → = access link between entries

They speculate that the motivation for separate entries is acquisitional, in that learning a new word, whether it is related or not to one already learnt, requires the creation of a new memory representation. If this is true, it should be true of suffixed forms too; however Stanners et al. do not make this clear. See 5.2 and chapter 6 for more on this general problem.

5.1.3.2 Access

The major questions which arise in the investigation of how morphologically complex words are recognised are when and how such a

136 *Morphology and mind*

word is decomposed into its separate morphemes. A model of the lexicon which includes full independent listings for all words would not require decomposition at all; however, there is no psycholinguistic evidence for this position, and much against it, as evidenced in the sampling above. In addition, the formulations discussed in the rest of this chapter have at least one feature in common: the recognition that, *at some point*, morphological decomposition can occur, at least to the extent that internal structure in words can be realised in some way.

The only detailed theory of access to morphologically complex words is the Affix-Stripping Model developed by Taft and his associates (Taft, Forster and Garrett 1974; Taft and Forster 1975, 1976; Taft 1979, 1981[4]). The model is claimed (Taft 1979) to be compatible with both the Search and Logogen models. The Cohort Model deals explicitly only with the accessing of simple monomorphemic forms, and although some work has been carried out on prefixing and suffixing (Tyler and Marslen-Wilson 1986; Tyler *et al.* 1988), the predictions of the model have only barely been articulated within that programme of research. I shall attempt to follow through on these predictions in the next section, and assess which model offers the most promising account of the problem.

Before embarking on a review of the Affix-Stripping Model and alternatives to it, two points should be made. Firstly, it is not unlikely that the major problem in processing morphologically complex words is presented by *prefixes*, rather than suffixes. As we have seen, (i) processing starts at the onset of the word and proceeds sequentially; (ii) access to the lexical entry seems to require access to the stem. With suffixes, the stem is located in initial position, therefore allowing normal processing in accordance with (i) and (ii) until the suffix is encountered, when presumably it is processed separately and combined with the stem, or prompts the processor to access a unitary representation of the stem + affix. With prefixes, however, the first element of the word to be encountered is the affix, causing problems for both features (i) and (ii). This asymmetry matches the one found by H&G (Hawkins and Gilligan 1988) in the cross-linguistic affix distribution data and exploited in Cutler *et al.*'s (1985) explanation (and noted also in work on complex word recognition in French by Segui and Zubizarreta (1985) and Colé, Beauvillain and Segui (1989)). Given the context of our enquiry, it is, naturally, with prefixes that the present section is primarily concerned (although, of course, I do not wish to suggest that the scores are all in on suffixes).

The second point, which only now becomes *especially* significant, is

Understanding affixes 137

that, thus far, we have been virtually ignoring the difference between reading and listening. The constraint of temporally sequential processing of the input is far more acute in the aural modality than in the orthographic, for obvious reasons (in the latter, but not in the former, all parts of the stimulus are simultaneously present in real time). In what follows, this distinction will become critical in deciding on the correct model of lexical access in auditory speech processing, which is the primary concern of this chapter.

Let us now examine the Affix-Stripping Model, and assess its success in modelling what we know about access to prefixed words. Based on results from an ingenious set of experiments, Taft and Forster (1975) proposed a model of lexical access which featured a set of mandatory procedures designed to establish the internal complexity of the input word. The key decision in the procedure was to determine whether the word was prefixed or not. This model has been most influential in the field, since it was the first model which articulated predictions for access to affixed words with some degree of sophistication. In what follows, I briefly outline the experimental foundation of this model, and then summarise the model itself. A discussion of the considerable problems and counter-evidence which the model must confront concludes the section.

The experiments were nearly all carried out in the written modality; however, the results yielded have often been applied to spoken word recognition too, and some later experimentation by Taft and his associates addressed the auditory domain (Taft and Hambly 1986; Taft, Hambly and Kinoshita 1986), without resulting in any modification of the model (though Taft (1988) raises the possibility of a potential weakening of the model on the basis of further speech data: see below). In their Experiment I, Taft and Forster (1975) presented subjects with real, bound stems such as **juvenate* (from *re+juvenate*) and also 'pseudostems', such as **pertoire* (from *repertoire*). Real stems, on a lexical decision task, took longer to reject as nonwords than pseudostems, indicating that real stems, even when bound, are 'directly represented in the lexicon'.

In Experiment II, they found that stems with both bound *and* free readings (e.g. *card* ($card_N$ and $dis+card_V$) and *vent* ($vent_N$ and $pre+vent_V$)) yield longer RTs than real stems which are free only, but only when the bound reading is more frequent. When the bound reading is less frequent, then there is no difference. These results are taken to indicate (i) that the bound stem readings are directly represented, accounting for the interference in RTs; and that (ii) items are accessed via a frequency-directed search, as in Forster's

138 Morphology and mind

model (5.1.1.3 above). So, for example, *card* would take as long as *coin*, because the free reading of *card* is more frequent than the bound (i.e. *card* is more frequent than *discard*), is equal in frequency to *coin*, and is therefore encountered first. On the other hand, *vent* will take longer than *fist* (same frequency), because the bound reading is more frequent than the free (i.e. *prevent* is more frequent than *vent*), therefore it will be encountered first and must be rejected before the free reading is located.

Experiment III revealed that real stem nonwords (with an inappropriate prefix, e.g. **de+juvenate*) yielded longer RTs than pseudostem nonwords (e.g. **depertoire*). This result was taken to reflect the extra step of locating a stem entry for **dejuvenate*, whereas for **depertoire*, no such stem is found, and so no check for whether the *de-* prefix is appropriate need be carried out. To account for all these results, they propose that the processor must follow a number of procedures in ordered stages, which they represented in a flow chart, given here as (19).

An additional result from an earlier study (Taft, Forster and Garrett 1974) should also be mentioned here: they found no difference in decision RTs for prefixed words (e.g. *re+juvenate*) and monomorphemic words (e.g. *somersault*), as predicted by the model in (19).

(19) The Affix-Stripping Model (Taft and Forster 1975)

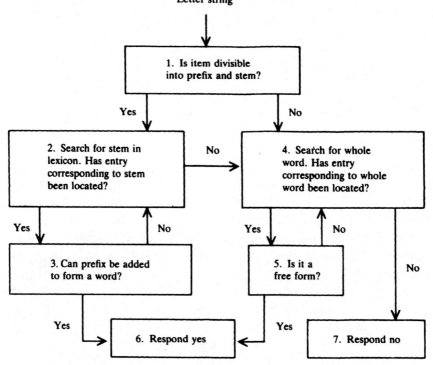

Understanding affixes 139

The appropriate steps for the various target words are given below:

(20)   a. juvenate (real prefix stripped):   1–4–5–4–7
         pertoire (pseudoprefix stripped):   1–4–––––7

      b. vent (frequency: bound > free):   1–4–5–4–5–6
         card (frequency: free > bound):   1–4–5–––––6

      c. dejuvenate (real stem, nonword):   1–2–3–2–4–7
         depertoire (pseudostem, nonword): 1–2––––––4–7

      d. rejuvenate (prefixed word):   1–2–3–6
         somersault (monomorphemic word): 1–4–5–6

The number of steps necessary for reaching the word/nonword decision is reflected in the RTs recorded in the experiments.

Taft's model has been much criticised in the experimental literature, on both methodological and theoretical grounds. Rubin, Becker and Freeman (1979) argued that subjects might have been employing a special decomposition strategy in Taft and Forster's experiments, because the test materials were heavily biased towards having prefixes. Rubin *et al.* tested two sets of materials, one with Taft and Forster's proportion of prefixed words, the other with a proportion reflecting that found in a text count. No differences were found between prefixes and pseudoprefixes in the latter context.[5]

In a series of experiments on Dutch complex forms of various types, Bergman and Eling (1984) identified factors which complicate Taft's model at the very least, and revealed some evidence which runs directly contrary to certain essential aspects of it. In a lexical decision task using written materials, they found, *contra* Taft, that Italic prefixed words were slower than controls, and that moribund Italic forms were slower than current ones. Germanic prefixed forms were, however, as fast as controls, in line with Taft's predictions. In further experiments, no differences were found between suffixed and pseudo-suffixed words, against the predictions of Taft's model. Their general conclusions were that *some* prefixed forms are processed with more difficulty than non-prefixed controls, but that suffixed forms are not more difficult. The particular 'step by step' results of Taft and Forster (1975) were not replicated. They also challenged Taft and Forster on theoretical grounds, questioning whether all the stages in the flow chart in (19) will take the same computational resources. Taft, by simply counting the steps involved as a metric of computational complexity, ignores this problem (which is part of the

140 *Morphology and mind*

greater metaphorical abstraction issue noted throughout this review).

Jarvella and Meijers (1983), measuring RTs to same/different judgements on stems and inflections in Dutch words, found that same stem judgements were faster than same inflection judgements, even in prefixed words; however, forms with bound stems (retaining in the past tense the *be-*, *ver-* etc. prefixes) took longer than those with free stems (taking the regular *ge-* past tense prefix). A discrepancy in RTs is not predicted by Taft's model, as both types should follow the same route (viz. 1–2–3–6) through the flow chart. In addition, Jarvella and Meijers found that both prefix types took longer than non-prefixed forms, again contrary to Taft's findings (cf. (20d)).

Another set of experimental results which run contrary to the Taft model are the French data mentioned earlier (Segui and Zubizarreta 1985; Colé, Beauvillain and Segui 1989). In experiments using the lexical decision task, these studies investigated the priming effects of morphological context (in items presented prior to the target word) in the earlier study, and the effects of surface and cumulative root (morphological family) frequency in the later study, in both prefixed and suffixed forms. The studies revealed context and frequency effects for suffixes but not for prefixes, and on the basis of this evidence these investigators were led to conclusions running directly contrary to Taft's prefix-stripping hypothesis:

> Processing from left to right requires the subject to access the root first in the case of suffixed words. Accessing the root morpheme entails accessing a morphological family of words. Subsequently, a new matching of the terminal properties of the signal with one of the members of this family takes place. We may hypothesize that it is this matching procedure which is speeded up in the case where words of comparable morphological structure *root + affix* are presented successively. . . . As for prefixed words, it is our contention that no matching procedure will be called for in lexical access, given that the affix in this case precedes the root: i.e. *there is no root accessing that precedes access to the whole word*. (Segui and Zubizarreta 1985: 770; my emphasis)

> The role of cumulative root frequency will be more important for the recognition of suffixed words than for prefixed words. Only suffixed words should be accessed preferentially via their root morphemes. *Because in prefixed words the affix precedes the root, they cannot be accessed via their root.* Consequently, latencies to prefixed words should be uniquely or principally affected by the surface frequency of the whole word form. (Colé *et al.* 1989: 4; my emphasis)

Understanding affixes 141

The experimental results which, needless to say, confirmed these hypotheses, are not only narrowly relevant to the question of morphological decomposition under discussion in this section; they are also of great relevance to the larger issue of the suffixing preference, as we shall see below.

An issue which is raised in both Bergman and Eling's and Jarvella and Meijers's studies is that of the heterogeneity of affix types. Very few experimenters take into account the fact that all prefixes are not equal. Within a given speaker's 'morphological competence', some prefixed forms may no longer be analysable, i.e. may be lexicalised, others may be completely transparent, whereas still others may lie at some intermediate stages. This observation will be examined in greater detail below and in chapter 6; suffice it to say now, though, that a unitary model such as Taft's is fundamentally flawed by virtue of its inability to recognise that different affix types may be treated by the processor in different ways (cf. Smith 1988). For the purposes of the present discussion, however, this problem will be temporarily shelved.

A further argument can be levelled at Taft, this time only if his model is advocated also for the auditory modality. The problem here is that prefix-stripping does not take into account the temporal nature of speech input. The experiments which form the empirical basis of the Affix-Stripping Model were almost all on the processing of the written form, but, as Marslen-Wilson has shown (1983), this might use very different mechanisms from those used in auditory lexical access. In phoneme-monitoring experiments, subjects were asked to respond as soon as they detected a phoneme given in advance. The phoneme was placed at roughly equidistant points in a three-syllable word in separate trials. Hearers process temporally from word onset, as we have seen, and, in addition, there is much evidence to suggest that they can only identify the phoneme when the phonological information in the lexical entry is accessed (i.e. upon word recognition) (cf. e.g. Morton and Long 1976). RTs should, then, decrease the later the phoneme occurs in the word, since the more that is heard of the word, the greater the likelihood that it has already been recognised or is about to be recognised. This is, in fact, what happened.

In a second experiment, Marslen-Wilson used the same procedure for written stimuli, in which a letter, rather than a phoneme, was to be detected. Here the letter in initial position was detected first, but there was no difference between the other positions. This suggests that written words are not processed strictly left to right in English,

142   *Morphology and mind*

and so we may conclude that any results from written modality experiments should not be automatically assumed to be relevant for spoken word processing. In the prefix-stripping model we can see that there is a sense in which the eye can 'skip' the prefix in written words, because it can perhaps be processed simultaneously, whereas in auditory input the hearer *must* wait for the prefix to get out of the way, if he or she knows that it is a prefix at all. The exact implications of the modality dichotomy in this area remain to be worked out, although it should be noted that Taft himself has acknowledged the possibility (1988: 664) that affix-stripping may not occur in the auditory domain.

Finally, a criticism from a very different source. In H&G, we have seen convincing demonstration that there is an overwhelming preference for suffixing over prefixing across languages. Given, then, that there is a universal tendency towards suffixation, it would seem rather perverse that the human processing mechanism, itself innate and therefore universal, would require hearers to first attempt to identify a prefix, *obligatorily*, in *every* input word, before they do anything else: nothing in the acoustic signal signifies categorically that a prefix is present (morphological bracketing is only a descriptive convention of linguists, and rarely has any phonological analogue[6]); in any case, it is clear that initial processing of the acoustic input must normally achieve contact with a form representation before morphological, or any other content-linked interpretation can begin (see 5.2.1). Finally, note that such a dysfunctional system would be *particularly* odd for languages which are exclusively suffixing (and these are many – cf. the data cited in chapter 2) or even predominantly suffixing, and yet these make up the majority of human languages.

Note that none of the criticisms levelled here at Taft's model constitute rejection of the notion of morphological decomposition *per se*; they are, rather, arguments largely against the particularly restrictive ordered steps in (19). The problem with the current state of research is, however, that not enough empirical evidence is available to support a more plausible model of access to *spoken* prefixed forms. Much more work in this area is needed if we are going to resolve the problems posed by Taft's model and the reactions against it in the literature. A new interest is beginning to develop, however, in this central issue in word recognition; the beginnings of such work are introduced in the next section, and the experimentation reported in chapter 6 and Hall (1987)[7] makes a further contribution.

5.2 MORPHOLOGICALLY COMPLEX WORDS IN A COHORT-BASED MODEL

So far we have been thinking of lexical entries as theoretical linguists do, as bounded units in which various types of information about words are listed, rather as in an orthographic dictionary. From a process point of view, however, we must consider the temporal dynamics of access and the type of architecture this entails in the mental lexicon. Since the mental lexicon is the central point of interface between sound and meaning, one important distinction that needs to be made is between the representation of form and content, a distinction that will be of great importance in the development in this section of a model of access to morphologically complex words; we must also specify the nature of the association or mapping between these representations.

Another issue is the role of input monitors (the 'low-level' devices responsible for activating lexical entries on the basis of matching incoming sensory input) and their relationship with lexical entries, which has been overlooked in previous work. This is particularly important in the context of the recognition of prefixed words: in the Cohort Model, the input monitors responding to the initial stretch of a prefixed word should trigger the activation of a cohort containing all words with that prefix and all other stem-initial words which match the sensory input (Tyler *et al.* 1988). If input monitors responding to the speech signal are restricted to main entries as opposed to subentries (as assumed in Marslen-Wilson 1987 and Lahiri and Marslen-Wilson 1990), then this implies that prefixed forms must be main entries too and so be independent of their associated stem entries (in line with Stanners, Neiser and Painton (1979) – cf. 5.1.3.1). We must, then, reassess the role of input monitors in the accessing of morphologically complex lexical entries.

Finally, given the questionable claims of the Affix-Stripping Model, and new evidence from the auditory domain carried out within the Cohort framework (Tyler *et al.* 1988), we must attempt to resolve the morphological decomposition issue. As in the previous section, I aim to ease exposition by separating as far as possible issues of representation from issues of access; again, though, the distinction cannot be maintained at all points in the analysis.

5.2.1 Representation

As a first stage in unravelling the representation issue, let us, in place of the dictionary-style listings we employed in (17) and (18) earlier,

144 *Morphology and mind*

conceptualise lexical entries not as separate boxes containing lists of related forms and information about them, but instead as connected representations of form and content, as in the simple case schematised in (21). I assume that the form representation contains information about the phonological form of the item, and that the content representation contains information about its syntactic properties and linguistic aspects of its semantic structure. I make no specific claims here about the nature of content representations, but will assume Lahiri and Marslen-Wilson's (1990) framework for an abstract, underspecified representation of lexical *form* in which only unpredictable, non-redundant, segmental-featural information is represented.

(21) Representation of the head of a lexical entry

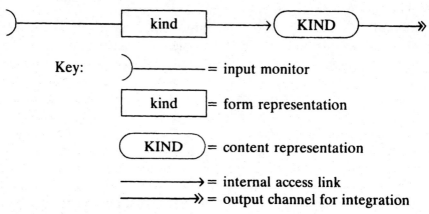

At its simplest, then, a lexical entry is a form representation and its associated input monitor, linked with a content representation and its associated output channel for integration purposes at the sentential level. As its iconic representation here suggests, the input monitor can be thought of as a cognitive 'satellite dish' tuned in to a particular ordered set of acoustic cues matching a unique structural representation in the mental lexicon. On responding, the input monitor triggers the activation of its associated form/content representations (thereby placing the lexical unit in the cohort of candidates for recognition). Of course, what is given in (21) is not the complete picture. When related forms are included, according to the model developed below, the representation becomes far more complex. As we have seen in earlier sections, there are, no doubt, activation links between semantically associated content representations (e.g. *kind* may be linked with *generous*). And, given the homophony of the form /kaind/, we may expect a second internal access link to a separate content

Understanding affixes 145

representation which itself is linked, in turn, with lexical entries for the nouns *type*, *sort*, *genus*, etc. Finally, we are ignoring completely here aspects of representation and access which may be involved in the *production* of words, and in processing in the *orthographic* modality.

Let us now turn to the rather more controversial question of the representation of morphologically complex words. First, the relatively straightforward case of suffixes. (22) shows a schematic formulation of a suffixed form, *kindness*, and its relationship with its related stem entry, *kind*. The stem is the privileged entry at both form and content levels – it is the 'head' of the lexical entry;[8] *kindness*, however, is a dependent entry or *sub-entry*, specified for form and content only when this differs from the main entry. Access to the content of sub-entries requires access to the main entry, i.e. the content of the sub-entry is available postlexically for integration only on access to the content of the main entry, as indicated by the lack of a direct output channel to the sentential level from the sub-entry, and, instead, a junction with the stem output channel at which the combined reading is made. The precise location of the combined reading computation is not crucial to the argument here: with regard to that phase of the recognition process, the diagram in (22) should be viewed as a schematic approximation only.

Also, the assumption implicit in the use of the word 'sub-entry' and in the representation of affixes in (22), that the affix is specified anew in each relevant stem entry (in (22) that *-ness* is exclusively associated with *kind*), is not a necessary one: it is highly probable that such redundancy is avoided and that there is only one sub-entry for each affix which is shared by all the stem entries with which it may be concatenated. For example, the form representation of *-ness* in *kindness* may be shared with other stem entries like *happy* (*happiness*), *fair* (*fairness*), etc. The formulation of the affix entry in (22) may therefore be viewed as part of a much larger network of access links between stem representations and their respective output channels. Although this does not affect the course of the central argument developed here, it should be borne in mind that in numerous respects where existing evidence is lacking, the diagrams employed are oversimplifications, which can only be corrected to a useful degree of refinement by an extensive programme of further research.

In the Cohort Model as currently formulated (i.e. on the basis of access to morphologically simple words) it is assumed that lexical entries have only one input monitor associated with them, the consequence of this being that prefixed forms would be obliged to

(22) Suffix representation

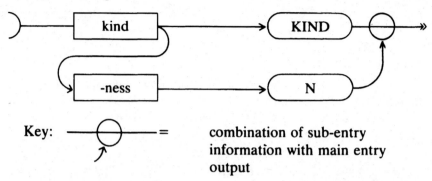

Key: ─○─ = combination of sub-entry information with main entry output

have separate lexical entries, regardless of the degree of phonological and/or semantic overlap between prefixed and bare stem form. An alternative view would be that lexical entries may have any number of input monitors, the number being determined by the shape of the onsets of morphologically related forms. (23) and (24) illustrate the two possibilities. In both, the input monitors for *kind* and *unkind* will respond to different input, and the forms will enter different cohorts. In (23) they belong to different lexical entries and are connected by activation links rather than access links, as *generous* is linked to *kind* (or as *doctor* to *nurse*). In (24), however, they are members of the same lexical entry, capturing the essential similarity with suffixed forms. Most of the evidence cited in the previous section (notably the experiments of Segui and Zubizarreta (1985) and Colé et al. (1989)) points to this alternative as the correct one, as does the massive redundancy in representation entailed by the restriction of one input monitor per lexical entry. It is, then, the conceptualisation in (24) that we shall assume henceforth.

(23) Prefix representation: separate head entry formulation

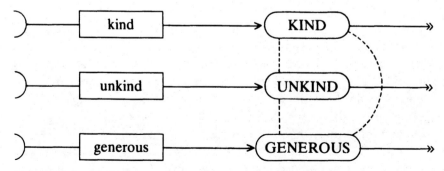

We now turn to the place of inflection in this formulation. We must first draw a distinction between regular and irregular (suffixed)

(24) Prefix representation: sub-entry formulation

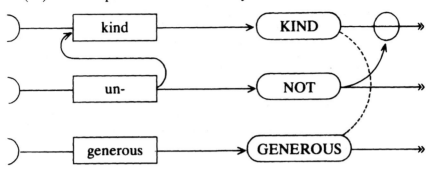

Key: ◯ ◯ = activation link between entries

inflection, where the former refers to inflection by suffixation which does not distort the form of the stem prior to its uniqueness point (i.e. the point at which it departs phonologically from all other words), and the latter refers to inflection which *does* distort the form of the stem in this way (either by stem modification (*run/ran*) or by suppletion (*go/went*)). In order to accommodate the difference observed (Stanners, Neiser, Hernon and Hall 1979; Kempley and Morton 1982 etc.) between the processing of regular and irregular inflections and derivations, where the regular inflections are found to be more effective primes than irregular inflections or derivations, we may propose that regularly suffixed inflected forms do not have separate sub-entries, but that irregular inflected forms *do*, and that these have input monitors associated with them. We then have a picture like (25), showing regular inflection, and (26), showing irregular inflection (these are, note, a compromise between the representational systems schematised in (17b) and (18)). Suppletion will pattern exactly as in (26), although *run* and *ran* may be linked by an activation link at the form level, whereas *go* and *went*, for example, patently will not.

(25) Representation of regular inflections

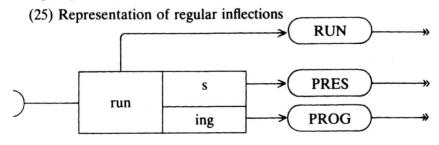

(26) Representation of irregular inflection

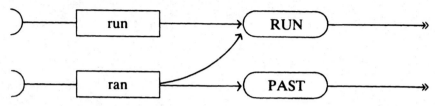

This predicts that irregular inflections require access to both the main entry and sub-entry, as do derived items. This is compatible with the finding in the experimental literature that irregular inflections and prefixed forms involve similar access delays compared with simple stems. The model also predicts that regular *prefixed* inflections in languages that have them, should subject the word to the same delays as irregular inflection and derived prefixation. No experimental results pertinent to this prediction are available, as far as I am aware. Note from (25) and (26) that in this formulation of inflectional representation, the sub-entries have direct output channels to the sentential level. This is intended to reflect the syntactic, sentence-level nature of the content of inflectional morphemes, compared with the essentially semantic, lexically-internal nature of most derivations. This formulation is consistent, then, with linguistic models of theoretical morphology which place the locus of inflectional processes in the syntax or at least *after* the output of word formation rules (recall the discussion in chapter 3).[9]

Before moving on to discuss the on-line process of affixed word recognition within the cohort framework, let me note one general point about lexical representation which will become very important later on. In all the models discussed, storage of prefixed forms requires more complicated internal structure than suffixed forms (unless the unlikely 'total redundancy' ('full listing') hypothesis, where related words have separate, autonomous lexical entries, turns out to be correct). Whether the model assumes separate lexical entries for prefixed forms (like Stanners, Neiser and Painton 1979) or a single full lexical entry with separate input monitors (like the model proposed here), prefixes will always necessitate more storage complexity than suffixes, given the assumption of a phonologically organised lexicon (or at least a lexicon with a phonological dimension of organisation), since prefixes, unlike suffixes, radically alter the initial portion of the word, the index to its phonological address, thus requiring separate input monitors. This storage distinction between prefix and suffix will be taken up again in more detail in chapter 6.

5.2.2 Access

Returning to the particular view of the lexicon assumed in the Cohort Model, what are its predictions for the actual on-line process of recognition of morphologically complex words? The hypothesis would seem to be that, for prefixed words like *rerun*, for example, access will be made to the main lexical entry *via* the sub-entry form representation. Only with access to the *stem* content representation will syntactic and semantic information about the whole word be made available for integration purposes, unless we assume duplication of all stem information in the sub-entry, thereby rendering the concepts of sub-entry and separate entry for derived forms indistinguishable from each other. I hypothesise, then, that the internal structure of the prefixed form (*if* such structure is part of the speaker's competence) is *realised* during processing by the successive accessing of the sub-entry and the stem entry.

Note that successive access does not entail prefix *stripping* as proposed in Taft's model. Stripping implies the creation of a new cohort for stem recognition on stripping of the prefix form, as represented in (27), where the prefix form information is not used in the accessing of the stem. Taft's conception predicts that, in spoken word recognition, not even subcategorial frame information is used to narrow down the identity of the stem. In the affix-stripping flowchart ((19) above) the inclusion of stage 3, requiring a check on the appropriateness of the affix–stem combination, implies that subcategorial information can only be used *after* stem recognition. Recall that in nonword experiments (Taft and Forster 1975), an inappropriately prefixed real stem (e.g. *dejuvenate*) was slower to reject than a prefixed pseudostem (e.g. *depertoire*). This they explained by the extra step necessary in locating the real stem and determining the inappropriateness of the prefix. In a model in which subcategorial information *is* made available, e.g. through an access link to the input monitors of appropriate stems, as in (28), exhaustion of these links (i.e. arrival at an empty cohort state) should be enough to reject the input as a nonword, without the need to identify the stem and then check to see whether the affix can be combined.

Notice that in the strong version of stripping (27), the bound morpheme is treated at the form level almost as a separate word, the availability of whose content is contingent upon recognition of the word which follows it. This implies that no information associated with the affix can become available to the system before stem recognition – the affix is put 'on hold' until the stem is accessed.

(27) Prefix stripping (strong version)

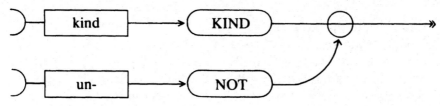

(28) Prefix stripping (weak version)

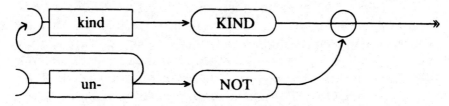

In contrast to stripping, the model proposed here envisages that access to the stem and hence recognition of the form of the whole word entails successively accessing prefix and stem in a single incremental process, with continual monitoring being transferred automatically from sub- to main entry as soon as stem information is received. Thus, only one cohort is involved in the access process. The transfer from sub- to main entry is represented in our diagrams by the direct access link between prefix and stem at the form level, by-passing the stem input monitor (cf. (24)). We will henceforth make a distinction, therefore, between 'realisation' and 'decomposition' of internal structure, where both refer to the successive accessing of separately represented internal components of the word, but only the latter requires the active decomposing process of *stripping*, i.e. the initiation of a new access process (cohort creation) for each internal component.

The exact temporal effects of prefixed word access are hard to determine even within a reasonably well-articulated processing model. Taft's model predicts that prefixed words will take no longer than simple words, since the same number of processing steps is required. This, as I have already suggested, is an over-simplistic metric for the computational and consequently temporal cost of prefix access. It would seem more likely that stripping would involve extra cost and would therefore retard processing (a conclusion reached by Henderson, Wallis and Knight 1984). Clearly, the Taft model predicts that word recognition *cannot* occur before the recognition point for the bare stem in prefixed words, since prefix and stem are processed separately in this model and acoustic information available from the prefix is not used in stem access. This prediction differs from that of a cohort-based model incorporating multiple input monitors per lexical entry, which would hold that processing should proceed initially in a strictly temporal, incremental fashion on the basis of acoustic input alone. There should, then, be no delay in form access attributable to stripping; indeed, it is predicted that access to the stem of the prefixed form should normally occur before the recognition point for the stem alone, since extra acoustic input is available in the former case, namely, in the form of the prefix. This prediction is incorporated into the model presented here in the form of the access link from prefix to stem entry (cf. (24)).

In an experiment designed to distinguish between these two predictions, Tyler *et al.* (1988) presented prefixed words and their corresponding bare stem forms to subjects in a gating task, a task which, it is thought, taps the *form* access phase. If the prefix were stripped à la Taft, then the recognition point should be the same for the bare stem as for the prefixed stem. If processing proceeds on the basis of the accumulating acoustic input alone, then the recognition point in the prefixed stem should be before that of the bare stem. The results of the experiment showed the latter, as represented schematically in (29).

(29) Tyler *et al.* (1988) findings

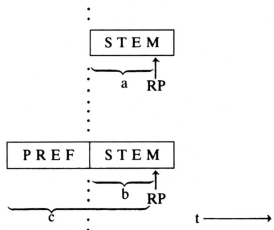

Key: RP = Word Recognition Point
        a = Input necessary for bare stem recognition
        b = Input necessary for prefixed stem recognition
        c = Input necessary for prefixed word recognition
        t = time

152 *Morphology and mind*

In the prefixed case, the RP is earlier in the stem than when the stem stands alone (i.e. b<a), suggesting that the prefix acoustic input is used to access the whole word. If we measure from the beginning of the *word* in each case, however, we see that the prefixed word takes longer to recognise in absolute terms (i.e. c>a). Tyler *et al.* (1988) claim that this is due to a length effect (i.e. longer words typically take longer to recognise, and naturally prefixes add length to the stem), rather than that any extra processing load is involved in the process of morphological realisation, although no data yet exist to decide between these positions. In any event, extra processing times are measured from word onset for prefixed forms (cf. also the results of Jarvella and Meijers 1983, and Bergman and Eling 1984, reported above). We may attribute this to one or more of the following: (i) cohorts take longer to clear when (especially, productive) prefixes occur before the stem (i.e. due to phonological redundancy)[10]; (ii) extra time is taken to access the stem entry once the prefix sub-entry has been isolated (i.e. morphological realisation has a computational cost which translates into a cost in real time); (iii) the extra length of prefixed words leads to longer RTs. Currently, the data needed to decide which is correct are not available.

5.2.3 Opacity

Before concluding this section we must return to the question of the idealisation assumed throughout this discussion that the form of the stem is totally redundant in sub-entries, and so is only listed in the main entry, requiring form access to prefixed words to occur there rather than in the sub-entry where the form of the prefix is listed. This conceptualisation is idealised since, as we saw in the last chapter, affixed forms *do* sometimes modify the form of the stem, i.e. the phonological relationship between affix and stem is often opaque, so we cannot necessarily assume the smooth transition between sub- and main entry which simple collocation would imply.

Recall that the form representations I am assuming in this model are abstract and underspecified, explicitly registering only non-redundant, marked, unpredictable information. It follows from this that some allophonic and allomorphic variation, since it is not registered in underlying representations, will have no effect on matching executed by the input monitors (cf. the discussion of Lahiri and Marslen-Wilson's study of Bengali nasalisation in 5.1.1.1). For example, prefixation provoking intervocalic voicing of stem-initial consonants would have no effect on access if voice was not specified

Understanding affixes 153

in the form representation of the stem entry. Any unpredictable modifications, however, would seem to require separate representations, as I now illustrate.

From the point of view of the lexical processing mechanism, the crucial factor with opacity in affix–stem combinations (in cases where variation is *not* subsumed by the postulation of underspecification) is the temporal location of the point at which the modified form begins to vary from the unaffixed main stem representation, specifically whether it occurs before or after the critical uniqueness point. Presumably when the stem is modified in an unpredictable fashion *before* its uniqueness point, we must posit a full representation of affix + stem at the form level, and a separate input monitor to permit form access. For prefixes this is perhaps in effect not such a grave problem, since, cross-linguistically, prefixed forms *do* seem to retain the stem form *intact* as compared with suffixed forms, as we saw in chapter 4, which means that perhaps the idealisation is not often going to be far from reality. When the prefix *does* modify the stem in a fashion not neutralised by underspecification, i.e. when the affix + stem combination involves a stem modification which involves a mismatch between surface form and stored underlying form, we must assume that the lexical entry patterns are exactly as in the cases of irregular inflection, i.e. with a separate full form representation in the sub-entry.

For suffixes, however, it seems that modification of the stem is far more prevalent. Modification of the stem *after* uniqueness point will perhaps not necessitate a separate full listing; e.g. if the uniqueness point for *except* occurs at the /p/, then the stem in the suffixed form *exception* will already have been recognised by the time it diverges phonologically from the head entry representation. In such cases we may postulate that stem modification information is listed along with the suffix in the sub-entry and that a mismatch after stem recognition transfers continued monitoring to the sub-entry until recognition of the full form occurs. In cases where the stem modification occurs *before* stem uniqueness point, e.g. in *regression*, where stem *regress* is isolated at the /s/ because of competition with *regret* up to that point, then we might propose that the full form of the suffixed word must be listed in the sub-entry, again requiring a separate input monitor: cf. (30) and (31) for what these two types of case might look like.

154 *Morphology and mind*

(30) Opaque suffix representation (modification subsequent to stem UP)

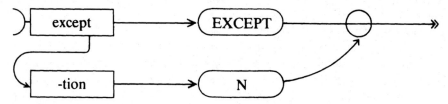

(31) Opaque suffix representation (modification prior to stem UP)

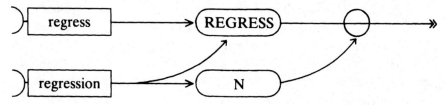

Here we are seeing the gradual diachronic movement from transparent to opaque combinations, i.e. from bimorphicity to monomorphicity, in action. When the *meaning* of the combination cannot be computed from content access to both prefix and stem (which occurs in the main entry), then fully-specified content must also be listed in the sub-entry. Once this transfer has been completed, the stem entry has nothing to contribute and so access links will be severed and the sub-entry will attain full, independent lexical entry status: cf. (32)–(34) for a schematic representation of the steps involved. (32) shows the lexical entry in which *profess* and *professor* are transparently linked at both form and content levels (*professor* simply means 'one who professes'): this presumably reflects the state of affairs obtaining at some stage in the history of English now over. (33) represents a subsequent stage, at which the forms are still related in the morphological competence of the speaker, but the meanings are no longer seen as connected. In (34) we see the ultimate stage, where *no* morphological relationship is perceived as obtaining. It is

(32) Lexicalisation process: stage I

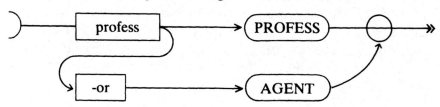

Understanding affixes 155

an empirical matter as to which ((33) or (34)) correctly represents the competence of individual speakers of present-day English.

(33) Lexicalisation process: stage II

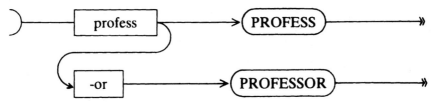

(34) Lexicalisation process: stage III

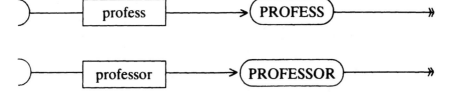

We return to 'micro-historical' processes involving the restructuring of lexical entries in chapter 6, but in the meantime will restrict ourselves to the transparency idealisation, and assume stem form redundancy in prefix sub-entries.

5.2.4 Some conclusions

Although the available data do not all converge on one solution to the problem of access and representation of affixed words, I think the empirical evidence presented in earlier sections, and the logic of the model offered in this section, do strongly suggest at least the following points, however:

(35) a. Lexical entries are organised according to temporal phonological coding from onset for access purposes, but are semantically directly wired to the central conceptual systems for production.

b. Lexical entries are headed by pairs of stem form and content representations, and contain all related forms, when the relation is part of the speaker's morphological competence.

(i) Regularly suffixed inflected forms are listed as part of the main stem entry.

(ii) Irregularly inflected or prefixed inflected forms and all derived forms are listed in sub-entries.

156   *Morphology and mind*

c. Representation of prefixes entails more storage complexity than representation of suffixes, since the key initial portion of the word is altered in the former case but not in the latter, thus requiring a separate input monitor (suffixes may require separate input monitors and full word representations at the form level when divergence from the form listed in the stem entry is unpredictable, given underspecification, and occurs *before* stem uniqueness point).

d. Access to the combined semantic interpretation of the word depends on access to the stem, therefore requiring a realisation of internal structure during processing, but isolation of the form of the input word may be achieved entirely in a sub-entry, in the case of opaque prefixation, irregular inflection, or suffixation as specified in (c). Decomposition, i.e. affix-stripping as conceived by Taft, is not required.

e. Prefixes delay lexical access to form representations, because (i) the presence of a productive affix before the stem postpones the recognition point, (ii) extra computational resources are needed to access the stem after the prefix sub-entry, and/or (iii) prefixes add length to the word, and longer words take longer to access. Suffixes do not delay access to the main stem entry, but may delay access to some types of syntactic and/or semantic information.

In addition, as I argued in 5.1.1.4 above, despite limitations, the Cohort Model constitutes a closer approximation at the observed optimal nature of the lexical processor than do either the Logogen or Search Models, or any blend of the two, and the predictions of the cohort-based model for prefixed forms, as articulated here, seem to fit the available data very well as far as they go. On many questions, however, we must await further research, particularly on prefixed forms and in languages maximally removed from English, before ultimate resolutions can be provided.

5.3 A PROCESSING EXPLANATION FOR THE SUFFIXING PREFERENCE

5.3.1 The Cutler *et al.* processing account[11]

On the basis of an array of evidence of the order of that presented in the review in the first part of this chapter, Cutler *et al.* (1985) present an explanation for the suffixing preference which has as its mainstay the notion of 'order of computation' in the processing of morpho-logically complex words. They claim that:

> The stem favors the most salient beginning position of a word, and the affix the less salient end position, because in the computational process of determining the entire meaning of a word from its parts, the stem has computational priority over the affix. (p. 748)

This computational priority is satisfied by the processor in that 'the preferred order of computation is ... stems first, affixes second' (p. 749). They claim that affixal information is primarily syntactic – it contributes to the building of a syntactic representation of the input, whereas stem information is primarily lexical/semantic. According to Cutler *et al.*, then, the logical order of computation puts stems first as a natural consequence of the 'meanings' or 'functions' of affixes in relation to the stem. So, according to them, case marking, the function of which is to encode sentence-level relationships, will be unusable until the noun to which it refers is known and can be integrated into its sentential context. Similarly, internal to the word, affixes such as *-ness* (as in *sadness*), with the meaning 'the abstract quality of x' will be unusable until x (the stem meaning) is known: 'the effect of the suffix cannot be determined without knowing what stem it has combined with' (p. 749).

The second set of arguments presented by Cutler *et al.* depend on the notion of the *redundancy* of affixes. Firstly, phonological redun-dancy: affixes belong to a closed set and are commonly monosyllabic, exhibiting, therefore, 'less phonological diversity than do stems'. So, Cutler *et al.* argue, 'prefixed words will be less informative in the most salient initial portions than will equivalent words carrying the same information in a suffix' (p. 750), and access to the stem will therefore be delayed in the former case in comparison with the latter; in terms of the Cohort Model, the set of candidates in a cohort generated for a prefixed word will take longer to clear, since in the initial stages there are *many* words, all sharing an identical initial sensory coding (cf. note 10). The second type of redundancy referred to by Cutler *et al.* is that of the syntactic information contained in affixes. It might be that much of this information is predictable from prior sentential context, whereas stems are rarely predictable. It would follow from this, then, that the more informative element should go first, i.e. the stem, and of course this could explain the suffixing preference.

Cutler *et al.*, however, find these redundancy arguments neither 'as simple or as compelling as the computational order argument'. The

158 *Morphology and mind*

phonological redundancy argument, they claim, itself assumes the computational order argument, since the delay that prefix redundancy entails is a delay in access to the stem information, rather than the affix information, and this should only be dispreferred by the processor if stems are preferably processed *before* affixes. For the syntactic/semantic redundancy argument, they claim that, in fact, 'most affixes are not predictable most of the time'. They observe that the affix category which always occurs word finally in H&G's sample is case, which encodes quite fundamental sentential information (especially in free word order languages) and is therefore not predictable from prior context.

The experimental evidence Cutler *et al.* cite to motivate their argument is of two sorts. The first suggests that the onset is psychologically the most 'salient' position in the word, on the basis of word recognition experiments using initial fragments as cues (such as those discussed above, e.g., Grosjean 1980; Nooteboom 1981), mispronunciation tasks in which onsets are distorted (such as Cole 1973; Marslen-Wilson and Welsh 1978), and a variety of other findings supporting the importance in processing, storage, and recall of the portion of the word before its uniqueness point. The second set of experimental results cited to support their argument suggest that affixes are represented in the mental lexicon and are identified and dealt with separately *at some point* in processing. The findings reported in 5.1.3 above constitute a sampling of the type of evidence appealed to.

Cutler *et al.*'s explanation of the cross-linguistic affix data goes, then, as follows. A number of principles describe the pattern of the data presented in chapter 2; these are, as we have seen, the HOP on the one hand, and eleven counterprinciples to this on the other, for which they then propose a processing explanation. The explanation holds that: processing takes place in real time and is therefore subject to temporal constraints, as modelled, for example, in Marslen-Wilson and Tyler's cohort formulation; also, processing is optimally efficient and therefore an attempt is made to decode the input as rapidly as possible. So, given that the beginnings of words precede the ends of words (and are therefore received by the processor earlier) it would be reasonable to expect that language structure would adapt to the requirements of the processor, and place the most salient information at the beginning of the word, which, they conclude on the basis of the experimental evidence cited above, *is* the most psychologically salient position. Next, given that the processor (at some point) recognises the difference between stems and affixes, and, more importantly, that

Understanding affixes 159

stems are preferably processed before affixes because they contain the most immediately important (and possibly least predictable) information, then we would expect language to reflect this preferred computational order and so prefer suffixing.

5.3.2 Problems with the Cutler *et al.* account

Although the general claims of the Cutler *et al.* (1985) processing account make sense and seem highly plausible given the amount of supporting evidence, there are problematic areas which require revision or abandonment if we are to satisfy the conditions on linguistic explanation set out in chapter 1. The most serious problem is the assumption that a processing explanation can be given without due attention to the problem of 'linkage', i.e. without specifying just *how* the psychological principles involved could actually cause language structure to accord with them (cf. Clark and Malt 1984; Bybee 1988). In terms of the historical account of the origin of affixes outlined in chapter 4, we must ask how processing considerations could 'block' the fusion of two free items into one bound + one free stem. We must also address the fundamental historical problem of opacity, which is not acknowledged in the Cutler *et al.* model. Chapter 6 provides a way of examining these complications, but in the meantime I make some observations about problematical areas of Cutler *et al.*'s processing account itself, and assess its adequacy as an explanatory hypothesis for the suffixing preference.

Up until recent years, the literature on lexical access has been plagued by a considerable degree of vagueness about the precise specifications of the internal operations and time course of the access process. Marslen-Wilson and Tyler are perhaps the first scholars in the field to examine lexical access at a level at which precise observations can be made about various stages in the process and the nature of their temporal sequencing. Earlier, and, alas, still much *current* work did not distinguish, for example, between access to the form of the word, i.e. initial isolation of the lexical item, and access to the content of that isolated item. This distinction has consequences for the time course of lexical processing, as demonstrated by Grosjean (1980) and Tyler and Wessels (1983), for example, in their gating experiments.

Although in the Cutler *et al.* proposal the form/content access stages are not explicitly recognised, it is clear that the computational order argument is an argument about *content* access: recall their reference (p. 748) to 'the computational process of determining the entire

160 *Morphology and mind*

meaning of a word from its parts' (my emphasis). When they state that 'simply recognizing prefixed words is no more difficult than recognizing monomorphemic words' (pp 745–6), they are talking in terms of access to *form* in the lexicon (although they admit that this is delayed in comparison with suffixed words due to prefix phonological redundancy).

As we saw in the review sections above, little is known about how and at what stage the *content* of a prefix is usable in the comprehension process. The evidence presented here and in Cutler *et al.* demonstrates only the optimality of earliness of stem recognition: this does not necessarily imply, as Cutler *et al.* suggest, that affixes found before the stem will be unusable, i.e. that the processor has to put them 'on hold' until the stem content is available for integration at the higher utterance level. This would, recall, match the strong predictions of affix-stripping as conceived by Taft. As we have seen, however, Cutler *et al.* do not seem to assume stripping at the form level as in Taft's model. It seems common sense that prefix content *might* be of use in the construction of an utterance representation, and inflections would potentially seem to be *especially* informative, given their essentially syntactic nature: as we saw in chapter 3, they are seen by many linguists as operating post-lexically, and for this reason they have been represented as having independent output to the syntactic level in my cohort-based model. Case, for example, which is prefixed only rarely, often expresses information crucial to the correct interpretation of a noun in the utterance string. There is no experimental evidence that I am aware of which suggests that the component of the processor concerned with syntactic representation cannot exploit this information and insert an N node, with the appropriate case, in the parse tree being built, regardless of the lexical content of the stem. No ordering of these information units has been shown to be *necessarily* preferred, as Cutler *et al.* assume.

What the evidence *does* point to is the optimality of the processor's operations. This optimality is realised through early access to the (morphologically simple or complex) word, and we have seen that prefixed words tend to delay access to the form of the stem, the key to the word. There is no evidence to suggest that one type of information encoded in words is valued more highly than another: the only vital goal seems to be rapidity in the transduction process which maps sound on to meaning, and at the point of contact between the two, the mental lexicon, it appears that prefixes inhibit this process, at least from the narrow point of view of the lexical processing device. This difference between arguments based on the computational order

Understanding affixes 161

preferred by the syntactic and lexical processors, and the preferred time course of lexical processing may seem slight, given our current understanding of access to content representations; however, what we *do* know does not seem to justify the stronger assumption entailed by Cutler *et al.*'s order of computation hypothesis.

In relation to this, Cutler *et al.*'s argument about the syntactic/semantic redundancy of affixes, downplayed in their discussion, does enjoy some support from experimentation on the predictability of *suffixes* in English, conducted by Tyler and Marslen-Wilson (1986). Using the gating method as a measure of the on-line point of lexical access, they demonstrate that subjects may 'synthesise' suffixal morphology if the previous syntactic context is strong enough. So, for example, in the following sentences subjects were able to produce the *-ing* suffix on the verb *correspond* in (36) before they actually heard it, whereas their performance in sentences such as (37) was far more erratic:

(36) Peter and Janet were old friends. For many years they had been regularly *corresponding/correspondence* with each other.
(37) Alice was getting worried. The only news she had received was through *corresponding/correspondence* with her uncle.

Perhaps, then, given the optimal on-line temporal nature of lexical processing, syntactic/semantic redundancy does contribute to the dispreference for prefixing associated with the processing mechanism, since it suggests that some affixes may, in fact, be completely redundant, and if they are located prior to the stem they simply delay recognition. Such evidence would support the weaker argument which appeals only to earliness of stem access; it is neutral with respect to the order of computation logic.

Finally, I should point out that it is not guaranteed that the processing factors appealed to by Cutler *et al.* will necessarily account for *all* of the data brought together in H&G's sample. Bybee (1988) suggests that in addition to the sort of explanation favoured here, there are at least two other possibilities. The first is that it might be the case that grammatical material tends to be postposed, whether it is bound or not (i.e. independently of any resistence to prefixing), leading to more suffixation, since it is grammatical (lexically empty) material which tends to undergo affixation. Comrie's (1980) data on Mongolian (cf. chapter 4) might constitute such a case. However, I am not aware of any principle, linguistic, psycholinguistic or other, which would motivate the hypothesis, and, at present it is untestable; if correct it would not, in any case, 'explain' the data, but rather shift

162 *Morphology and mind*

the need for explanation elsewhere (conceivably to the level of syntactic as opposed to lexical processing).

The second possibility is that morphemes cannot become fused with free lexical neighbours unless they enjoy exclusive adjacency, for instance it could be that adverbs and the possibility of Subj–Aux inversion are blocking the fusion of English auxiliaries with following verbs. Kahr (1976) has proposed, at least for a limited number of languages and for only one grammatical function (namely case), that preposed morphemes, in her examples prepositions, do not reduce to prefix status because other elements intervene between preposition and noun. However, the crucial cross-linguistic evidence needed to establish whether this explanation generalises to a significant number of languages and morpheme functions is not yet available, and again, the need for explanation would only be shifted, this time to account for the asymmetry in adjacency between preposed and postposed morphemes and the potential stems to which they may become bound. An actual counter-example to Kahr's claim is evidenced in French, where intervening elements such as negative *ne* and proclitic object pronouns are not blocking the current drift towards fusion between the subject pronoun and the verb (Ashby 1980).

Nevertheless, it may well be that such factors are involved in the suffixing preference, and it is to be hoped that the extent of their potential involvement will soon be measurable. The possibility of their involvement is not, however, a motivation for abandoning the investigation of processing factors which, in the absence of counter-evidence, constitute the only major convincing account of the phenomenon.[12]

5.4 CONCLUSION

In this chapter, I have attempted to provide a psycholinguistic framework for assessing Cutler *et al.*'s processing explanation of the suffixing process, by reviewing the major assumptions made in the field about word recognition and the mental lexicon, before going on to tackle the less straightforward area of the representation of, and access to, morphologically complex words. I have stressed that considerable care needs to be taken in interpreting the results of experimentation in this area, and have attempted to clarify matters by constructing an explicit model of access and representation from which specific predictions can be made and tested. The surface result of such explicitness may be increased complexity in what is already a complex area – a can of worms within a can of worms; however, this

Understanding affixes 163

complexity is hopefully offset by a corresponding decrease in the level of vagueness with which the literature is plagued.

I ended the chapter with a discussion of Cutler *et al.*'s explanation of the suffixing preference, and with promises of even closer inspection of the issues, to be undertaken in chapter 6. We can see that although Cutler *et al.*'s account seems to fit pretty consistently with the state of our current knowledge of the processing of affixed words, it does not offer a place for the diachronic facts presented in chapter 4. The next chapter provides this linkage, as well as clarifying aspects of the processing account, and addressing some issues placed so far 'on hold'.

6 A micro-analysis of historical change

So far we have discussed the psychological explanation for the suffixing preference in rather general terms, without appealing to any direct experimental data, and without integrating it fully with the diachronic facts discussed in chapter 4. In this final chapter I attempt to pinpoint the exact historical locus of the engagement of the dispreference, and in so doing refine the explanatory hypothesis itself, by examining the cognitive events which lie at the root of the diachronic account. The material in this chapter constitutes, then, an attempt to investigate the mental processes involved in a putative historical change. This will perhaps be viewed by some as premature and over-ambitious given our current state of knowledge and experimental techniques; the account may also at times seem to rely too heavily on (informed) speculation to carry the hypothesis forward. I believe, however, that the cohesiveness of the resulting theory and the lack of persuasive alternatives justify this 'micro-analysis' of historical change.

Before embarking on the main discussion, a few words about the empirical work reported in this chapter. Collecting psychological data in any domain is a considerable challenge both methodologically and logistically. It is especially so when the mental processes we are interested in are not only removed in terms of direct observability, but also in terms of time and space: the putative processing dispreference for prefixes must have taken place in many languages all over the globe during long stretches of time, many now over, some still in progress and presumably yet to come.

To carry out a full psycholinguistic investigation we would need to examine comprehension *and* production of prefixed words in a variety of language types, especially in systems where there is exclusive prefixing, inflectional prefixing, or initial mutation (see note 9, chapter 5). Data from many languages is a goal to be aimed at in

A micro-analysis of historical change 165

order to find ultimate answers; however, the necessary prerequisite of this is to study one or two languages in great depth, with a view to determining the appropriate procedures and constructing a sufficiently articulate and constrained model from which to make predictions. The experimentation documented in 6.2 below (and additional work reported in Hall (1987)) was designed as a first step in this process.

6.1 REFINING THE HYPOTHESIS

Viewing the suffixing preference from the integrated psycholinguistic/ historical vantage point afforded by the discussion in chapters 4 and 5 allows us to take a much closer look at the process of affix development in terms of how the resistance to fusion with potential prefixes word-initially actually goes to work in the real-time history of languages as they are learnt, spoken and understood. We also take up here in greater detail two issues touched upon in those earlier chapters but not resolved, partly because our account had not yet achieved the necessary degree of sophistication. As a result of the advances made below, we will be in a position to shed more light on the problems of economy of lexical representation, left off in chapter 5, and of secondary sources of affixation, introduced briefly in chapter 4. Unfortunately, however, given the limited scope of this study, neither can be dealt with in a fully satisfactory fashion here.

6.1.1 The flirting process

Let us first look at the historical process of affix creation from the perspective of language as a socially shared system rather than as knowledge stored in the mental grammars of individuals, as in the conception implicit in the work of most typologists and historical linguists (cf. 4.1). We know that change in a language as a social system occurs very gradually, starting with a tentative structural reanalysis (or sound change, or whatever) in a small number of language acquirers/speakers which gains ground from one synchronic slice to each successive one, until it becomes a dominant pattern in the language (cf. Chen and Wang 1975). Some attempted reanalyses (provoked for whatever reason) will actually fail to become established within speakers' grammars, or will fail to survive in the analyses of future generations, and so will fail to endure as part of 'the language'.

The dispreference for prefixing may be instantiated therefore in the

166 Morphology and mind

following way: a free morpheme, for example a causative full verb like 'make', in some language, will gradually lose all its specific, idiosyncratic meanings and become general (and, to a certain extent, redundant or at least predictable in many contexts) when it stands typically before free morphemes of some lexical category (in our example, before adjectives). According to the account of affix development advanced in chapter 4, the causative verb will start to reduce phonologically as well as semantically, and will be a candidate for prefixation on following adjectives.

From the perspective of individual speakers' cognitive systems, we may then hypothesise the following diachronic/psycholinguistic process: a significant number of language acquirers, on encountering the semantically general and partially phonologically reduced causative morpheme, will, given sufficient triggering conditions for the dispreference (i.e. the linguistic scenario sketched in chapter 4 and the lack of counter-preferences of greater force, amongst other factors) either (i) analyse it first as a free stem and subsequently reanalyse it as a bound prefix, only to revert to the original analysis, or, (ii) analyse it first as a prefix and then reanalyse it as a free form. In both cases, the result will be a rejection of the bound analysis, because on comparison, according to our hypothesis, the free analysis has a processing advantage, as suggested in chapter 5. If the reduced morpheme were in *post*-adjective, i.e. *suffix*, position, the affix analysis or reanalysis would be more likely to be retained, since the psycholinguistic disadvantages accrued are not so grave. Reanalyses and subsequent rejections are amply demonstrated in research on child language acquisition, particularly internal to the word (cf. e.g. Bowerman 1982).[1]

The hypothesised universal psycholinguistic dispreference for prefixing must, it seems, be instantiated in particular languages word by word by a mechanism which, given the right conditions, 'blocks' the fusion of potential prefixes with free stems. The essential triggering conditions are present at the point where the first tentative reanalysis of a pair of free forms as one bound + one free form takes place in the mental lexicon. This phase, I suggest, is characterised by a 'flirting' process, in which a semantically and phonologically decayed free form attempts to become bound to (i.e. 'flirts' with) a full free form on which it depends and with which it is habitually contiguous. When the dispreference is triggered with sufficient strength, the pressure for a bound analysis is challenged and the form does not reduce as far as affix status. The postulation of the existence of rejected potential prefixes finds support in the observation that grammatical functions located in preposed position are more often expressed as free lexical items than when postposed, where they more frequently find expression as affixes (cf. 4.3). If at subsequent stages the word order has changed and the originally preposed semantically impoverished form occurs *after* the free form, then the pressure for it to be rebuffed is no longer so great (cf. the Mongolian case discussed in chapter 4). It is clear that immediately prior to fusion, the potential prefix is fuller both semantically and phonologically than at any subsequent point, and so on initial reanalysis as an affix it will be most disruptive to processing. It must be at this stage that the dispreference is engaged, i.e. that the would-be prefix is rebuffed. That rebuffing should be simultaneous in many individuals follows naturally from the fact that these flirting structures have reached a critical state in the shared synchronic system as a result of the ongoing reduction process, namely in that they have reached a point of semantic and phonological weakness which renders them liable to become bound morphemes, as demonstrated in chapter 4.

Let us try to formalise this hypothesis using the vocabulary and schematic representations of the psycholinguistic model of morphologically complex words introduced in chapter 5. What characterises flirting forms is the instability of the morpheme combination and the tentative nature of the bound analysis. We may hypothesise that this representational instability requires *decomposition* of internal structure during the access process rather than simple *realisation*, which is effected in the case of established forms (cf. 5.2). We may formalise the notion of flirting, then, by expressing it as in (1) and (2). The unestablished flirting prefix and suffix forms are represented as subentries to the main lexical entry headed by the stem, but, unlike the established prefix and suffix forms (recall (22) and (24) in chapter 5), there is as yet no direct access link between sub-entry and main entry form representation. During the access process, decomposition of the stripping variety is required, i.e. each unestablished sub-entry has an input monitor associated with it, and access to the combined form requires the operation of both sub-entry and main entry input monitors in both cases, i.e. the generation of two cohorts. The transitional, unstable status of the flirting forms is, therefore, reflected in the co-existence of the free and bound features associated with them: like pairs of free items, they require the activation of two cohorts, but like bimorphemic items they are represented in a single lexical entry.

168   *Morphology and mind*

(1) Hypothesised structure of lexical entry containing flirting prefix form

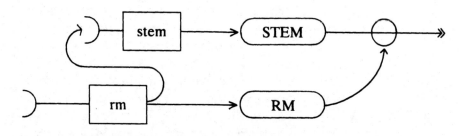

Key: rm = reduced morpheme
              (form representation)
         RM = REDUCED MORPHEME
              (content representation)

(2) Hypothesised structure of lexical entry containing flirting suffix form

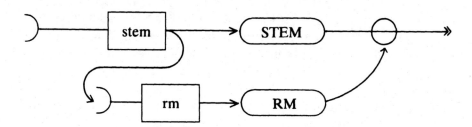

Ultimate retention of the bound reading involves, for suffixes, the loss of the input monitor associated with the sub-entry, and, for prefixes, the redirection of the access link directly to the main entry, i.e. bypassing the input monitor. This restructuring of the lexicon will occur on a progressive, case-by-case basis, with permanent links being implemented as each appropriate collocation of reduced morpheme and stem is encountered, rather than in one simultaneous mass linking process between the reduced morpheme form representation and *all* appropriate stems. Reanalysis of bound morphemes as free forms involves, for both pre- and postposed morphemes, the severing of access links, i.e. removal from the stem lexical entry.

Pursuing this hypothesis, we now need to address two critical issues: (i) precisely what decomposition means in the context of the lexical access model outlined in chapter 5; and (ii) precisely what it is

A micro-analysis of historical change 169

in this formulation which leads to the typical retention of the suffix reading, but the rejection of the prefix reading. Let us examine the processing consequences of the formulations in (1) and (2) for prefixes and suffixes in turn.

In the recognition of a particular unestablished prefixed form, the initial acoustic input of the reduced morpheme will provoke the generation of a cohort by the responses of the input monitor(s)[2] associated with each instantiation of this morpheme in unestablished sub-entries. All other items which match the sensory input will also respond and enter the cohort. On recognition of the *form* of the reduced morpheme, all other items will drop out of the cohort, leaving only the lexical entries in which the reduced morpheme is represented. The termination point of this cohorting process will be determined by the isolation of a single *form*, as in a conventional cohort, but, unusually, with *multiple* membership of the cohort in terms of activated lexical entries. This is because the reduced morpheme will be analysed as a prefix on *numerous* stems heading *numerous* lexical entries.

In its turn, the sensory input associated with the initial stretch of the stem will be received by the processor. This will cause a second cohort to be generated, however, this time only the input monitors corresponding to heads of lexical entries activated by recognition of the reduced morpheme will respond: i.e. the second cohort will be restricted to entries still activated by the previous one. Access to the form of the combined morpheme pair will occur when only one stem form remains in the cohort, and subsequently the combined content will be computed. What I am hypothesising is, then, a new type of selection process which occurs *internal* to lexical entries, i.e. which is contingent on previous activation by separate input monitors within the same lexical entry. Recall that the association of more than one input monitor with a lexical entry was proposed in 5.2, where it was independently motivated to account for established prefix access.

For the recognition of unestablished *suffixed* forms, the process is different in a number of respects. The initial sensory input from a particular stem will provoke the generation of a cohort in the usual way, and access to the stem form will succeed when only one item remains. Subsequent input from the postposed reduced morpheme will in this case not generally cause the creation of a second cohort because the only input monitors responding (cf. note 2) will be those associated with sub-entries of the previously recognised stem, i.e. almost invariably only the reduced morpheme itself. The concept of a

170 *Morphology and mind*

single member cohort is vacuous, since unitary membership defines the termination of the lexical discrimination process.

Items from other lexical entries which match the sensory input will not become activated, as they would in conventional lexical access – this follows from the assumption that access links within lexical entries have priority, i.e. that matching *within* the lexical entry is exhausted before a new cohort for a new input word is entertained. If this were *not* the case, access to *established* suffix sub-entries where the stem is not modified by the suffix would be contingent upon new cohort generation, to which free items matching the suffix form might trigger responses: e.g. *purify* would be subject to the same processing procedure as *pure efficiency*, i.e. involving two complete 'jobs' by the lexical processor (see below), which patently cannot be the case. The processes hypothesised to be involved in the recognition of flirting forms are obviously *not* the same as the processes involved in the successive recognition of two contiguous free forms, since recognition is accomplished internal to one lexical entry, and the lexical processor reaches *one* termination state, not two.

Thus, our question (i) above is resolved, and we are in a position to address question (ii), namely why is it that the advances of would-be prefixes are preferably rebuffed, but those of would-be suffixes generally accepted? I.e. why is there a suffixing preference? As we have seen, a comparison of the processes involved shows that entertaining a flirting prefix should require two cohorts, whereas entertaining a flirting suffix should require, in effect, only one. Also, we saw in the discussion of Tyler *et al.*'s (1988) experiment reported in chapter 5, that decomposition of established prefixes should entail delayed access to the stem, i.e. recognition should occur after the necessary input required for the stem alone, *plus* the input corresponding to the prefix, since the prefix input is not used to constrain cohort membership. In the case of unestablished, prefixed flirting forms, the second cohort, the one generated for stem recognition, although reduced in membership (since membership is limited to entries containing the reduced morpheme sub-entry) *will* contain more than one member, since the general applicability of the reduced morpheme to more than one stem is what contributes to its susceptibility to affixhood, and so a similar delay in stem access should be expected. In the case of would-be suffixes, stem access is completely unaffected, and no extra computational cost is involved. Thus, if our hypothesis is correct, we can conclude that a prefix (re)analysis entails greater cost to the lexical processor than a suffix (re)analysis, at the point at which the (re)analysis takes place.

6.1.2 Objections and exceptions

At this stage in the argument we are in a position to answer a possible objection to our proposed processing explanation for the suffixing preference, which has been laid to one side until the appropriate argumentative tools became available. The question is: why should we suppose that one complex word in a morphological relationship is harder to process than two simple ones in a syntactic relationship? I.e. is the historical process of affix creation not just shifting processing complexity from the syntax to the morphology, rendering any argument based on potential *increases* in complexity meaningless?

The answer lies in the postulation of *modularity* in the language processing system. Just as many theorists in current mentalistic frameworks of grammar (e.g. Chomsky 1981) have stressed the modularity of distinct spheres of grammatical knowledge, which has the effect of placing restrictions on the degree of access between distinct knowledge sources, so within most models of mind, including those concerned with linguistic processing, modularity has been adopted to some degree or other. In his seminal work *The Modularity of Mind*, for example, Fodor (1983) presents a strong modularity theory for cognitive processing capacities, which features the 'impenetrability' of modules, i.e. the inaccessibility of the internal state of one module to any other module, and Frazier (1979, 1987b; Frazier and J. D. Fodor 1978) has specifically adopted such a strong theory to characterise processes like sentence parsing which are *internal* to the linguistic capacity. Likewise, Katz, Boyce, Goldstein and Lukatela (1987) have argued for modular processing of syntactic and semantic information in the spoken word recognition process, and Gibson and Guinet (1971) made similar claims for word recognition in the written modality.

Marslen-Wilson and Tyler (e.g. 1980, 1987; Marslen-Wilson 1987), on the other hand, adopt an interactive processing model, but one which nevertheless assumes completely autonomous (therefore interpretable as modular) initial processing of the sensory input in a bottom-up fashion. Their model also implicitly recognises two other autonomous processes, one concerned with word recognition and one dedicated to sentence parsing (cf. Marslen-Wilson 1987: 98 ff.). A review of Marslen-Wilson and Tyler's work within the Cohort Model (cf. e.g. 5.1.1.1) demonstrates convincingly the untenability of a strong 'impenetrability' thesis, at least as far as lexical processing is concerned; however, this in no way weakens the commonly accepted position that there are two independent processing modules for the

172 *Morphology and mind*

lexicon and the syntax, with two independent tasks (cf. Frazier 1987b). Experimentation supporting the Cohort Model does not seem incompatible with this position (or with an even stronger modular position, as Frazier (1987b: 304) points out).

The task of the modular lexical processor is to recognise words in the input string: it terminates each 'job' on successful recognition of a word, and then returns to its initial state, ready to begin monitoring for the next word. The task of the parser is to build a syntactic parse of the sentence on the basis of information from the lexicon made available by the lexical processor (e.g. categorial, subcategorial and selectional details) and from the grammatical knowledge source (e.g. X' requirements, binding constraints): it terminates each 'job' on successful construction of a parse tree for the sentence, which serves semantic interpretation of the utterance in its discourse context. This is pretty standard theorising about the processing of input strings, and is generally consistent with most models: i.e. despite differences concerning how penetrable the various modules are, and how their interaction is organised temporally (i.e. sequentially or in parallel), most investigators would agree that there *do* exist different tasks, and these tasks *are*, in a sense, *delegated* to distinct subcomponents of the processing mechanism as a whole, rather than being executed by some super-processor (cf. the papers in Garfield (1987) for extended discussion).

It follows from this, then, that what is best for the lexical processor is not necessarily best for the syntactic parser and vice versa, and that because the two are independent, they will not necessarily co-operate to find a solution of common benefit: as has been noted throughout this book, principles of language organisation and use will as often be in a relationship of opposition as they are in one of complementarity or conspiracy. The reason for this, I contend, lies in the fact that many principles are associated with distinct *modules* of the representative and functional mechanisms of the language capacity, i.e. linguistic principles have a limited, local motivation and a limited, local domain of application.

It appears that in the case of cross-component (syntax to morphology) reanalysis that we are discussing, namely where two formerly free morphemes in a syntactic relationship are reanalysed as a single bimorphemic word listed in the lexicon, what we have is an increase in complexity for the lexical processor, in that the successful completion of a single 'job' (the only task of any processing module) is made more difficult in these cases: this then conflicts with the ease-of-processibility principle applicable in the domain of the lexical

A micro-analysis of historical change 173

processing module. And it is highly improbable that such a principle would or could lead to a pressure to restrict the *number* of 'jobs' (in effect to prefer shorter sentences in terms of the number of words they contain). Hence we can conclude that the lexical processor is *not* likely to prefer one job (the bound reading) to two (the free reading).

An objection based on this observation, namely that the processing dispreference is meaningless if complexity is merely shifted to another processing area rather than increased overall, is now simply answered, then, by recognising a modular interpretation of language representation and use, specifically: (i) that parsing a sentence for syntax is executed by a module distinct from the one which recognises words; (ii) that distinct modules have their own independent tasks and domains of applicability; and (iii) that principles of linguistic organisation and use are often associated with particular modules, sharing their restricted domains of applicability.

Another (rather unfair) objection that has been levelled at the processing explanation is that it sheds no light on the observation that some languages *do* employ prefixes (approximately 10 per cent of the languages in H&G's survey employ *only* prefixes). If, according to the foregoing discussion, the syntactic parser is not the source of a principle which may oppose the dispreference for prefixes, by preferring complex single words to simple word pairs, is it in fact possible, then, to locate such a principle, and thus account for the existence of prefixes in language? In responding to this question we must stress once more that many principles, some competing, some complementary, some conspiring towards the same effect, can be involved in determining the form of language, both at a universal and a local (language-specific) level. It is, then, hardly surprising that we should find exceptions to the type of linguistic regularity favoured by one particular module of the enormously complex language faculty, i.e. in our case that we do find prefixes in large numbers, despite the principled preference for suffixing. Osgood (1966: 302) argues the general point succinctly in the following passage:

> I have been a walking pincushion for the barbs of linguists who have gleefully blunted my probes for psycholinguistic universality with counter-points of 'exceptions'. ... The point is that scientific laws are not merely honored by their exceptions – they are literally manufactured out of their exceptions. Exceptions reflect interactions among the whole set of functional laws. Language Z does not display regularity X *because* laws 1, 2, and 3 operate in one way under condition alpha and quite differently under condition

174 *Morphology and mind*

beta. In other words, it is the nonuniversal, *statistical* universals that are most interesting to a science of language behavior. Out of the complex patterning of nonuniversal (but lawful) phenomena we will draw forth the underlying principles of a science of language.[3]

Now, of course, I cannot claim to be able to identify conditions alpha and beta in the relatively few languages of H&G's corpus (or elsewhere) which manifest an impressive array of sturdy prefixes, and until I can, the exceptions remain an unsolved part of the jigsaw puzzle, and a principle (or principles) accounting for them remains elusive. Having conceded this, however, I should stress that the exceptions in themselves, by virtue of their comparative rarity in the languages of the world, in no way constitute a disconfirmation of the explanatory hypothesis advanced to account for the majority of the data. Serious study of their resistance to the pressures involved in determining this majority pattern is therefore not essential to the main direction of the argument developed here.

Nevertheless, before resuming our central theme, let me highlight one important principle that may oppose the prefixing dispreference, in that it demands the creation of affixes irrespective of whether these are realised in prefix or suffix position, i.e. it is blind to position. I can, however, supply no rationale as to why this principle should be dominant over the suffixing preference in some cases and not in others (i.e. why prefixes are sometimes tolerated but more often not). Recall that we spent most of chapter 4 discussing how some words tend to lose their semantic specificity and become general, relational in nature, gradually losing, as a consequence, their fullness of phonological form, and becoming, ultimately, candidates for treatment as bound morphemes on words with which they are habitually contiguous, regardless of their position in relation to the future stem. This reduction tendency is played out in the successive analyses made by children in the acquisition of the languages to which they are exposed.

The child is equipped with certain preprogrammed knowledge, much of it expressible as grammatical principles, all of it universal. Most of the *lexical* knowledge inherent in the particular language to which the child is exposed must be acquired *without* the aid of built-in choices and guiding principles, but even without these the child is not completely blind: it is likely that the functional architecture required for lexical entries is genetically programmed to some degree of specificity, including facilities for sub-entries, and that the architecture of the

A micro-analysis of historical change   175

lexical processor is almost completely genetically determined. We assume also that learning and categorisation strategies like Slobin's (1985) operating principles are available, which direct the child to analyse data in as simple a manner as possible.

When segmenting the input string into words, then, the child is quite likely to treat flirting morphemes as affixes, independently of what the processing modules might have to say about it, since the child, in its segmentation routines, will attempt to group like units with like, and will list regularly co-occurring units *together* (cf. the operating principles of Slobin cited in 3.3). Hence, it might be that innate strategies for *learning* yield principles which may oppose the processing principles which result in a dispreference for prefixing: *regardless of whether they are pre- or postposed*, some morphemes are gradually assigned more general, relational meanings by children seeking simplicity in the input data; subsequently these morphemes have on successive reanalyses been eroded to such an extent, first semantically and then phonologically, that the child's lexical processor is inclined to treat them as *part* of the words with which they habitually co-occur, given the innate learning principles and strategies that are bound to apply.

Finally, it should be stressed again that, very often, language-particular contingencies will override universal functional pressures, as would be the case for the suffixing preference if the suggestions made by Comrie (1980) in his discussion of the Mongolian data (cf. 4.3), or those more general proposals made by Bybee (1988) (cf. 5.3.2). could be substantiated. Other cases of this nature, in which, for example, *social* factors seem likely to render structural analyses impervious to functional pressure, will be addressed in 6.1.4 below.

6.1.3 Simplicity of representation

The bound prefix analysis may also be rejected by the acquirer for reasons of simplicity of representation within lexical entries. Simplicity of representation is a factor often invoked in the explanation of language change and in deciding between analyses provided by alternative grammars. It is observed to be a central principle of mental organisation, and underlies strategies employed in the process of grammar construction (or discovery) by the child. In language change instantiated at the acquisition stage, explanations may be provided, according to Harris (1982: 11), by appealing to simplicity as part of speakers' preferences (or strategies):

176 *Morphology and mind*

... unconsciously to organise their linguistic material (like so many other aspects of their experience) coherently, economically and consistently ... linguistic change is often a response to this preference, which may thus be said to cause the change in question.

Lightfoot's Transparency Principle (1979: 121–41), for example, elevates this observation into a principle of universal grammar which limits the class of possible changes in syntax by constraining the complexity of derivations which the introduction of new rules may involve (cf. Chomsky's 'least effort' principles discussed in chapter 1).

Recall that in the discussion of representation models in chapter 5 it was suggested that prefix representation entails more storage complexity than suffix representation in a phonologically organised lexicon, since prefixing disturbs the uniformity of the 'address' of the lexical entry, as represented by the initial acoustic specifications of the stem. So, for example, suffixing -*ness* to *kind* to produce *kindness* requires the simple addition of a sub-entry to the main entry *kind*, whereas prefixing *un-* to *kind* to produce *unkind* requires the addition of a separate input monitor as well. In the case of *inflection*, suffixes only entail an extension to the main stem entry, whereas prefixes require separate sub-entries with the associated input monitor and access link. In the same way, however, that the *access* cost of prefixes must be assessed at the flirting phase, so we must examine *representational* costs in terms of the stage at which the level of such costs could influence the balance between bound and free analyses. It is clear that representational costs could only become a factor once a decision is made to retain the bound reading, i.e. at the conclusion of the flirting process, since only at this point does the asymmetry between prefix and suffix representation reveal itself. Inspection of (1) and (2) above shows that equal representational complexity is entailed at the flirting stage, whereas the corresponding established form representations ((22) and (24) in chapter 5) show greater costs for the prefix form.

Note that the reanalysis of a free morpheme as bound will also entail greater redundancy in the representation of information in the lexicon. In a redundant model, in which affix representations are not shared between lexical entries but are duplicated in each entry, the redundancy is enormous, since instead of being contained in a single entry, the information associated with the morpheme must be represented in all the entries which contain stems to which the new

A micro-analysis of historical change 177

affix may become bound. In a more parsimonious model, where form and content is listed once and is linked with relevant head entries, there will still be increased redundancy and complexity, since at least some index, link, or address relating bound item to appropriate stems must be posited for each lexical entry involved, and idiosyncratic form and content features must also be listed explicitly in lexical entries. Affixes, then, appear to entail an extra cost in lexical memory resources in terms of both the complexity they imply in lexical entry representation *and* the redundancy of information stored in the lexicon as a whole. Prefixes entail *greater* representation costs than suffixes, as I have shown.

In the light of these remarks, we may find of some relevance the conclusions that Cowgill (1966: 131) draws with reference to a correlation between prefixes and polymorphemicity observed in his corpus of data from Indo-European languages:

> Tentatively, we can say that in I-E a high morpheme-to-word ratio appears to go with a high prefix-to-suffix ratio.... It [seems] possible that there may be some fundamental difficulty about prefixes compared with suffixes so that a high ratio of prefixes and prevalence of polymorphemic words are just two aspects of a basic trait of 'complexity', and a rise in one could be expected to entail a rise in the other.

Although we would need to assess Cowgill's hypothesis on the basis of a much broader cross-linguistic survey, it is consonant with the psycholinguistic argumentation applied here to the problem of affixation in languages, specifically from the point of view of the preference for simplicity of representation, since it follows naturally from our argument that polymorphemicity as well as prefixation will involve a very high degree of redundancy in the lexicon as a whole as well as complexity within individual lexical entries. What is problematic with Cowgill's hypothesis, however, is the question of why a morphologically 'complex' language in terms of polymorphemicity should typically tolerate *extra* complexity in the form of a high prefix-to-suffix ratio, and vice versa. A potential answer to this question lies in the postulation of some unitary general principle against complexity operating in language. Such a principle, if it failed to apply in one of these domains of morphological complexity, might fail to apply in both domains, resulting in many cases in a correlation between the two complexity types.

In what follows, the issue of representational complexity necessarily takes a back seat, since, to air once more a persistent problem,

178 *Morphology and mind*

it is difficult to see how such a hypothesis may be tested empirically, given current research techniques in psycholinguistics (cf. the paucity of conclusive research on lexical representation reported in chapter 5). The absence of deeper scrutiny in this important area in the present work, therefore, should not be interpreted as a repudiation of the logic of the representation argument, nor even as an indication of its weaker status as a potential explanatory principle, but rather as a reluctant and temporary shelving of empirical verification until some future stage of the research programme. In the light of this we will, therefore, continue to concentrate on the *processing* aspect of the psycholinguistic explanation for the remainder of the chapter.

6.1.4 Lexical reanalysis and borrowing

Now that we have a clearer conceptualisation of the type of mental processes likely to be going on in the original emergence of affixes through reduction and fusion processes in language, we are in a position to return to the problem of 'secondary' origins, namely lexical reanalysis (i.e. reanalysis internal to the morphology) and borrowing, left off in chapter 4.

Internal, lexical reanalysis can lead to 'new' affixes in at least two ways. New instances of affix–stem combinations can be created via back formation (e.g. English *pedlar* → *peddle + er*), and also through the substitution of new bound forms for old ones within the same morphological slots. This latter process occurs in inflection and derivation with simple replacement where equally productive forms compete (e.g. Eng *unaccountableness* → *unaccountability*) or where one form establishes dominance and squeezes out the competition (e.g. Eng plural -*s*). In inflection we also find the equivalent phenomenon of paradigm restructuring, often involving the pivotal third person singular form of verbs, as exemplified in Watkins's study of the pre-Celtic verb (Watkins 1962). Details of these processes are supplied in 4.1.1.

For both types of internal reanalysis, we may speculate along the following lines as to the applicability of the psycholinguistic principles which, according to our hypothesis, lead to a predominance of suffixes. The functional pressures which give rise to new combinations of prefix + stem via lexical reanalysis are presumably as strong as those which are involved in the semantic and phonological reduction of lexical items; the difference is that in the former, newly analysed prefixes are derived on the basis of analogy with existing bound morphemes already established in pre-stem position within the

A micro-analysis of historical change   179

same paradigm or subcategorial frame. So, the functional pressure which has already tolerated such prefixes over the demands of the processor will presumably prevail in new cases too, since only new *combinations*, and not new *prefixes*, are being created. In cases of flirting, however, the morpheme is not yet established as a bound element in *any* lexical entry and is therefore much more vulnerable to the processing pressure.

The pressure for simplicity of representation is equally unlikely to work against prefixation in internal reanalysis processes, because usually what is involved is *levelling* within paradigms, or generalisation across subcategorial frames, both of which lead to greater simplicity of representation, in that variety in the number and type of affix representations is normally reduced in paradigm restructuring, and less ambiguity results from back formation (the incidence of pseudo-affixation (cf. chapter 5) is reduced).

The introduction of affixes to a language via borrowing is a different matter, because it is partly social in its motivation and occurrence, unlike the psychological–internal case of lexical or cross-component (i.e. syntax → morphology) reanalysis. The process of borrowing is innovation under what Itkonen calls *social control* (Itkonen 1983: 211):

> Linguistic change ... may ... be viewed as (rational) collective action. The collective aspect is provided by *social control*, which manifests itself in the fact that only innovations not exceeding certain strict limits will have a chance of being accepted. The same goes for the eventual survival of mental grammars abduced by children. The linguistic community could be said to act as a 'rationality filter' on innovations and abductions. The end result is that the community as a whole seems to change its language. On closer inspection, however, this turns out to be an aggregate of innumerable individual actions performed under social control.

It is difficult to see how, as he seems to be claiming, *all* change may be viewed in this way. Certainly the reanalysis of a free form as bound is not performed under social control, i.e. subjected to some social filter, since the change involved occurs internally, with no immediate external (i.e. social) manifestation, as a result of the state of the reduced morpheme in individual speakers' lexicons. The physical manifestations of this type of reanalysis, although observable to diachronic linguists, are not going to be so to contemporary members of the speech community: phonological fusion itself is not necessarily a diagnostic of bound morpheme reanalysis (cf. Bybee's examples

180   *Morphology and mind*

with English *have*, chapter 4), and in legitimate cases of reanalysis, it will not usually occur until later generations when the affix analysis is firmly implanted in the language. The prohibition on intervening free morphemes, a real diagnostic of affix status, is, as negative evidence, equally unavailable. The change in the language is, then, 'an aggregate of innumerable individual actions', but these actions are performed independently of each other, below the level of consciousness, and almost simultaneously, and are therefore *not* subject to social control.

Most cases of internal lexical reanalysis, either of affix addition or of substitution, will also lack any immediate external reflex, although, unlike the cross-component reanalyses, some *will* have more immediate consequences for speech production. We can see this in back formation, for example with the emergence in English of the verb *orate*, a result of the reanalysis of *-or* as an agentive in the word *orator*, a word previously treated as monomorphemic in English. We are perhaps seeing a reflex of paradigm restructuring in the emergence of /sɛz/ (from third person *says*) as first person form in some varieties of English. Such reanalyses will therefore spread from speaker to speaker through lexical diffusion, and be subject to social control, although not to the degree that borrowing entails, as I now argue.

Unlike the other types of affix creation, borrowing (e.g. English-*esque* from French) will spread under strong, often conscious, social control, usually becoming accepted as a consequence of the prestige of the supplier language (Malkiel 1966: 331) or the non-availability in the native tongue of forms associated, for example, with some newly-introduced skill which the supplier language may furnish. It is quite likely that internal pressures such as the psychological ones discussed above may be overridden by the social pressures involved in borrowing, considering the heightened level of consciousness of the latter, the former being completely automatic and inaccessible to conscious control. So, it is unlikely that affixes introduced from another language will be subject to the pressures which result in a suffixing preference when conflict with the stronger social pressures is involved.

What, then, will be the impact of these secondary sources of affixation on the cross-linguistic distribution of affixes as prefixes or suffixes? With the current lack of sophistication in crosslinguistic affixation data, it is very difficult to answer this question. According to the speculations above, lexical reanalysis should not affect the distribution very much since most reanalyses of this sort only replace old affixes with new ones in the same positions or extend

A micro-analysis of historical change   181

the number of affix combinations within a particular subcategorial frame. Borrowing, however, may sway the distribution away from the native pattern (which has its origin in the reduction of free morphemes), although here it is necessary to consider which type of language we are dealing with, and how much borrowing is involved. With regard to the second of these considerations, it is clear that the proportion of borrowed bound morphemes varies greatly from language to language, but research on word formation has shown that it is minimal in comparison with the degree of free morpheme borrowing. Fleischmann (1977), for example, offers the following general principle: '... the more *lexical* an item is, the greater its potential for transfer; the more *grammatical* it is, the less likely it is to be borrowed' (p. 274). We may conclude, then, that since bound morphemes have low lexical content and often high grammatical content (particularly so in H&G's data, which, recall, consist almost entirely of inflectional categories), then the proportion of borrowed morphemes in any given sample is likely to be low, and consequently will not confound too greatly the principles which are posited to determine the dominant distribution pattern.

The existing distribution of affix positions in a language may also be a factor in determining the degree of borrowing. For instance, it is possible that a predominantly prefixing language would preferably not introduce borrowed suffixes, and that an *exclusively* prefixing language would be even more unlikely to do so, whereas a language with roughly equal numbers of prefixes and suffixes might borrow either type, or an exclusively or predominantly prefixing language might quite happily entertain more prefixes. That is, it may be easier for a language to accommodate borrowings which conform to its own basic pattern, in a similar way to the processes by which borrowed forms are often *made* to conform at the phonological level (cf. Lehmann 1978: 402). Comrie (1980), recall, discusses the case of affixes of person-and-number in Mongolian languages, which evolved via reduction from postposed rather than preposed nominal and genitive pronouns, yielding suffixes (cf. 4.3 for details). He suggests that this might be because the Mongolian languages are predominantly or exclusively suffixing, i.e. that the existing structure of the system might impose conformity. Bybee (1988), however, criticises this view, arguing that it

> implies that speakers in some sense 'decide' on suffixes rather than prefixes, as more appropriate for their language. This would mean

182 *Morphology and mind*

that the typology of a language is manifested in individual grammars in such a way that it may come into play during the creation of new structures. (p. 356)

Fleischmann's (1977) study, however, which examines reflexes of the Graeco-Latin suffix *-aticú* in Romance languages, leads her to speculate that borrowing of affixes most probably occurs between genetically related languages, with the borrowed form replacing a parallel or cognate affix – i.e. prefix for prefix, suffix for suffix. In borrowing, then, Bybee's worries may not apply, if analogical processes which identify similarities between form and/or function, such as those found between cognate forms, determine the probability of affix transfer, rather than explicit knowledge of typology:

We find that parallel (even cognate) suffixes existed in the various Romance languages surveyed, all of which were distinctly less productive amd more restricted functionally than Gallo-Romance *-age*. With this in mind, plus the fact of formal similarity and functional overlap of the parallel suffixes, it is not surprising that *-age* effectively took over the activities of its cognates.

We may, perhaps, infer from the above that transfer of suffixes is most likely to occur among genetically related languages. Once the borrowed suffix was introduced, it was no doubt at varying levels of consciousness felt by speakers to be akin to their own reflexes of *-ATICÚ*, which understandably facilitated the replacement of the native by the imported suffix and the eventual transfer of functions. (p. 276)

If this is the case, we would again not expect borrowing to have any significant confounding effect on the dominant pattern of affix positions in the languages in the H&G survey.

Of course, we cannot be sure that borrowing accounts for so little of the distributional data until we see some statistics taken from diachronically-informed cross-linguistic surveys. Indeed, we know that the native English distributional pattern, for example, has been significantly skewed by the introduction of Latin prefixes, and, if we consider the manner in which affixes are borrowed, we can see that the native pattern may not, in fact, exert much pressure. Fleischmann (1977: 275) points out that

prefixes and suffixes are never borrowed directly; as a rule they are extracted as detachable morphemes only after a number of words in which they occur have been borrowed. Once Spanish, Portuguese, Italian and English had adopted a series of words in

A micro-analysis of historical change 183

-*age* from French, only then could speakers become conscious of the nature of this suffix and begin using it analogically in coining new derivations from their own native lexical stock.

So, in fact, affixes only arrive in the language as baggage accompanying a full lexical item; their introduction is dependent on the introduction of the particular words with which they are associated, and these words are taken on first as unanalysed wholes, without regard for their internal structure, i.e. for their compatibility with native morphological patterns. In a further twist, however, it is possible that the existing native pattern (or, if Fleischmann is correct, the existence of cognates), does exert an influence by constraining the analysis and extraction of the affix once the full word has been borrowed.[4]

Despite the speculative nature of much of the discussion in this section, I think we can conclude with reasonable confidence that secondary sources of affixation, namely internal lexical reanalysis and borrowing, are largely impervious to the psycholinguistic constraints on affix position posited in this book, but that they have not had a profound effect on the distribution of affixes in H&G's language sample since they are marked and relatively rare in comparison with the cross-component (i.e. reduction from syntax to lexicon) source. In any case, where they *do* occur it is possible that they tend to reinforce the existing (native) pattern, rather than conflict with it, thus bolstering rather than confounding the existing (native) system, i.e. that predicted by the HOP-suffixing preference interaction.

6.2 TESTING THE HYPOTHESIS

The dispreference for prefixing is, then, instantiated historically at the flirting stage, when the new prefix is semantically transparent enough and phonologically intact enough to remain as a free lexical item. It is at this stage, I hypothesise, that the main force of the explanans is located, i.e. that the processing pressure blocks prefix reanalysis. Testing this hypothesis empirically presents a great number of problems: as I pointed out in the introduction to this chapter, historical phenomena are not very amenable to experimental probing. This is because: (i) the number of languages involved is huge, and experimenting on a representative sample would be a colossal logistical undertaking; (ii) the phenomena involved are extremely difficult to pin down in particular languages at particular synchronic states (since most diachronic studies are written, of

184 *Morphology and mind*

course, retrospectively, i.e. after the phenomena they report, and those that *do* chronicle ongoing changes (e.g. the work on French reported, for example, in Ashby (1980) and Champion (1980), cf. chapter 4) do not undertake cognitive micro-analyses); (iii) psycholinguists have not yet developed methodologies sensitive enough to establish with any great degree of confidence the internal state of lexical entries (as we have seen in chapter 5).

What we *can* do, however, is look for relevant evidence by attempting to model the cognitively interpreted diachronic process as closely as possible using current English (or other language) stimuli. Logically, the results of such inquiry will only be indirectly relevant to the historical process we are interested in, but in so far as their relevance is defined by the closeness of the match between the actual historical process and the current process employed to model it, we can justify to a greater or lesser extent their status as evidence for the hypothesis being tested. I believe that the stimuli described below *are* very close to the flirting forms discussed in the last section, and so experimental data concerning them can be quite confidently employed in support of the explanatory hypothesis for the suffixing preference.

6.2.1 Novel forms

The stimuli I identified as best candidates to model the flirting process are the most newly and transparently prefixed forms in current English, i.e. *novel* combinations of prefix + stem. Examples include: *untile* ('I have just decorated the bathroom. Of course, he doesn't like the wall, so I've got to untile it'); *re-ambush* ('They ambushed us on the way to Vera Cruz, and we were re-ambushed on the way back'); *pre-eclipse* ('Will you join me for a pre-eclipse cocktail?'); *de-moss* ('I have to de-moss the garden wall this afternoon').[5] Prefixes in novel combinations are close to the flirting prefix forms in that they do not assimilate phonologically with the stem, they retain equal stress, have a fully transparent semantic reading, attach only to free stems, and are productive in word formation rules. They are also not yet established as prefix + stem forms, i.e. although their component morphemes are both known and established in the language, their combination is unfamiliar to hearers. For this reason they should require decomposition during processing at both form and content stages.

Let us compare the two types in terms of the representational format introduced in chapter 5. There it was suggested that stripping may be conceived of in two ways, repeated here in (3) and (4) (from (27) and (28) in chapter 5). (3) represents Taft's strong conception of stripping, where processing of the stem is entirely independent of any affix information, and the affix must be kept 'on hold' until stem form recognition; (4) represents the weaker version of stripping with subcategorial information directly employed in terms of the access link to the stem input monitor from the prefix form representation.

(3) Prefix stripping (strong version)

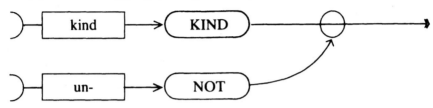

(4) Prefix stripping (weak version)

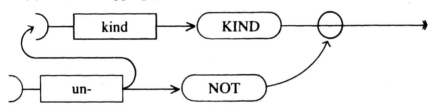

The hypothesised structure of a lexical entry with flirting prefix ((1) above), is identical to the conception in (4); however, since novel forms are completely unfamiliar, it is unlikely that subcategorial information will be encoded in access links. If (4) proves to be the correct representation for novel forms, as this suggests, the closeness of modelling should nevertheless still be sufficient, considering that what we are interested in is the distinction between availability and non-availability of prefix *form* information in access to the critical stem entry, i.e. one cohort vs. two cohorts. As I argued in 6.1.1, it is in the very nature of prefixes (especially new, therefore productive, ones) that they combine with many stems, and so there will still be competition from other stem candidates, even taking into account subcategorial constraints. For our narrow concerns, then, I would argue that novel form lexical representation does match flirting form representation to a degree to which generalisations from one to the other may be made.

Two differences from other perspectives should be mentioned here: (i) the prefixes in novel combinations *are* established as *prefixes* in the language; and (ii) they typically have a non-redundant (though

186 *Morphology and mind*

still highly general, relational) meaning. However, with regard to (i), presumably the age of the prefix in the language is not a feature that in itself has any consequence for learners (who, after all, are not etymologists). That contemporary subjects will analyse novel forms as containing prefixes because they recognise the forms *as* prefixes is not fundamentally different from acquirers analysing reduced morphemes as bound prefixes and generalising this to subsequent occurrences, at least as far as the processing mechanisms are concerned. In both cases the processor is dealing with a morpheme analysed as a prefix which is fully transparent and is appearing in novel combinations, and in both cases the only restructuring of the lexicon required is the positing of an access link between on the one hand (in flirting) the existing form representation of the reduced morpheme and the form representations of the free forms to which it may become bound, and on the other hand (in novel forms) the existing prefix form representation and the form representation of the particular stem involved. Although in the former case, many new links are posited (and in the latter case only one), this array of links is patently not implemented in the system at one go: links will be formed progressively on a word-by-word basis as appropriate collocations are encountered by the lexical processing mechanism.

The problem of (ii) can be met for present purposes by sidestepping it. In the experimentation reported below, investigation of the processing of novel forms is carried out using the gating task, which is confidently thought to reflect accessing of *form* only. This, then, means that the semantic content of the prefix is not a factor in the results obtained. Investigation of the semantic implications of flirting forms, perhaps in contrast to established forms, must await further investigation.

6.2.2 Experimental evidence

6.2.2.1 Rationale

The hypothesis to be tested in this experiment was that novel prefixed forms disrupt lexical access more than established prefixed forms by requiring decomposition of form, as hypothesised for the flirting prefix forms in the last section. The experimental paradigm adopted was that used by Tyler *et al.* (1988) in their investigation of the accessing of prefixed forms in English, summarised in chapter 5. Recall that those experimenters found that recognition points in prefixed stems fell *earlier* than those in the corresponding bare stems,

(5) Experimental predictions

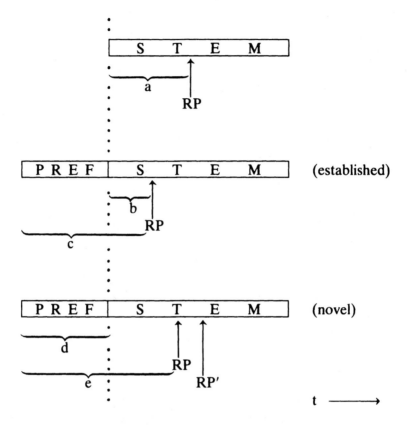

Key: RP = Hypothesised Word Recognition Point
(Weak hypothesis)
RP′ = Hypothesised Word Recognition Point
(Strong hypothesis)
a = Input necessary for bare stem recognition
b = Input necessary for established prefixed stem recognition
c = Input necessary for established prefixed word recognition
d = Input corresponding to length of prefix
e = Input necessary for novel prefixed word recognition
t = time

suggesting that accessing of form did not entail stripping of the prefix. The present experiment was a follow-up to that experiment, adding a degree of refinement to the controlling of variables in the selection of

188 *Morphology and mind*

prefixed forms, and also, critically, adding the novel form condition, not previously examined in the laboratory.

For this experiment, it was predicted that, in accordance with the processing model outlined in chapter 5, the internal structure of the novel forms would be decomposed, reflected by RPs falling roughly at the same point in the stem in both prefixed and bare stem conditions, i.e. (e − d) = a in the schematic representation in (5). A stronger prediction was that extra processing load may be involved, since decomposition involves new cohort formation, and the affix is left 'on hold', entailing some computational cost. We might expect that this indirect computational route for stem access would have an effect on the time course of the access process, over and above that required for the accumulation of the necessary sensory input from both prefix and stem. Recall that it is this factor which I proposed as a possible explanation for the longer time taken to recognise established prefixed words in absolute terms in the Tyler *et al.* experiment (i.e. c > a in (5)). If this is so, we would expect the RPs for novel forms consistently to fall significantly *beyond* the RPs for their corresponding bare stems, as a result of the cost of decomposition. This point is schematically represented as RP′ in (5).

The established prefixed forms to be tested alongside the novel forms were all fully transparent combinations in terms of phonological fusion, semantic compositionality, and productivity (see Hall 1987 for details of how these parameters may be categorised). I selected these forms so that all variables could be kept constant except for the 'novelty' factor, since it is this factor which distinguishes the status of prefixes at the 'flirting' and 'post-flirting' stages of their development. These controls were also included so that we could assess the validity of the Tyler *et al.* results, using a controlled set of prefixed forms (the stimuli set in the Tyler *et al.* experiment was uncontrolled for opacity, length etc.).

6.2.2.2 *The experiment*[6]

I chose the gating paradigm (Grosjean 1980; Tyler and Wessels 1983) as the best option for investigating novel prefixed form recognition experimentally. The procedure is well-suited to our purposes since it taps specifically into the *form* access stage of the word recognition process, and is designed to measure the point within the word at which the form of the whole word is isolated from all others in the mental lexicon. The results of a gating experiment could also be directly compared with those of Tyler *et al.* (1988), and be used to test

A micro-analysis of historical change 189

the robustness of their findings, which have provided the basis for much of the argumentation here.

In the gating task subjects hear successively larger fragments of the target word, starting from its onset, and after each fragment they attempt to identify the word. The successive increments, or 'gates', are of 50 msec (except for the first which is 100 msec) so the point within the word at which it is recognised can be estimated to within 50 msec. Two measures of this point are used. The first, known as the Isolation Point (IP), is calculated as the number of gates needed by the subject to identify the word correctly and not subsequently to change his or her mind. The second measure, known as the Recognition Point (RP), is the point at which the subject isolates the correct word and is 80 per cent confident of his or her response (subjects rate their confidence on a scale from 1 to 10 for each guess they make). The RP is usually subsequent to the IP, although they can occur together, i.e. if 80 per cent confidence is reached on first isolating the word, and without subsequent retracking.

In designing the stimuli words to be used in the experiment, it was necessary to have some form of objective criterion for judging that novel forms would, in fact, be unfamiliar to subjects, and that established forms would be familiar. Accordingly, then, I designed a pretest to select both test sets, using 200 words of varying degrees of (intuitively judged) familiarity. Of these, sixty were intended as novel forms, using transparent readings of the following productive prefixes: *un-*, *re-*, *non-*, *pre-*, *de-*, and *ex-*.[7] Bisyllabic as well as monosyllabic stems were used, because it was very important that subjects were not able to predict the length of the word in advance on the basis of a regular pattern in previous words presented, since this reduces the number of possible candidates and hence distorts RPs. All prefixes were checked (Marchand 1969; Bauer 1983) for phonological, syntactic and/or semantic restrictions on the stems to which they could attach, so that the novel combinations could reasonably be called 'legal' according to English morphological rules. Each novel form was also checked with a panel of independent judges to confirm that it did have a semantic reading and was potentially usable in some conceivable context.[8] The established forms included in the pretest comprised the ten most transparent forms from the Tyler *et al.* (1988) stimuli set plus twenty others.[9] No stem was used in both novel and established conditions.

The pretest items and 110 fillers[10] were presented in random order to subjects, who were instructed to listen carefully to the words and for each one rate it on a scale of familiarity from 1 to 10, where '1'

190 *Morphology and mind*

indicated that they had *never* come across the word, and '10' indicated that they came across it *very* frequently. The twenty lowest-scoring words from the novel class and the twenty highest-scoring from the established class were selected for inclusion in the main experiment.[11] Pretest items are listed in Appendix 1, and final test sets, with pretest familiarity means, appear in Apppendix 2.

In the experiment proper, subjects were presented with gated fragments of the established class and novel class test items, in both bare stem and prefixed stem conditions. The first fragment was 100 msec long and subsequent fragments 50 msec. No subject heard both prefixed and bare versions of the same stem. For each subject and for each item, the following data were recorded: (i) candidate words produced after each gate, (ii) degree of confidence for these words on a scale from 1 to 10.

6.2.2.3 *Results and analysis*

For each test item per subject, Isolation Points (IPs) were calculated in terms of the number of gates needed to identify the correct item without subsequently changing it. The number of subsequent gates needed to reach 80 per cent confidence were then added to calculate Recognition Points (RPs). The mid-mean[12] number of gates per item was then calculated, and this was transformed into a msec measure of both IP and RP (recall that first gate = 100 msec and subsequent gates = 50 msec). Following the Tyler *et al.* (1988) technique, the msec IP and RP measures were then expressed as percentages of the stem length.[13] This percentage measure was used because the bare stem is not an identical acoustic match with the stem as it appears in the prefixed form (the latter is typically shorter than the former) and so direct comparisons in terms of raw msec measures would be invalid.

IPs and RPs as percentages of stem length, henceforth IPPs and RPPs, were then compared for each stem and its corresponding prefixed form in both novel and established conditions. The predictions were (i) that established prefixed forms would have IPP/RPPs occurring *earlier* than in the bare stem forms, and (ii) that novel prefixed forms would have IPP/RPPs occurring (a) *at the same point as* or (b) *after* those in the bare stem forms. The results are tabulated in (6) and (7), and inspection of these tables shows that the predictions (i) and (ii)(b) were confirmed, at least on the IPP measure.[14]

(6) IPP means

	Established	Novel
Bare stem	54	57
Prefixed stem	30	65

(7) RPP means

	Established	Novel
Bare stem	73	77
Prefixed stem	47	76

6.2.3 Discussion

The results of the experiment strongly support the hypothesis that novel prefixed forms significantly disrupt access to lexical form, at least on the IPP measure. That the RPP measure is not significant is hardly surprising, since gating reflects recognition of form, and in novel prefixed words, although the component parts are familiar, the combination is not (this is what defines the class). Subjects are obviously going to be hesitant to assign high confidence to the identification of such forms, since they have never heard them before. The fact that some items from the novel class never reached 80 per cent, or reached it only after the last gate, attests to the fact that RPs are not good indicators of form access for this class, whereas IPs are, since they show at which point the form of the novel combination is isolated, regardless of confidence.

The results show a significant delay in the isolation of prefixed novelly combined stems over their bare stem counterparts, rather than the equity which would be expected if decomposition of the prefix and access to the word via the stem entailed no extra processing cost. They therefore constitute support for the stronger of our two original hypotheses, namely that decomposition involves extra processing load, since it requires a new access process (new cohort creation) initiated at the morpheme boundary between prefix and stem, instead of one single continuous access process starting at word onset.

If the processing of novel prefixed forms closely reflects the processing of flirting prefixed forms, as I reasoned in the last section, then these experiments can be claimed to have revealed some evidence for the processing dispreference for prefixing. What the results show is that decomposition of bound morphemes in front of

192 *Morphology and mind*

the stem, in the isolation of form if not also of meaning, does indeed lead to a delay in the accessing of the stem over and above that militated by the actual length of the prefixed morpheme. This supports the hypothesised asymmetry between flirting prefixes and suffixes detailed in section 6.1.1, where access to a flirting suffix does not affect stem access. These data can therefore be interpreted as strong preliminary support for the psycholinguistic explanation of the suffixing preference.

With regard to the established transparent class, the experiment confirmed the Tyler *et al.* (1988) results: there was no significant difference between the IPP/RPPs in both prefixed and bare stem conditions, suggesting that prefixed words, once established in the lexicons of hearers, are not decomposed, at least for form, and that they are recognised in the same way as non-prefixed words, by gradual accumulation of sensory input regardless of morpheme boundary until enough input is received to distinguish the form from its competitors. This evidence is consistent with the model advanced in chapter 5, in which morphological boundaries are *realised* during access, but do not signal the completion of a single access phase, i.e. isolation of a form in the cohort (as occurs in affix-stripping). The finding in Tyler *et al.* that prefixed forms take longer overall, i.e. measuring from *word*, rather than *stem* onset, is confirmed in the present experiment, suggesting again that the phonological redundancy of prefixes, particularly productive transparent ones, cannot be ruled out as a contributory factor in explaining the dispreference for prefixes; however, given the identification of the *locus* of the dispreference revealed by the historical/psychological micro-analysis reported in the previous section, it is unclear *how* such a factor could influence the cross-linguistic affix distribution.

6.3 CONCLUSION: A UNIFIED EXPLANATION OF MORPHOLOGICAL REGULARITY

What I have tried to achieve in this book is a synthesis of knowledge from various areas of cognitive linguistic science and other language-related areas, in an effort to show how such an interactive approach, unifying the formal/functional divide, can lead to significant findings about the role of language use in the determination of cross-linguistic regularities in form. I chose to look at morphology, from a cognitive perspective, and particularly at the distribution of affixes. Two major features of the distributional pattern were examined: the preference for suffixes over prefixes, and the correlation between affix position

A micro-analysis of historical change   193

and syntactic head position. The explanation given for the suffixing preference was one which appealed to principles of language processing, as suggested by Cutler *et al.* (1985), tempered by principles of diachronic change. These latter principles also supplied an explanation for the head/affix correlation.

The logic of the historical account of affix creation indicates that processing can only wield an influence on the language at the stage at which change is implemented. Accordingly, this stage was subjected to a 'micro-analysis' in an effort to isolate the cognitive events involved. This revealed a historical scenario which could be modelled and empirically tested using stimuli from current English. The experimental results reported here yielded strong preliminary confirmation of the explanatory hypothesis.

I believe that this research has gone some way towards identifying a 'strong' psychological constraint on language, as defined by Clark and Malt (1984) who proposed four criteria for such constraints: (i) *empirical grounding*, (ii) *structure independence*, (iii) *theoretical coherence*, and (iv) *linkage*. In the area of empirical grounding, all the facts are not yet in. Cutler *et al.* (1985) report a lot of suggestive but indirect psycholinguistic evidence, and the experimentation in chapter 6 represents a beginning, but this must be followed up with more specific experimentation, especially on languages other than English, before we can be completely confident. Also, more extensive and detailed cross-linguistic research is needed, specifically with a view to determining the pervasiveness of the historical tendencies discussed in chapter 4. However, the constraint on affixation advanced here *is* independent of the facts it seek to explain, i.e. the explanans is external to the descriptive apparatus employed to characterise the explanandum. It is also fully consistent with broader theoretical claims about language comprehension and diachronic change, as our micro-analysis has shown. Finally, a major purpose of this work has been to stress the importance of what Clark and Malt call 'linkage', the dynamic processes by which explanandum is linked to explanans, and it is the achievement of this that perhaps constitutes the major development here on previous accounts of the suffixing preference.

In this study, distributional regularities of human morphological systems were subjected to a detailed explanatory analysis from the perspective of mind. I believe that the fruits of such an extended discussion have their own intrinsic merit and interest within the study of language. In striving towards this narrow goal, however, I have constantly been trying to support and justify my plea for a unified,

194 *Morphology and mind*

interdisciplinary approach to explanation in linguistics. I hope that the demonstration of what can be achieved through this approach will encourage a greater number of scholars from diverse fields to participate in the study of language as an integrated cognitive system.

Appendices

APPENDIX 1: PRETEST MATERIALS

Novel forms (n = 60)

un-	hitch	brass	thorn
plush	clench	urban	fur
crude	latch	fragile	grit
mild	tilt	routine	moss
tag	wedge	acrid	feather
tile	dent		
rig	jam	*pre-*	*ex-*
buoyant	lodge	chat	clown
drastic	patch	pledge	tramp
pious	blend	jail	duke
vivid	audit	mount	coach
jagged	comfort	trim	pimp
agile	portray	wax	chaplain
	ambush	eclipse	guardian
	migrate	filter	merchant
re-			athlete
darn	*non-*	*de-*	marshal
hoist	vague	turf	gypsy

Established forms (n = 30)

mis-	interpret	*un-*
guide	understand	hook
represent		just
pronounce		kind

196   *Morphology and mind*

ripe	*pre-*
clean	historic
happy	
cover	*dis-*
pleasant	trust
	like
re-	mount
write	prove
marry	

From Tyler et al (1988)

rebuild	asleep	misfortune
rethink	prejudge	enlarge
defrost	prearrange	
adrift	amoral	

Fillers (n = 110: 30 'unfamiliar', 80 'familiar')

'Unfamiliar'

placebo occident morganatic furlong hendiadys heterodox plosive
scansion plethora avuncular maniple counterpane polymath epistaxis
hubris meritricious doxology roborant riparian sagum pabulary
ontogenesis spikelet monomark monkish hantle cresset libate
volumetric obtest

'Familiar' (non-prefixed)

twist photograph lamp ski paper turmoil cushion bassoon shelf
cashier tranquil forge establish coffee tower bat strategy letter
ambulance vehicle falcon jump question bid follow standard crest
massive opportune glass secret mutton pen cottage fly burn coat light
balustrade average play escalate senile mascot perpendicular stipend
platoon frill walk chisel fraught phone address stencil portend dome
erratic conundrum omnipotent card

'Familiar' (prefixed)

remainder deference persuade pretend prevent request inmate
exterminate concur remain distort engulf resit research impure
degenerate subway ex-wife anti-hero non-toxic

APPENDIX 2: TEST ITEMS WITH PRETEST FAMILIARITY SCORES

Novel Forms (n = 20)

Item	Mean	Standard Deviation
unplush	1.08	0.2763
untile	1.08	0.2763
undrastic	1.00	0.0000
unvivid	1.08	0.2763
redent	1.00	0.0000
reambush	1.08	0.2763
recomfort	1.18	0.3857
rejam	1.27	0.4454
remigrate	1.27	0.4454
non-vague	1.08	0.2763
non-brass	1.08	0.2763
non-acrid	1.18	0.3857
prepledge	1.08	0.2763
prejail	1.18	0.3857
prechat	1.08	0.2763
pre-eclipse	1.18	0.3857
exclown	1.08	0.2763
extramp	1.18	0.3857
expimp	1.18	0.3857
demoss	1.27	0.4454

Established forms (n = 20)

Item	Mean	Standard Deviation
misrepresent	5.27	1.4827
misinterpret	6.36	1.6109
misunderstand	7.36	1.1499
misfortune	5.91	1.3787
mispronounce	4.90	1.2398
unjust	6.00	1.4142
unkind	7.64	1.3666
unclean	5.91	2.2342
unhappy	7.91	1.6211
uncover	6.73	1.9582
unpleasant	7.54	0.9875
unripe	4.91	2.1931
dislike	7.64	1.4316
disprove	6.36	1.3666
distrust	6.27	1.9112
rebuild	5.45	1.4993
rethink	5.82	2.0810
defrost	6.09	1.3787
enlarge	6.73	2.0041
prehistoric	4.73	0.9621

Notes

1 EXPLANATION IN LINGUISTICS

1 From amongst the many books and articles which take issue with him on this question, the following is a more-or-less representative selection. In Hutchinson's (1974) view, there has been much confusion between descriptivism and mentalism in Chomsky's framework; Bach (1974), Bever (1974), and Clark and Haviland (1974) address from differing perspectives (and in differing degrees of sympathy) the need to investigate performance factors in the explanation of linguistic regularities; Givón (1979), Itkonen (1983), Julia (1983), and Derwing *et al.* (1980) are impassioned critiques of the narrowness of the Chomskyan perspective; Lieberman (1984) subjects Chomsky's innatist position to strong criticism on evolutionary–biological grounds; Piaget and his followers (Piaget and Inhelder 1969; Karmiloff-Smith 1979) and, more recently, the connectionists (e.g. Arbib, Conklin and Hill 1986) take issue with Chomsky's position on the central problem of language acquisition.

2 I shall have little more to say on the latter two areas of cognitive linguistic science, although they are of crucial importance to the success of the collective research programme (see Gardner 1987, chapters 6 and 9, for further discussion).

3 A serious lack of clarity about the locus or level of explanation is generally exhibited by researchers seeking explanations for language. This causes much confusion in both formal and functional camps, and especially in debates between them. When 'formalists' deny the influence of functional factors on the form of grammar, it is not always clear whether they are thinking in terms of phylogeny (i.e. the evolution of the species) as well as diachrony/ontogeny. Similarly, when 'functionalists' advance their hypotheses (see 1.3) they do not often specify at what level (and how) the functional pressures might have applied.

4 The fact that Hawkins provides an X-bar interpretation for CCH implicitly endows it with explanatory status; however, this interpretation is not a component of the principle itself, which remains purely descriptive. In 3.2.1 and 3.3.2 I show how this descriptive/explanatory distinction in the status of CCH has important implications for the affix/head correlation.

5 Within the universal–typological approach to language, explanation of data from external sources is playing an ever more important role. For

Notes 199

example, Keenan and Comrie (1977) offer a tentative psycholinguistic explanation for their Accessibility Hierarchy for relative clauses, and in a subsequent publication, Keenan and S. Hawkins (1987) actually test this explanatory hypothesis. Papers in Butterworth *et al.* (1984) and Hawkins (1988), and Cutler *et al.* (1985) itself, are clear examples of the heightened awareness in some quarters of the goal of explanation within the universal-typological school. Much of this work is valuable and interesting, and simply cannot be handled, on either the descriptive *or* the explanatory level, within an explanatory framework for language as limiting as the formal generative one.

2 MORPHOLOGICAL REGULARITY

1 Greenberg notes (1966: 93) that 'there are probably no languages without either compounding, affixing, or both. In other words, there are probably no purely isolating languages. There are a considerable number of languages without inflections, perhaps none without compounding and derivation.'

2 In this study we are not principally concerned with cases of discontinuous affixation such as (i) *intercalation*, e.g. in Semitic languages, where the value of the vowel slots of a word constitute a morpheme, and this is intercalated into a consonantal template which constitutes the stem; (ii) *circumfixing*, where the stem appears inside the affix – i.e. elements of the affix precede and follow the stem; or (iii) *infixing* where the affix appears inside the stem. The rarity of such structures has a ready psycholinguistic explanation, namely the processing complexity associated with discontinuous elements (e.g. verbs with particles, sentences with centre embedding, fillers and gaps) because of the necessity to pass over the first element without assigning an interpretation to it (and hence adding to memory load), or because the first element may be perceived as a complete entity, thus causing a 'garden path' analysis.

3 Comrie (1980: 94, note 3) points out a couple of rare exceptions.

4 The corpus of 203 languages consists of three samples: *Leon Stassen* (113 languages) recording for Ns: case, definiteness, indefiniteness; and for Vs: tense, aspect, person, negation. *Revere Perkins* (40 languages) recording only for Vs: tense, aspect, mood, person, negation, voice, valence, causativity. *Gary Gilligan* (50 languages) recording for Ns: case, gender, plurality, possession, definiteness, nominalisation; and for Vs: tense, aspect, mood, person, negation, voice.

5 In the figures given in the text, we are ignoring the fourth column, i.e. cases where neither prefixes nor suffixes are used in a language; however, it is perhaps significant that a large number of head-initial languages do not encode the functions recorded in the H&G sample as affixes. As we shall see in chapter 3, head-initial languages are more likely than head-final languages to yield prefixes, and these seem to be dispreferred cross-linguistically.

6 Ochs (1982) demonstrates quite strikingly the need for sociolinguistic awareness when determining basic word order. She shows that the basic word order proposed by previous linguists for Samoan (VSO) was, in fact, based on male informants using a formal register, but that this did not

200　*Morphology and mind*

reflect the majority word order VOS, employed by female speakers and the informal register. Admittedly, such cases are going to be rare, and in this particular case, head ordering was not affected; however, that a word order may be misreported due to sociolinguistic factors further motivates the need for explicit criteria in judging basic word order.

7 Note that there is no necessary correlation between productivity and frequency: in language x, affix f might occur on twenty words and affix g on only five, but these five may be twenty times more frequent than each of the words to which f may be attached. Consequently, f will have a 'frequency factor' of twenty and a 'productivity factor' of twenty, whereas g will have a 'frequency factor' of 100 but a 'productivity factor' of only five.

3 AFFIXES AND HEADS

1 See Jackendoff (1977) for a full account of how the X' system was motivated by the lexicalist hypothesis.

2 In the X' component of Chomsky's model, the inflectional features are associated with an abstract 'INFL' or 'I' node in the syntax which appears as sister to VP (V''), dominated by a constituent INFL' or I' (=S). The form of the inflectional morphology is dictated by some variant on the traditional affix-hopping rule (Chomsky 1981: 256; cf. Chomsky 1989 for extended discussion).

3 The PrPr does not exclude the possibility of inflectional rules applying in the lexicon, and Borer notes that this is necessary in some cases, e.g. when inflections appear within compounds, such as *sales manager training* and *profits tax law*.

4 Note that some prefixes in English seem to behave as heads in some constructions and not in others. In the first couple of examples in (22), *dis-* acts as head, whereas in the following, it is the stem which acts as head (in that its categorial features percolate to the word level):

$$[\text{dis-}] + [\text{agree}_V] \quad \rightarrow [\text{disagree}_V]$$
$$[\text{dis-}] + [\text{loyal}_A] \quad \rightarrow [\text{disloyal}_A]$$
$$[\text{dis-}] + [\text{advantage}_N] \rightarrow [\text{disadvantage}_N]$$
$$[\text{dis-}] + [\text{interest}_N] \quad \rightarrow [\text{disinterest}_N]$$
$$[\text{dis-}] + [\text{passionate}_A] \rightarrow [\text{dispassionate}_A]$$

In order to account for this we may postulate two homophonous prefixes dis_1- and dis_2-. Such a move is not unmotivated: an examination of the semantics of *de-* and *dis-* prefixes in English (Hall 1983) shows that the non-head variety of *dis-* is restricted to two semantic classifications, namely (i) when it means 'opposite of X' (where X = stem), e.g., in *disagree, disloyal, disadvantage*; and (ii) when it refers to 'absence of X', e.g. in *disinterest* and *dispassionate*. In only one other semantic classification is *dis-* a non-head, and here only in a single idiomatic case, closely related to the 'opposite' reading (*distributary* with the prefix meaning '(physical) reversal of'); in all other classifications, *dis-* determines the word as verbal. We may therefore propose two types of *dis-*, which correspond (with only one exception) with semantic classifications; one which is assigned the category V and one which is unmarked for category. This is sketchy, since

Notes 201

the semantic classifications do not seem to fall into two neat head and non-head supercategories; however, the correspondence with semantic factors is suggestive. Zwicky (1985) presents similar cases of suffixes which seem to act sometimes as head, sometimes as non-head, e.g. *-ful*, head in *careful, hopeful, beautiful*, but non-head in *handful, cupful, pocketful*. The semantic distinction here is very clear: in *careful* the suffix means 'having the quality X' and is [-ful$_A$]; in *handful* the suffix means approximately 'quantity of capacity of X' and is [-ful$_u$].

An alternative approach might be to retain a single morpheme *dis-*, and specify that the semantics determines headship. Section 3.1.2 deals with semantic approaches to headship, and concludes, however, that they are inadequate; it would therefore be a most *ad hoc* move to allow semantic factors to play a role here beyond providing, as they do, independent evidence for the existence of two or more prefixes which share the same form but differ in head status.

5 One feature of this formulation which might seem to pose problems is that the head (X) is obligatory (the optionality of P and Q being indicated by parentheses) thus maintaining its essential identity with the syntactic notion of head (recall Lyons's observation discussed in 3.1.1.1). In both Williams and Selkirk, however, the notion of headless words is entertained to account for exocentric compounds like [in$_P$] + [step$_V$] → [instep$_N$] and [bare$_A$] + [back$_N$] → [bareback$_{ADV}$]. For Selkirk such forms present us with a choice between the following structures:

(a) i.   or   ii.

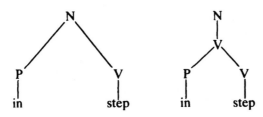

(b) i.   or   ii.

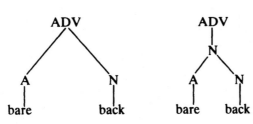

However, in the (ii) variants it seems that the category immediately dominating the terminal nodes – i.e. the V in (a)ii and the N in (b)ii – is determined for Selkirk by the RHR – without independent motivation. It is unclear what *could* motivate category selection in such constituent trees. Of course, the same problem is faced with bare stems, e.g., [fall$_V$] → [fall$_N$], [light$_A$] → [light$_V$], [axe$_N$] → [axe$_V$]. Apparently, these examples contradict Lyons's observation that heads are obligatory. The only alternative

202 *Morphology and mind*

is to specify phonologically null elements which bear syntactic features, so for example [fall_N] would be allowed by the independently motivated compounding rule N → V + N, as in the following pair:

(c) i.   cf. ii.

Exocentric compounds like *instep* or *bareback* could be formed like other three-member compounds as shown in the following:

(d) i.   cf. ii.

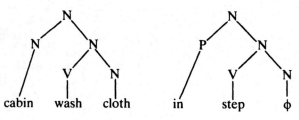

(e) i.   cf. ii.

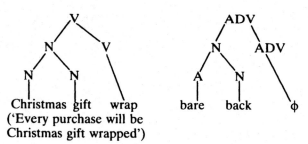

('Every purchase will be
Christmas gift wrapped')

There is considerable motivation in both current syntactic and phonological theory for postulating phonologically null elements. In Chomsky's syntactic model, for example, there are at least three types of phonologically null NPs: NP traces, variables (i.e. Wh traces) and PRO (Chomsky 1981); in grammatical paradigms there are often gaps which, though phonologically unrealised, have grammatical features associated with them. In autosegmental phonology the need for segments without feature matrices is seen in reduplicative affixation, where phonologically empty segments are affixed which then 'borrow' feature matrices from the stem (cf. Marantz 1982). See note 9, chapter 5, for discussion of how such elements may be handled in language processing.

6 Doug Pulleyblank (p.c.) points out that phrases such as 'run the gauntlet' *are* semantically headed, since 'running' is involved, but the metaphor still requires an interpretation not available from general semantic rules.

Notes 203

7 = 'domain' < OE *dom* = 'fate, destiny' (*Shorter Oxford English Dictionary* (1973), [*SOED*]). Marchand (1969: 262) gives an alternative (and more plausible) gloss in the context of combinations such as *kingdom*, *Christendom*, *earldom*, *martyrdom*, etc., viz. 'jurisdiction, state, statute'. In Middle English it acquires the meaning of 'territory' for *kingdom* and other forms.

8 = 'make' < Fr *-fier* < Lt *facere* = 'make' (*SOED*).

9 In the abstract, mathematical approach to learnability theory taken by Wexler and Culicover (1980), the notion of syntactic head plays a very significant role. They claim that 'it is important that the classically central linguistic notion *head* is central ... to learnability theory' (p. 486), and they exploit it to the utmost as a constraining characteristic on rule domains in their theorems.

10 Williams (1987: xi–xii) suggests that the identification of affixes in acquisition is unlikely to be the result of parameter setting, as the HOP would seem to assume. Rather, it is probably served by nothing more than the detection of a statistical regularity by some sort of 'low-level induction device'.

4 THE DIACHRONIC LINK

1 Givón's original formulation (p. 401) of (3) and (4) confusingly labels the output of the reanalysis as 'np' rather than 'pp' (here pre- or postpositional phrase) and labels the postposition in (4) as 'prep'. I have corrected these labellings here.

2 Although the languages in the H&G corpus do maximally reflect the wide distribution of language families in the world, details of their genetic relations are not taken into account in this calculation, and so the quantification of languages here and in other parts of this paper can only give a rough approximation of actual genetic variation (it is possible, for example, that the 76 languages appealed to here are all genetically related, although even if this were so (and it is most unlikely), they still as a body speak against the SOV/Mod-N claim).

3 It should be noted here that although I adopt Givón's claim for the origin of affixes, it is not necessary to accept the stronger claim that current morpheme order allows us always to reconstruct previous syntactic order. There are a number of counterexamples to this prediction (cf. e.g. Comrie 1980; Green 1976; Bybee 1985), yet these do not weaken the model described here, since the basic word order at the time of affixation is only one of many factors which influence the reduction of full words to affixal status (cf. also the discussion in chapter 2 of problems in establishing basic word order and also the language examples discussed in the final section of this chapter).

4 Assimilation is not the only weakening process that occurs at word endings upon suffixation: consonant loss, in order to maintain preferred syllable structure, is also attested, for example in Korean (cf. Hyman, 1975: 162):

/əps # ta/	→	[əp+ta]	'there is no'
/nəks # to/	→	[nək+to]	'the soul also'
/anč # kəra/	→	[an+kəra]	'sit!'

204 *Morphology and mind*

5 Chomsky (1959: 202–3) finds Greenberg's argument 'very dubious on empirical grounds', since it would predict the predominance of word orders such as NNV, V Aux, and sentence-final pronouns, which is not the case. He prefers instead an explanation based on the observation that 'in regular conditioned sound changes, the conditioning factor is far more frequently a sound which follows than one which precedes' – i.e. the preponderance of regressive assimilation argument. What Chomsky fails to realise is that there are going to be many principles, psychological and otherwise, which influence the form of language, and that many of these are going to be in conflict with each other, so that one cannot reject a hypothesised organising principle of language on the basis of its inapplicability in some domains (cf. 6.1.2). Further, many principles will *coincide* in their effect due perhaps to some higher level contingency, thus, as we have seen in this chapter, Greenberg's information processing principle and Chomsky's preferred assimilation principle are in fact *both* reflexes of the temporal nature of spoken language production and comprehension, and both conspire to the same end: a preference for suffixes over prefixes.

5 UNDERSTANDING AFFIXES

1 RP (recognition point) is distinguished from IP (isolation point) which refers to the point at which the word is first correctly identified, regardless of confidence, and UP (uniqueness point) which refers to the point at which, theoretically, the word diverges in form from all other competing words (as calculated phonemically using a suitable lexical database).
2 Tyler's (1984) *post hoc* study of subjects' responses in Tyler and Wessels's (1983) gating experiment provides strong evidence for the Cohort Model's claims about the structure of the initial cohort, specifically that subjects *do* initially produce a large set of responses which is reduced as more of the sensory input is received. And, as predicted by the model, the degree of context provided *is* found to reflect the rate at which isolation of a unique set member is achieved.
3 Henderson (1985) is a useful if quirky summary of research in this area, and raises a number of interesting questions regarding both methodology and theory.
4 Taft (1988) contains a brief review of this research.
5 Taft (1981) countered this by arguing that subjects are not likely to have employed a prefix-stripping strategy if they knew that most of the words were prefixed and, as Rubin *et al.* (1979) suggest, they can alternatively access the forms *without* stripping. Taft also identified an empirical flaw in the experiment: the 'no difference' results in the text frequency materials can themselves be attributed to a special strategy, for in Rubin *et al.*'s materials, no prefixed words were nonwords. So, if this was realised by subjects, then the lexical decision task could be performed without complete processing.
6 Although Hyman (1985, 1987) gives examples of African languages which phonologically mark the stem.
7 Hall (1987) reports preliminary experimentation not included here.
8 Not to be confused with the unrelated grammatical sense of *head* used in chapter 3.

Notes 205

9 Boyce, Browman and Goldstein (1987) report some data from the rare phenomenon of initial mutation, in their case in Welsh, which have a ready interpretation in the context of the approach to inflectional representation advocated here. Inflectional categories in Welsh may be realised by variation in the initial phoneme, the legacy of an earlier rule of progressive assimilation from preceding items. Boyce *et al.*'s results from experiments using the priming technique suggest that mutated variants share lexical entries with their associated base forms, much as in the prefixed form representation hypothesised in (24). The priming observed (base for mutated form, mutated form for base, mutated form for related mutated form) is significantly less than for identity priming, suggesting a lack of the close association found in regular affixed inflection, as in English.

What is most interesting is that these priming differences do not appear to be due to phonological form variation, since with forms in an inflectional mutation context which do not actually mutate (e.g., /b/ → /b/ in aspirate mutation contexts, whereas /p/ → /f/ in the same contexts), the same priming differences are observed. The authors suggest a solution involving an autosegmental approach to morphological representation (cf. McCarthy 1981; Marantz 1982) and two 'dimensions' of access, one lexical and one morphological.

Their conclusions, although lacking in detail, seem quite consistent with the model proposed here. Their dimension of lexical access seems functionally equivalent to our *form* access stage, and their dimension of morphological access may be viewed as a part of our *content* access stage. Their results may then be quite easily captured by the model proposed here if we conclude that non-mutating forms in mutating contexts are accessed in the same way as zero-derived and zero-inflected forms in English (see note 5, chapter 3), where form access will be through the stem/base form, but morphological processing at the content access stage will require access to a non-phonologically represented sub-entry. Access to the sub-entry will be triggered by encountering a mis-match with morphological features listed in the main entry. The zero-morpheme entry will then be an entry at the *content* level only, as represented in (a) for English and (b) for Welsh. In the Welsh example, the word *brawd*, 'brother', is shown with some morphological feature *i* in the sub-entry, representing the relevant mutating context.

(a)

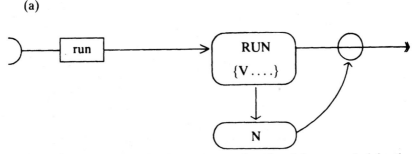

This conceptualisation will thus account for the delay revealed in the Welsh priming results for items of the same form but different morphological content. I know of no experimental data which bear on this view of

206 *Morphology and mind*

(b)

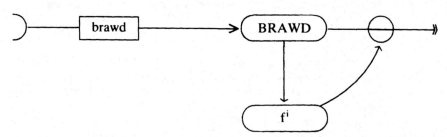

English zero-morphemes: it provides an interesting area for further research.
10 The size of the word-initial cohort *per se* should not have an effect on word recognition point, since the determinant of isolation is the distribution of syntagmatic acoustic specifications rather than any paradigmatic quantification of alternative candidates; however, the probability of extended syntagmatic redundancy (and hence later recognition point) increases as the pool of candidates is enlarged. So, for example, although it is possible that a two-word initial cohort might lead to recognition at the *end* of the target word if the two only differ in, say, their final consonant, whereas a thirty-word cohort might be reduced to one after only the first CV sequence, it is clear that the greater the number of candidates, the more likely one or more of them is going to share acoustic features with the target for a longer stretch of the input string.
11 A later version of this paper has appeared as Hawkins and Cutler (1988). It does not differ essentially from the original version.
12 I am encouraged here by Martinet (1964: 197) who opines that 'the difficulties experienced in identifying all the circumstances which may have influenced the genesis of a linguistic change should not deter the search for an explanatory analysis'.

6 A MICRO-ANALYSIS OF HISTORICAL CHANGE

1 In apparent contrast to this view, Bybee and Slobin (1982) argue, on the basis of a comparative study of attested changes in the English past tense system and elicited innovations from different age groups, that: 'both socially and linguistically ... older children and adults are in control of morpho-phonemic change' (p. 37). The type of change exemplified by the free → bound reanalysis is, however, of a very different order from the type of change considered by Bybee and Slobin. These authors acknowledge that the evolving grammatical systems of small children are the locus of changes attributable to universal principles, such as operating principles (Slobin 1985 – cf. 3.3); as we have seen in chapter 4, the move towards phonological reduction and eventual morphologisation is motivated by general universal principles rather than language-particular factors. In addition, it occurs *internal* to individual speakers, and has no immediate social manifestation: cf. the discussion in 6.1.4. Thus, I believe we can quite confidently conclude that small children, 'not yet under the influence

Notes 207

of an internalized language-specific system' (Bybee and Slobin 1982: 37), are the source of the (ultimate) origin of affixes.

2 According to the least redundancy hypothesis, a single listing of a bound affix will be linked with multiple stem entries, in which case only one input monitor will be involved.

3 I should, in the light of Osgood's invocation of functional laws, reiterate here my acceptance of the fact that some, perhaps many universals, especially those reflecting a portion of our genetic endowment, may derive from nothing more than pre-existing neural structure, and thus *may* have no relation to any 'functional law', linguistic or otherwise (cf. chapter 1).

4 An anonymous Routledge reviewer points out that the native pattern of affixing cannot *block* identification of affixes in non-native position if a sufficient number of words of this type are borrowed. In the reviewer's words: '. . . if speakers happen to borrow (unanalysed) a reasonably large number of prefixed forms, by the time that they realise that there are prefixes, would it not be too late? What could they do – not notice the prefixes? – unborrow the words?' This is fair criticism, and so perhaps we should restrict ourselves to claiming that native structure might positively *facilitate* affix identification in borrowed words which match native position, even when perhaps relatively few such words have been borrowed, whereas the native pattern might *inhibit* affix identification in non-native position until some critical number of such forms have entered the lexicon.

5 Evidence that novel combinations are not just artefacts of the psycholinguistics laboratory can be seen in the naturally-occurring example contained in the comments of the Routledge reviewer quoted in footnote 4, this chapter (viz. *unborrow*). Tom Lehrer introduces his troop song for a Third World War as a bit of 'pre-nostalgia' (since there will be no one around to reminisce *after* the war).

6 I gratefully acknowledge the help of Dr Lorraine Tyler and Dr William Marslen-Wilson and their colleagues at the MRC Language and Speech Group, Department of Experimental Psychology, University of Cambridge, in generously accommodating me in their laboratory and making its facilities available to me. Subjects were drawn from the laboratory's Subject Pool. Each subject was paid for their participation; no pretest subject participated in the experiment proper.

7 The semantic readings and resultant syntactic categories employed were as follows (with established examples):

un-:	not x (A); reverse process of x (V) (unkind/untie)
re-:	x again (V) (rebuild)
non-:	characterised by absence of x (A) (non-alcoholic)
pre-:	before x (A); x before (V) (pre-war/predate)
de-:	remove x from (V) (descale)
ex-:	former x (N) (ex-lover)

208 *Morphology and mind*

8 The mean frequency of stems used in the novel class was 10 per million (Francis and Kučera 1982), and for prefixed stems, of course, the frequency is 0; for established forms the mean frequency for bare stems was 197, and for prefixed stems, 10. The disparity between novel and established bare stem frequency is large; however, since the crucial comparisons in this experiment are between identical stems, frequency should not be a factor.

9 The existing Tyler *et al.* gating data on these words were not used; the forms to be used in the experiment were in fact re-gated, to ensure uniformity.

10 In addition to the 90 transparently prefixed forms (60 novel + 30 established), 110 'filler' items were included. Fillers are intended to obscure any patterns in the test stimuli to prevent the development of special strategies (conscious or unconscious) by subjects. The fillers were therefore designed to be spread along a continuum of familiarity, crudely reflecting frequency of occurrence in the spread of language uses, in that there were fewer 'unfamiliar' forms than 'familiar' (30 vs. 80 respectively). The 'familiar' fillers covered a wide range of syllable lengths and frequency scores in the Francis and Kučera (1982) count, whereas the 'unfamiliar' fillers were largely bi- or trisyllabic and were mostly not listed in the Francis and Kučera count. See Appendix 1.

11 Mean scores for the novel forms ranged from 1.08 to 1.27. For the established class, means ranged from 4.73 at the lowest end up to 7.91 at the highest. Appendix 2 lists the means for each item.

12 Mid-means are means calculated after an equal proportion of data points has been removed from both the top and the bottom of the original data set: in this case a standard 25 per cent was removed from each end. Mid-means are a better indication of central trend since they exclude extreme responses from the analysis.

13 Mean length of stems (in msec) was as in the following table:

	Established	*Novel*
Bare	619	556
Prefixed	581	559

Mean length of prefixes was 191 msec for established forms and 257 msec for novel forms. Notice that in the established condition, stem length is considerably shorter when prefixed, whereas in the novel condition it is unaffected. These figures are consistent with the claims in chapter 4 about reduction in form being correlated with degree of establishment in the lexicon. They also support the claim that novel forms match the hypothesised structure of flirting forms in terms of phonological transparency between prefix and stem.

14 Separate ANOVAs were performed to establish whether the novelty factor (i.e. novel vs. established) accounted for variance in a significant portion of the data, using IPs and RPs as well as IPPs and RPPs. The results were highly significant ($p<0.0001$ in all cases; for IP, $f(1, 38) = 22.88$; for RP, $f(1, 37) = 21.76$; for IPP, $f(1, 38) = 37.17$; and for RPP,

f(1, 38) = 22.28). Two-tailed paired t-tests were then performed in *post hoc* analyses to establish whether the differences in IPP/RPPs in each condition were significant. The earliness of established prefix IPP and RPPs was highly significant ($p < 0.0001$ in both cases). In the novel class the prefixed form IPPs were significantly later than the stem IPPs ($p < 0.01$), however the RPPs were not significantly later ($p > 0.5$).

Bibliography

LI = *Linguistic Inquiry*
JVLVB = *Journal of Verbal Learning and Verbal Behavior*

Andersen, H. (1973) 'Abductive and deductive change', *Language* 49,4, 765–93.

Anderson, S. R. (1980) 'On the development of morphology from syntax', in J. Fisiak (ed.), *Historical Morphology*, The Hague: Mouton.

—— (1982) 'Where's morphology?', *LI* 13, 571–612.

Antinucci F., A. Duranti and L. Gebert (1979) 'Relative clause structure, relative clause perception, and the change from SOV to SVO', *Cognition* 7, 145–76.

Aoun, J. (1985) *A Grammar of Anaphora*, Cambridge, Mass.: MIT Press.

Arbib, M. A. and J. Hill (1988) 'Language acquisition: Schemas replace universals', in J. A. Hawkins (ed.), *Explaining Language Universals*, Oxford: Basil Blackwell.

——, E. J. Conklin and J. C. Hill (1986) *From Schema Theory to Language*, Oxford: Oxford University Press.

Archangeli, D. (1984) *Underspecification in Yawelmani Phonology*, unpublished Ph.D. dissertation, MIT.

Ashby, W. J. (1980) 'Prefixed conjugation in Parisian French', in H. J. Izzo (ed.), *Italic and Romance: Linguistic Studies in Honor of Ernst Pulgram*, Amsterdam: John Benjamins.

Bach, E. (1974) 'Explanatory inadequacy', in D. Cohen (ed.), *Explaining Linguistic Phenomena*, New York: Hemisphere Publishing Corporation.

Badecker, W. and A. Caramazza (1989) 'A lexical distinction between inflection and derivation', *LI* 20, 1, 108–16.

Bauer, L. (1983) *English Word-formation*, Cambridge: Cambridge University Press.

Benveniste, E. (1968) 'Mutations of Linguistic Categories', in W. P. Lehmann and Y. Malkiel (eds), *Directions for Historical Linguistics: A Symposium*, Austin, Texas: University of Texas Press.

Bergman, M. and P. Eling (1984) 'The recognition of morphologically complex words', paper presented at the EPS–NPF Conference, Amsterdam, July 1984.

Berlin, B. (1972) 'Speculations on the growth of ethnobotanical nomenclature', *Language in Society* 1, 51–86.

Bibliography 211

Berwick, R. C. and A. S. Weinberg (1984) *The Grammatical Basis of Linguistic Performance*, Cambridge, Mass.: MIT Press.

Bever, T. G. (1970) 'The cognitive basis for linguistic structures', in J. R. Hayes (ed.), *Cognition and the Development of Language*, New York: Wiley.

—— (1974) 'The ascent of the specious or, there's a lot we don't know about mirrors', in D. Cohen (ed.), *Explaining Linguistic Phenomena*, New York: Hemisphere Publishing Corporation.

Bopp, F. (1974 [1820]) *Analytical Comparison of the Sanskrit, Greek, Latin, and Teutonic Languages, Shewing the Original Identity of their Grammatical Structure*. Edited by E. F. K. Koerner as Amsterdam Classics in Linguistics 3. Amsterdam: John Benjamins.

Borer, H. (1984) 'The projection principle and rules of morphology', in C. Jones and P. Sells (eds), *Proceedings of NELS* 14, Amherst, Mass.: University of Massachussets GLSA.

—— and K. Wexler (1987) 'The maturation of syntax', in T. Roeper and E. Williams (eds), *Parameter Setting*, Dordrecht: Reidel.

Bowerman, M. (1982) 'Reorganizational processes in lexical and syntactic development', in E. Wanner and L. R. Gleitman (eds), *Language Acquisition: The State of the Art*, Cambridge: Cambridge University Press.

—— (1988) 'The "No negative evidence" problem: How do children avoid constructing an overly general grammar?' in J. A. Hawkins (ed.), *Explaining Language Universals*, Oxford: Basil Blackwell.

Boyce, S., C. P. Browman and L. Goldstein (1987) 'Lexical organization and Welsh consonant mutations', in *J. Memory and Language* 26, 419–52.

Bresnan, J. (ed.) (1982) *The Mental Representation of Grammatical Relations*, Cambridge, Mass.: MIT Press.

Brown, R. and D. McNeill (1966) 'The "tip-of-the-tongue" phenomenon', *JVLVB* 5, 325–37.

Butterworth, B. (1983) 'Lexical representation', in B. Butterworth (ed.), *Language Production, Volume 2: Development, Writing and Other Language Processes*, London: Academic Press.

——, B. Comrie and O. Dahl (eds) (1984) *Explanations for Language Universals*, Amsterdam: Mouton.

Bybee, J. L. (1985) *Morphology: A Study in the Relation between Meaning and Form*, Amsterdam: John Benjamins.

—— (1988) 'The diachronic dimension in explanation', in J. A. Hawkins (ed.), *Explaining Language Universals*, Oxford: Basil Blackwell.

—— and M. A. Brewer (1980) 'Explanation in morphophonemics: Changes in Provençal and preterite forms', *Lingua* 52, 201–42.

—— and W. Pagliuca (1985) 'Cross-linguistic comparison and the development of grammatical meaning', in J. Fisiak (ed.), *Historical Semantics, Historical Word Formation*, The Hague: Mouton.

—— and W. Pagliuca (1987) 'The evolution of future meaning', in A. G. Ramat, O. Carruba and G. Bernini (eds), *Papers from the Seventh* International Conference on Historical Linguistics, Amsterdam: John Benjamins.

—— and D. I. Slobin (1982) 'Why small children cannot change language on their own: Suggestions from the English past tense', in A. Ahlqvist (ed.) *Papers from the Fifth International Conference on Historical Linguistics*, Amsterdam: John Benjamins.

212 *Morphology and mind*

Caramazza, A., A. Laudanna and C. Romani (1988) 'Lexical access and inflectional morphology', *Cognition* 28, 297–332.

Champion, J. J. (1980) 'A note on prefixed inflection in French', in H. J. Izzo (ed.), *Italic and Romance: Linguistic Studies in Honor of Ernst Pulgram*, Amsterdam: John Benjamins.

Chen, M. Y. (1973) 'Cross-dialectical comparison: A case study and some theoretical considerations', *J. Chinese Linguistics* 1, 38–63.

—— and W. S.-Y. Wang (1975) 'Sound change: Actuation and Implementation', *Language* 51, 2, 255–81.

Chomsky, N. (1959) Review of Greenberg (1957) in *Word* 15, 1, 202–18.

—— (1965) *Aspects of the Theory of Syntax*, Cambridge, Mass.: MIT Press.

—— (1970) 'Problems of explanation in linguistics', in R. Borger and F. Cioffi (eds), *Explanation in the Social Sciences*, Cambridge: Cambridge University Press.

—— (1972) *Language and Mind*, Enlarged Edition, New York: Harcourt Brace Jovanovich, Inc.

—— (1977a) *Essays on Form and Interpretation*, New York: North Holland.

—— (1977b) 'Conditions on rules of grammar', in R. W. Cole (ed.), *Current Issues in Linguistic Theory*, Bloomington, Indiana: Indiana University Press.

—— (1980) *Rules and Representations*, Oxford; Basil Blackwell.

—— (1981) *Lectures on Government and Binding*, Dordrecht: Foris.

—— (1986a) *Knowledge of Language, Its Nature, Origin and Use*, New York: Praeger.

—— (1986b) *Barriers*, Cambridge, Mass.: MIT Press.

—— (1989) 'Some notes on economy of derivation and representation', in R. Freidin (ed.), *Principles and Parameters in Comparative Grammar*, Cambridge, Mass.: MIT Press.

—— and H. Lasnik (1977) 'Filters and control', *LI* 8, 3, 425–504.

Clark, H. H. and E. V. Clark (1977) *Psychology and Language: An Introduction to Psycholinguistics*, New York: Harcourt, Brace, Jovanovich.

—— and S. E. Haviland (1974) 'Psychological processes as linguistic explanation', in D. Cohen (ed.), *Explaining Linguistic Phenomena*, New York: Hemisphere Publishing Corporation.

—— and B. C. Malt (1984) 'Psychological constraints on language: A commentary on Bresnan and Kaplan and on Givón', in W. Kintsch, J. R. Miller, and P. G. Polson (eds), *Method and Tactics in Cognitive Science*, Hillsdale, N.J.: Erlbaum.

Colé, P., C. Beauvillain and J. Segui (1989) 'On the representation and processing of prefixed and suffixed derived words: A differential frequency effect', *J. Memory and Language* 28, 1–13.

Cole, R. A. (1973) 'Listening for mispronunciations: A measure of what we hear during speech', *Perception and Psychophysics* 11, 153–6.

—— and J. Jakimik (1980) 'A model of speech perception', in R. A. Cole (ed.), *Perception and Production of Fluent Speech*, Hillsdale, N.J.: Erlbaum.

Company Company, C. (1983) 'Tiempos compuestos en el Español Medieval', *Nueva Revista de Filología Hispánica*, XXXII, 2, 235–57.

—— (1985) 'Los futuros en el Español Medieval: Sus orígenes y su evolución', *Nueva Revista de Filología Hispánica*, XXXIV, 1, 48–107.

Comrie, B. (1976) *Aspect*, Cambridge: Cambridge University Press.

Bibliography 213

—— (1980) 'Morphology and word order reconstructions: problems and prospects', in J. Fisiak (ed.), *Historical Morphology*, The Hague: Mouton.

—— (1981) *Language Universals and Linguistic Typology*, Chicago: University of Chicago Press.

Cooper, W. E. and J. Paccia-Cooper (1980) *Syntax and Speech*, Cambridge, Mass.: Harvard University Press.

Corbett, G. G. (1987) 'The morphology/syntax interface: Evidence from possessive adjectives in Slavonic', *Language*, 63, 2, 299–345.

Cowgill, W. (1966) 'A search for universals in Indo-European diachronic morphology', in J. H. Greenberg (ed.), *Universals of Language*, Cambridge, Mass.: MIT Press.

Cutler, A. (1980) 'Errors of stress and intonation', in V. A. Fromkin (ed.), *Errors in Linguistic Performance: Slips of the Tongue, Ear, Pen and Hand*, New York: Academic Press.

——, J. A. Hawkins and G. Gilligan (1985) 'The suffixing preference: A processing explanation', *Linguistics* 23, 723–58.

Dahl, O. (1979 'Typology and sentence negation', *Linguistics* 17, 79–106.

Derwing, B. L., G. D. Prideaux and W. J. Baker (1980) 'Experimental linguistics in historical perspective', in G. D. Prideaux, B. L. Derwing and W. J. Baker (eds), *Experimental Linguistics*, Ghent: E. Story-Scientia.

Dressler, W. V. (1986) 'Explanation in natural morphology, illustrated with comparative and agent-noun formation', in G. E. Booij and J. van Marle (eds), *Modular Approaches to Morphology*, special issue, *Linguistics*, 24, 3.

Fay, D. A. and A. Cutler (1977) 'Malapropisms and the structure of the mental lexicon', *LI* 8, 505–20.

Fleischmann, S. (1977) *Cultural and Linguistic Factors in Word Formation*, Berkeley: University of California Press.

Flynn, S. (1987) *A Parameter-Setting Model of L2 Acquisition: Experimental Studies in Anaphora*, Dordrecht: Reidel.

Fodor, J. A. (1983) *The Modularity of Mind*, Cambridge, Mass.: MIT Press.

——, T. G. Bever and M. F. Garrett (1974) *The Psychology of Language: An Introduction to Psycholinguistics and Generative Grammar*, New York: McGraw-Hill.

—— and Z. W. Pylyshyn (1988) 'Connectionism and cognitive architecture: A critical analysis', in S. Pinker and J. Mehler (eds), *Connections and Symbols*, Cambridge, Mass.: MIT Press.

Fodor, J. D. (1984) 'Constraints on gaps: is the parser a significant influence?', in B. Butterworth, B. Comrie and O. Dahl (eds), *Explanations for Language Universals*, Amsterdam: Mouton.

Foley, J. (1977) *Foundations of Theoretical Phonology*, Cambridge: Cambridge University Press.

Forster, K. I. (1976) 'Accessing the mental lexicon', in R. J. Wales and E. Walker (eds), *New Approaches to Language Mechanisms*, Amsterdam: North Holland.

—— and Chambers, S. (1973) 'Lexical access and naming time', *JVLVB* 12, 627–35.

Foss, D. (1969) 'Decision processes during sentence comprehension: Effects of lexical item difficulty and position upon decision times', *JVLVB* 8, 457–62.

Francis, W. N. and H. Kučera (1982) *Frequency Analysis of English Usage: Lexicon and Grammar*, Boston: Houghton Mifflin.

214 *Morphology and mind*

Frauenfelder, U. H. and L. K. Tyler (eds) (1987) *Spoken Word Recognition*, special issue, *Cognition* 25.

Frazier, L. (1979) 'On comprehending sentences: syntactic parsing strategies', unpublished ms., Indiana University Linguistics Club, Bloomington, Indiana.

—— and J. D. Fodor (1978) 'The sausage machine: a new two-stage parsing model', *Cognition*, 6, 291–326.

—— (1987a) 'Structure in auditory word recognition', in U. H. Frauenfelder and L. K. Tyler (eds), *Spoken Word Recognition*, special issue, *Cognition* 25, 1–2, 157–87.

—— (1987b) 'Theories of sentence processing', in J. L. Garfield (ed.), *Modularity in Knowledge Representation and Natural-Language Understanding*, Cambridge, Mass.: MIT Press.

Gardner, H. (1987) *The Mind's New Science: A History of the Cognitive Revolution*, with Epilogue, New York: Basic Books.

Garfield, J. L. (1987) *Modularity in Knowledge Representation and Natural-Language Understanding*, Cambridge, Mass.: MIT Press.

Gazdar, G. and G. K. Pullum (1982) *Generalized Phrase Structure Grammar: A Theoretical Synopsis*, Bloomington: Indiana University Linguistics Club.

Gibson, E. J. and L. Guinet (1971) 'Perception of inflections in brief visual presentations of words', *JVLVB* 10, 182–9.

Givón, T. (1971a) 'On the verbal basis of the Bantu verb suffixes', *Studies in African Linguistics* 2, 2, 145–63.

—— (1971b) 'Historical syntax and synchronic morphology: An archaeologist's field trip', in *Papers from the 7th regional meeting of the Chicago Linguistics Society*, Chicago: CLS.

—— (1979) *On Understanding Grammar*, New York: Academic Press.

—— (1984) *Syntax: A Functional-Typological Introduction*, Vol. 1, Amsterdam: John Benjamins.

Green, J. (1976) 'How free is word order in Spanish?' in M. Harris (ed.), *Romance Syntax: Syntactic and Diachronic Perspectives*, Manchester: University of Salford.

Greenberg, J. H. (1957) *Essays in Linguistics*, Chicago: University of Chicago Press.

—— (1966) 'Some universals of grammar with particular reference to the order of meaningful elements', in J. H. Greenberg (ed.), *Universals of Language*, Cambridge, Mass.: MIT Press.

—— (1980) 'Circumfixes and typological change', in E. C. Traugott, L. LaBrum and S. Shepherd (eds), *Papers from the Fourth International Conference on Historical Linguistics*, Amsterdam: John Benjamins.

Grosjean, F. (1980) 'Spoken word recognition and the gating paradigm', *Perception and Psychophysics* 28, 267–83.

Haiman, J. (1980) 'The iconicity of grammar: Isomorphism and motivation', *Language* 56, 515–40.

—— (1983) 'Iconic and economic motivation', *Language* 59, 781–819.

Hall, C. J. (1983) 'The semantics of *de-* and *dis-* negative prefixation in English', unpublished ms., University of York.

—— (1985) 'Morphology, syntax and logical form: Towards the resolution of a border conflict', in G. M. Gilligan, M. A. Mohammad and I. Roberts (eds), *SCOPIL 10: Studies in Syntax*, Los Angeles: USC.

Bibliography 215

—— (1987) 'Language structure and explanation: a case from morphology', unpublished Ph.D. dissertation, University of Southern California.

—— (1988) 'Integrating diachronic and processing principles in explaining the suffixing preference', in J. A. Hawkins (ed.), *Explaining Language Universals*, Oxford: Basil Blackwell.

Halliday, M. A. K. (ed. G. R. Kress) (1976) *Halliday: System and Function in Language*, London: Oxford University Press.

Harris, M. (1982) 'On explaining language change', in A. Ahlqvist (ed.), *Papers from the Fifth International Conference on Historical Linguistics*, Amsterdam: John Benjamins.

Hawkins, J. A. (1982) 'Cross-category harmony, X-bar and the predictions of markedness', *J. Linguistics* 18, 1–35.

—— (1983) *Word Order Universals*, New York: Academic Press.

—— (1985) 'Complementary methods in universal grammar: A reply to Coopmans', *Language* 61, 3, 569–86.

—— (1988) 'On explaining some left–right asymmetries in syntactic and morphological universals', in M. Hammond, E. Moravcsik and J. Wirth (eds), *Studies in Syntactic Typology*, Amsterdam: John Benjamins.

—— (ed.) (1988) *Explaining Language Universals*, Oxford: Basil Blackwell.

—— and A. Cutler (1988) 'Psycholinguistic factors in morphological asymmetry', in J. A. Hawkins (ed.), *Explaining Language Universals*, Oxford: Basil Blackwell.

—— and G. Gilligan (1988) [H&G] 'Left–right asymmetries in morphological universals', in J. A. Hawkins and H. Holmback (eds), *Papers in Universal Grammar*, special issue, *Lingua*.

Henderson, L. (1985) 'Toward a psychology of morphemes', in A. W. Ellis (ed.), *Progress in the Psychology of Language*, London: Erlbaum.

——, J. Wallis and D. Knight (1984) 'Morphemic structure and lexical access', in H. Bouma and D. Bouwhuis (eds), *Attention and Performance*, X, *Control of Language Processes*, London: Erlbaum.

Hoekstra, T., H. van der Holst and M. Moortgat (1981) *Lexical Grammar*, Dordrecht: Foris.

—— and J. G. Kooij (1988) 'The Innateness Hypothesis', in J. A. Hawkins (ed.), *Explaining Language Universals*, Oxford: Basil Blackwell.

Hoenigswald, H. M. (1966) 'Are there universals of linguistic change?' in J. H. Greenberg (ed.), *Universals of Language*, Cambridge, Mass.: MIT Press.

Hooper, J. B. (1976) *Introduction to Natural Generative Phonology*, New York: Academic Press.

Hopper, P. J. and S. A. Thompson (1980) 'Transitivity in grammar and discourse', *Language* 56, 2, 251–99.

Hutchinson, L. (1974) 'Grammar as theory', in D. Cohen (ed.), *Explaining Linguistic Phenomena*, New York: Hemisphere Publishing Corporation.

Hyman, L. (1975) *Phonology: Theory and Analysis*, New York: Holt, Rinehart & Winston.

—— (1985) 'Word domains and downstep in Bamileke-Dschang', *Phonology Yearbook*, 2, 47–83.

—— (1987) 'Prosodic domains in Kukuya', *Natural Language and Linguistic Theory*, 5, 311–33.

Itkonen, E. (1983) *Causality in Linguistic Theory*, London: Croom Helm.

216 *Morphology and mind*

Jackendoff, R. (1975) 'Morphological and semantic regularities in the lexicon', *Language* 51, 3, 639–71.

Jaeggli, O. (1977) 'Spanish diminutives', unpublished ms., MIT.

—— (1977) *X' Syntax: A Study in Phrase Structure*, Linguistic Inquiry Monograph Two, Cambridge, Mass.: MIT Press.

—— (1983) *Semantics and Cognition*, Cambridge, Mass.: MIT Press.

Jarvella, R. J. and G. Meijers (1983) 'Recognising morphemes in spoken words: Some evidence for a stem-organised mental lexicon', in R. Jarvella and G. B. Flores d'Arcais (eds), *The Process of Language Understanding*, Chichester: Wiley.

Jeffers, R. J. (1974) 'On the notion "explanation in linguistics"', in J. M. Anderson and C. Jones (eds), *Historical Linguistics II: Theory and Description in Phonology*, Amsterdam: John Benjamins.

—— and A. M. Zwicky (1980) 'The evolution of clitics', in E. C. Traugott, L. LaBrum and S. Shepherd (eds), *Papers from the Fourth International Conference on Historical Linguistics*, Amsterdam: John Benjamins.

Jensen, J. T. and Stong Jensen M. (1984) 'Morphology is in the lexicon!', *LI* 15, 3, 474–98.

Jespersen, O. (1924) *The Philosophy of Grammar*, London: G. Allen & Unwin.

Julia, P. (1983) *Explanatory Models in Linguistics*, Princeton: Princeton University Press.

Kac, M. B. (1980) 'In defense of autonomous linguistics', *Lingua* 50, 243–5.

Kahr, J. C. (1976) 'The renewal of case morphology: Sources and constraints', *Stanford Working Papers on Language Universals* 20, 107–51.

Kaisse, E. M. (1985) *Connected Speech: The Interaction of Syntax and Phonology*, Orlando, Florida: Academic Press.

Kanerva, J. M. (1987) 'Morphological integrity and syntax: the evidence from Finnish possessive suffixes', *Language* 63, 3, 498–521.

Karmiloff-Smith, A. (1979) *A Functional Approach to Child Language*, Cambridge: Cambridge University Press.

Katz, L., S. Boyce, L. Goldstein and G. Lukatela (1987) 'Grammatical information effects in auditory word recognition', *Cognition* 25, 235–63.

Keenan, E. L. (1978) 'Language variation and the logical structure of universal grammar', in H. Seiler (ed.), *Language Universals*, Tuebingen: Narr.

—— (1979) 'On surface form and logical form', *Studies in the Linguistic Sciences* special issue, Vol. 8, 2.

—— and B. Comrie (1977) 'Noun phrase accessibility and universal grammar', *LI* 8, 63–99.

—— and S. Hawkins (1987) in E. L. Keenan (ed.), *Universal Grammar: Fifteen Essays*, London: Croom Helm.

Kempley, S. T. and J. Morton (1982) 'The effects of priming with regularly and irregularly related words in auditory word recognition', *British Journal of Psychology* 73, 441–54.

Kent, R. G. (1936) 'Assimilation and dissimilation', *Language* 12, 245–58.

King, R. D. (1969) *Historical Linguistics and Generative Grammar*, Englewood Cliffs, N.J.: Prentice Hall.

Kiparsky, P. (1982) *Explanation in Phonology*, Dordrecht: Foris.

Klatt, D. H. (1980) 'Speech perception: A model of acoustic–phonetic analysis and lexical access', in R. A. Cole (ed.), *Perception and Production of Fluent Speech*, Hillsdale, N.J.: Erlbaum.

Bibliography 217

Kuno, S, (1974) 'The position of relative clauses and conjunctions', *LI* 5, 1, 117–36.

Lachter, J. and T. G. Bever (1988) 'The relation between linguistic structure and associative theories of language learning: A constructive critique of some connectionist learning models', in S. Pinker and J. Mehler (eds), *Connections and Symbols*, Cambridge, Mass: MIT Press.

Lahiri, A. and W. D. Marslen-Wilson (1990) 'The mental representation of lexical form: A phonological approach to the recognition lexicon', unpublished ms., Max Planck Institute for Psycholinguistics, Nijmegen.

Lass, R. (1980) *Explaining Language Change*, Cambridge: Cambridge University Press.

Lee, M. (1988) 'Language perception and the world', in J. A. Hawkins (ed.), *Explaining Language Universals*, Oxford: Basil Blackwell.

Lehmann, W. P. (1978) 'Toward an understanding of the profound unity underlying languages', in W. P. Lehmann (ed.), *Syntactic Typology: Studies in the Phenomenology of Language*, Austin, Texas: University of Texas Press.

Levinson, S. C. (1983) *Pragmatics*, Cambridge: Cambridge University Press.

Lieber, R. (1980) 'On the organization of the mental lexicon', unpublished Ph.D. dissertation, MIT.

Lieberman, P. (1984) *The Biology and Evolution of Language*, Cambridge, Mass.: Harvard University Press.

Lightfoot, D. W. (1979) *Principles of Diachronic Syntax*, Cambridge: Cambridge University Press.

—— (1982) *The Language Lottery: Towards a Biology of Grammars*, Cambridge, Mass.: MIT Press.

Lyons, J. (1968) *Introduction to Theoretical Linguistics*, Cambridge: Cambridge University Press.

McCarthy, J. (1981) 'A prosodic theory of nonconcatenative morphology', *LI* 12, 373–418.

McClelland, J. L. (1988) 'Connectionist models and psychological evidence', *J. Memory and Language* 27, 2, 107–23.

—— and J. L. Elman (1986) 'The TRACE model of speech perception', *Cognitive Psychology* 18, 1–86.

Malkiel, Y. (1966) 'Genetic analysis of word formation', in T. Sebeok (ed.), *Current Trends in Linguistics, Vol. III: Theoretical Foundations*, The Hague: Mouton.

Maran, La. R. (1971) 'Burmese and Jinghpo: A study of tonal linguistic processes', in F. K. Lehman (ed.), *Occasional Papers of the Wolfenden Society on Tibeto-Burman Linguistics*, Vol. IV, Urbana: University of Illinois.

Marantz, A. (1982) 'Re reduplication', *LI* 13, 3, 435–82.

Marchand, H. (1969) *The Categories and Types of Present-day English Word-formation*, Muenchen: Beck.

Marslen-Wilson, W. D. (1975) 'Sentence perception as an interactive parallel process', *Science* 189, 226–8.

—— (1983) 'Function and process in spoken word recognition', in H. Bouma and D. Bouwhuis (eds), *Attention and Performance* X, Hillsdale, N.J.: Erlbaum.

—— (1987) 'Functional Parallelism in spoken word-recognition', in U. H.

218   Morphology and mind

Frauenfelder and L. K. Tyler (eds), *Spoken Word Recognition*, special issue, *Cognition*, 25, 71–102.

—— and L. K. Tyler (1980) 'The temporal structure of spoken language understanding', *Cognition* 8, 1–71.

—— and L. K. Tyler (1987) 'Against modularity', in J. L. Garfield (ed.) *Modularity in Knowledge Representation and Natural-Language Understanding*, Cambridge, Mass.: MIT Press.

—— and A. Welsh (1978) 'Processing interactions and lexical access during word-recognition in continuous speech', *Cognitive Psychology* 10, 29–63.

Martinet, A. (1964) *Elements of General Linguistics*, Chicago: University of Chicago Press.

Meillet, A. (1958) *Linguistique Historique et Linguistique Générale*, Paris: Champion.

Meyer, D. E., R. W. Schvaneveldt and M. G. Ruddy (1975) 'Loci of contextual effects on visual word recognition', in P. M. A. Rabbit and S. Dornic (eds), *Attention & Performance* V, London: Academic Press.

Mithun, M. (1985) 'Diachronic morphologization: The circumstances surrounding the birth, death, and decline of noun incorporation', in J. Fisiak (ed.), *Papers from the Sixth International Conference on Historical Linguistics*, Amsterdam: John Benjamins/Adam Mickiewicz University Press.

Moore, T. E. (1972) 'Speeded recognition of ungrammaticality', *JVLVB* 11, 550–60.

Morton, J. (1969) 'The interaction of information in word recognition', *Psychological Review* 76, 165–78.

—— (1979) 'Facilitation in word recognition: Experiments causing change in the Logogen Model', in P. A. Kolers, M. E. Wrolstad and H. Bouma (eds), *Processing of Visible Language*, Vol. 1, New York: Plenum Press.

—— (1981) 'The status of information processing models of language', *Philosophical Transactions of the Royal Society of London*, 295, 387–96.

—— and J. Long (1976) 'Effect of word transitional probability on phoneme identification', *JVLVB* 15, 43–52.

Nooteboom, S. G. (1981) 'Lexical retrieval from fragments of spoken words: Beginnings versus endings', *J. Phonetics* 9, 407–24.

Ochs, E. (1982) 'Ergativity and word order in Samoan child language', *Language* 58, 3, 646–71.

Ohlander, S. (1976) *Phonology, Meaning, Morphology. On the Role of Semantic and Morphological Criteria in Phonological Analysis*, Göteborg: Acta Universitatis Gothoburgensis.

Osgood, C. E. (1966) 'Language Universals and Psycholinguistics', in J. H. Greenberg (ed.), *Universals of Language*, Cambridge, Mass.: MIT Press.

Peters, A. (1983) *The Units of Language Acquisition*, Cambridge: Cambridge University Press.

Piaget, J. and B. Inhelder (1969) *The Psychology of the Child*, New York: Basic Books.

Pinker, S. and P. Bloom (1990) 'Natural language and natural selection', unpublished ms., Department of Brain and Cognitive Sciences, MIT.

—— and A. Prince (1988) 'On language and connectionism: Analysis of a parallel distributed processing model of language acquisition', in S. Pinker

Bibliography 219

and J. Mehler (eds), *Connections and Symbols*, Cambridge, Mass.: MIT Press.

Pisoni, D. B. and P. A. Luce (1987) 'Acoustic–phonetic representations in word recognition', in U. H. Frauenfelder and L. K. Tyler (eds), *Spoken Word Recognition*, special issue, *Cognition* 25, 21–52.

Prideaux, G. D. (1980) 'In rejection of autonomous linguistics', *Lingua* 50, 245–7.

Pylyshyn, Z. W. (1984) *Computation and Cognition: Toward a Foundation for Cognitive Science*, Cambridge, Mass.: MIT Press.

Roeper, T. and E. Williams (eds) (1987) *Parameter Setting*, Dordrecht: Reidel.

Rosenberg, S., P. J. Coyle and W. L. Porter (1966) 'Recall of adverbs as a function of their adjective roots', *JVLVB* 5, 75–6.

Rubin, G. S., C. A. Becker and R. H. Freeman (1979) 'Morphological structure and its effect on visual word recognition', *JVLVB* 18, 757–67.

Rumelhart, D. E. and J. L. McClelland (eds) (1986) *Parallel Distributed Processing: Explorations in the Microstructure of Cognition* (2 vols.), Cambridge, Mass.: MIT Press.

Samuels, M. L. (1972) *Linguistic Evolution*, Cambridge: Cambridge University Press.

Savin, H. B. (1963) 'Word-frequency effect and errors in the perception of speech', *Journal of the Acoustical Society of America* 35.

Scalise, S. (1984) *Generative Morphology*, Dordrecht: Foris.

—— (1988) 'Inflection and derivation', *Linguistics* 26, 561–81.

Segui, J. and M.-L. Zubizarreta (1985) 'Mental representation of morphologically complex words and lexical access', *Linguistics* 23, 759–74.

Selkirk, E. O. (1982) *The Syntax of Words*, Linguistic Inquiry Monograph Seven, Cambridge, Mass.: MIT Press.

Shorter Oxford English Dictionary (1973) [*SOED*], Oxford: Oxford University Press.

Slobin, D. I. (1973) 'Cognitive prerequisites for the development of language', in C. A. Ferguson and D. I. Slobin (eds), *Studies in Child Language Development*, New York: Holt, Rinehart & Winston.

—— (1977) 'Language change in childhood and history', in J. Macnamara (ed.), *Language Learning and Thought*, New York: Academic Press.

—— (1985) 'Crosslinguistic evidence for the language-making capacity', in D. I. Slobin (ed.), *The Crosslinguistic Study of Language Aquisition*, Hillsdale, N.J.: Erlbaum.

—— and T. G. Bever (1982) 'Children use canonical sentence schemas: A crosslinguistic study of word order and inflections', *Cognition* 12, 229–65.

Smith, P. T. (1988) 'How to conduct experiments with morphologically complex words', *Linguistics* 26, 699–714.

Stampe, D. (1979) *A Dissertation on Natural Phonology*, unpublished Ph.D. dissertation, University of Chicago.

Stanners, R. F., J. J. Neiser, W. P. Hernon and R. Hall (1979) 'Memory representation for morphologically related words', *JVLVB* 18, 399–412.

——, J. J. Neiser and S. Painton (1979) 'Memory representation for prefixed words', *JVLVB* 18, 733–43.

Stemberger, J. P. (1985) *The Lexicon in a Model of Language Production*, New York: Garland.

220 Morphology and mind

Swinney, D. (1979) 'Lexical access during sentence comprehension: (Re)consideration of context effects', *JVLVB* 18, 645–59.

Taft, M. (1979) 'Recognition of affixed words and the word frequency effect', *Memory and Cognition* 7, 263–72.

—— (1981) 'Prefix stripping revisited', *JVLVB* 20, 289–97.

—— (1988) 'A morphological-decomposition model of lexical representation', *Linguistics* 26, 657–67.

—— and K. I. Forster (1975) 'Lexical storage and retrieval of prefixed words', *JVLVB* 14, 638–47.

—— and K. I. Forster (1976) 'Lexical storage and retrieval of polymorphemic and polysyllabic words', *JVLVB* 15, 607–20.

——, K. I. Forster and M. F. Garrett (1974) 'Lexical storage of derived words', paper presented at the First Experimental Psychology Conference, Monash University, May 1974.

—— and G. Hambly (1986) 'Exploring the cohort model of lexical representation', *Cognition* 22, 259–82.

——, G. Hambly and S. Kinoshita (1986) 'Visual and auditory recognition of prefixed words', *Quarterly Journal of Experimental Psychology*, 38A, 351–66.

Tyler, L. K. (1984) 'The structure of the initial cohort: Evidence from gating', in *Perception and Psychophysics* 36(5), 417–27.

—— and W. D. Marslen-Wilson (1986) 'The effects of context on the recognition of poly-morphemic words', *J. Memory and Language* 25, 6, 741–52.

——, W. D. Marslen-Wilson, J. Rentoul and P. Hanney (1988) 'Continuous and discontinuous access in spoken word recognition: The role of derivational prefixes', *J. Memory and Language*, 27 368–81.

—— and J. Wessels (1983) 'Quantifying contextual contributions to word-recognition processes', *Percection and Psychophysics* 34, 5, 409–20.

Ultan, R. (1978) 'The nature of future tenses', in J. Greenberg *et al.* (eds), *Universals of Human Language 3*, Stanford: Stanford University Press.

Vennemann, T. (1974) 'Topics, subjects and word order: From SXV to SVX via TVX', in J. M. Anderson and C. Jones (eds), *Historical Linguistics 1*, Amsterdam: North Holland.

Watkins, C. (1962) *Indo-European Origins of the Celtic Verb*, Dublin: Dublin Institute for Advanced Studies.

Wexler, K. and P. W. Culicover (1980) *Formal Principles of Language Acquisition*, Cambridge. Mass.: MIT Press.

Williams, E. (1981) 'On the notions "Lexically Related" and "Head of a Word"', *LI* 12,2, 245–74.

—— (1987) 'Introduction', in T. Roeper and E. Williams (eds), *Parameter Setting*, Dordrecht: Reidel.

Williamson, K. (n.d.) 'Consonant distribution in Ịjọ', unpublished ms., University of Ibadan.

Žirmunskij, V. M. (1966) 'The word and its boundaries', *J. Linguistics* 27, 65–91.

Zwicky, A. (1985) 'Heads', *J. Linguistics* 21, 1–29.

Index

'access' function 113–14, 122–3; *see also* word recognition

acquisition 3, 5, 7 15–22, 28, 30–2, 78–83, 106, 165–6, 175–6, 185–6, 198n, 203n, 206–7n; *see also* learnability, parameters

affix (*see also* head/affix correlation): functional categories of 44, 46–8, 56–60, 62–3, 69, 86–91, 93, 104–6, 108–11, 200–1n; ordering 28, 39, 57; affix-stripping 134, 136–43, 149–51, 156, 160, 167, 184–5, 192; *see also* decomposition, 'realisation'

'*affixum ex machina*' 85, 96

artificial intelligence 7, 19–22, 27

assimilation 99, 102–3, 184, 203–4n

autonomy: lexical 103, 134, 148, 154; of linguistic component 6, 7–8, 13, 15, 27; *see also* modularity

autosegmental phonology 205

auxiliary verbs 93, 104–6, 162

back formation 90–1, 178–80

behaviourism 21

binding 22, 172

borrowing 91, 179–83, 207n

case 57–8, 81, 157–8, 160, 162

causatives 166

'charges to language' 31, 107–8; *see also* Economy, Principle of

circumfixing 40, 110–11, 199n

Clarity, Principle of 107–8

clitics 88–9, 93, 110, 162

cloze values 115–16, 118

cognitive science 7, 27, 37, 113, 192–4

cohort, word-initial 119–20, 121, 125, 143, 144, 149–50, 152, 157, 167–70, 185, 188, 191–2, 204n, 206n

Cohort Model 101–2, 113–23, 124, 125, 127–8, 136, 143–56, 157, 171–2, 204n, 206n

competence, morphological 131, 141, 154, 155

compositionality, semantic 188

compounding 54, 62, 66–9, 89, 201–2

connected speech rules 97

connectionism 19–22, 123

content, lexical (*also* semantic) 103–4, 128–9, 142, 143–50, 159–61, 177, 181, 184, 186, 205n; *see also* form, lexical

contextual effects 115–19, 120–2, 123–4, 140, 157, 161

Cross-Category Harmony, Principle of (CCH) 23, 24, 72–3, 76, 79–80, 81–2, 95, 198n; *see also* head ordering

decay, phonological *see* reduction, phonological

decomposition 131, 135–43, 149–52, 156, 167–70, 184–8, 191; *see also* affix-stripping, 'realisation'

D(eep)-structure 5

derivation 46, 54, 55, 58–61, 88–9, 130, 133–5, 147–8, 155, 178; *see also* inflection

Dissimilation Principle 71–2

222 *Morphology and mind*

Economy, Principle of 108, 175–8, 179
evolution 5, 12–15, 18, 27, 30–2, 107
exceptions (*also* counterexamples, counterprinciples) 44, 46–7, 75–7, 110, 173–5
explanation: biological 3, 5, 12, 24, 26, 32, 36; causal 6, 8, 17, 25–6, 34–5, 36–7, 84; expository 17, 25, 36; formal 1–27, 29–32, 35–6; functional 1, 8–15, 16–18, 27–36, 37, 82; historical 24–6, 32, 74–7, 82, 84–111, 164–86; iconic 28–9; pragmatic 8, 28, 33–5; psycholinguistic 8–22, 24, 27, 28, 30–2, 78–83, 96–7, 101–2, 108, 110, 156–63, 164–94; semantic 28–9, 39, 103–7; unified approach to 36–8, 50, 51, 159, 192–4
explanatory adequacy 2, 9, 12–13, 17, 22, 25, 26–7

'flirting' 165–70, 176, 184–6, 191–2
form, lexical 103–7, 122–3, 128–9, 142, 143–56, 159–61, 177, 185–6, 188–91, 205n; *see also* content, lexical
full interpretation (FI) 10, 58
functional architecture 20–2, 174
fusion, phonological 85–9, 96, 103–4, 106–11, 159, 165–86, 188; *see also* reduction, phonological

gating 117–18, 122, 151, 159, 161, 188–92
Generative Phonology 24, 123

head: head/affix correlation 38, 40–8, 49–83, 109, 199n; Head First Preference (HFP) 78–9, 81; Head Ordering Principle (HOP) 43–4, 47–8, 49–50, 66, 73, 74–7, 85, 158, 183; lexical (*also* head of word) 49–83, 200–2n; ordering/serialisation of 22–3, 31, 40–1, 43, 49–52, 70–3; semantic 66–70, 200–1n; syntactic (*also* head of phrase) 4–5, 51–5, 56–7, 64–6, 69–70, 74–7, 86

idioms 68
'impenetrability' 171
incorporation 74–5
Inertial Development Principle 98
infixing 39–40
inflection 46, 52, 54–62, 65, 88–9, 130, 133–5, 140, 146–8, 153, 155, 160, 176, 178, 200n, 205–6n; *see also* derivation
information processing 106–7
innateness 15–22, 23, 29
'innovations analogiques' 89
input monitors 119–20, 143–7, 149, 151, 153, 156, 167–9, 176, 185
'integration' function 114, 120, 144, 145, 149, 160; *see also* word recognition
interactivity 15, 123, 171–2

learnability 79, 81–2
'least effort' principles 9–11, 13, 81–2, 101, 102–3, 107, 176; *see also* Economy, Principle of
lexical access *see* word recognition
lexical component 5, 51–70, 83, 97; *see also* mental lexicon
lexical decision 119, 124, 133, 134, 137–40, 205n
Lexicalist Hypothesis 53, 58–9
linkage 17–18, 26, 27, 33–5, 37, 38, 48, 76, 83, 159, 193
'Logic of Competing Variants' 93
Logical Form (LF) 5, 10
Logogen Model 113, 120, 123–5, 127–8, 129, 134, 136, 156

malapropisms 129
mental lexicon 80–1, 102, 103, 108, 112–63, 167–78, 185–6, 188, 192, 205–6n
'micro-historical' analysis 155, 164, 184, 192, 193
modality 105–6
modularity (*also* autonomy) 5, 6, 53, 123, 171–3

nasality 122
Natural Generative Phonology 98
Natural Phonology 98
Natural Serialisation Principle 71–3, 95

Index 223

negation 108
negative evidence 3, 11, 18–19, 180
neurosciences 5, 37, 60, 113
nonwords 119, 137–9, 149
novel (prefixed) forms 184–92, 195, 197, 207n

opacity, morphological 103, 141, 152–6, 159, 188; *see also* transparency
operating principles 78, 80–1, 175
'Order of Computation' 156–61
orthographic processing 112, 123, 125, 134, 136–7, 141–2, 145
overgeneralisation 18–20

paradigm restructuring 90, 178–80
parallel processing 19–22, 123, 172; *see also* connectionism
parameters (of UG) 3, 4–5, 11–12, 17, 18–19, 23, 30, 36, 78, 80
parsing (*also* sentence processing) 8–18, 22, 28, 30–1, 33, 160, 171–3
percolation 51–2, 54–5, 56, 59, 61–2, 63–6, 83
Phonetic Form (PF) 10
phonological strength 98–103
phonological weakness 98–103, 167
plural 89
polymorphemicity 46, 177
Positional Criterion 55–64, 66, 70, 77, 83, 201n
Postpositional Noun Modifier Hierarchy 94
potentiation 62–3
predictability 106–8, 153, 156, 157–8, 161, 166; *see also* redundancy
Prepositional Noun Modifier Hierarchy 93
priming 116–17, 124, 129, 133–5, 140, 147, 205n
processing *see* orthographic processing, parsing, production, word recognition
production 112, 125, 128–30, 145, 155, 164, 180
productivity 47, 184–5, 188, 192, 200n
Projection Principle (PrPr) 58–9, 200n

pseudoaffixation 139, 179
pseudostems 137–9, 149

rapid speech rules 97
reading *see* orthographic processing
'realisation' (of morphological structure) 149–52, 156, 192; *see also* decomposition, affix-stripping
reanalysis, lexical 89–91, 97, 103, 106, 154–5, 165–83, 206–7n
recognition point (RP) 118–19, 150–2, 156, 186–92, 204n
reduction, phonological 74–7, 83, 85, 88–9, 91, 97, 107, 162, 165–7, 178, 181
redundancy 102, 103–7, 108, 130, 145–6, 148, 152, 155, 157–8, 160–1, 166, 176–7, 185–6, 192, 206n; *see also* predictability
relevance 28, 39, 106
Righthand Head Rule (RHR) *see* Positional Criterion
rules, grammatical 8, 10, 16–17, 19–20, 24–6, 176

Search Model 113, 125–8, 129, 136, 137–8, 156
'selection' function (*see also* word recognition) 114, 169
selectional restrictions 52, 58–9, 172
Serialisation Principle 71–3
simplicity *see* Economy, Principle of
social control 179–80
Specified Subject Condition (SSC) 4
speech errors 129, 131–3
speech shadowing 115–16, 124
Stem First Preference (SFP) 80–1
stress 133, 184
subcategorisation 43, 52, 56, 58–9, 65, 78–9, 81, 90, 118, 149, 172, 179, 181, 185
suffixing: preference 23, 31, 35, 37–8, 40–8, 85–6, 91–7, 103, 106–7, 107–11, 136, 141, 142, 156–63, 164–94; Principle 48
suppletion 147
syntactic component 50–4, 56–9, 64–6, 68–70, 171–3, 176, 179; *see also* Universal Grammar

224 *Morphology and mind*

temporal control 130
tense 56–7, 105–6
thematic roles (*also* frames,
  restrictions) 52, 58–9, 69
'tip of the tongue' (TOT) State 132–3
trace (Theory) 3–4, 26, 29–30,
transitivity 33–5
transparency, morphological 141,
  152–5, 184, 186, 188, 189, 192; *see*
  also opacity
Transparency Principle 176

underspecification 123, 144, 152–3,
  156
uniqueness point 119, 124, 147, 153,
  156, 158
Universal Grammar (UG) 2–27, 29–
  32, 58–60, 82, 176
universals, typological 11, 22–3,
  27, 36, 39–48, 70–83, 84–5, 177,
  182

W-Syntax 53–5, 61–2, 63–7
word formation rules (WFRs) 59, 65,
  83, 148, 184
word frequency 121, 123–4, 125, 126,
  133, 137–9, 140
word order 45, 47, 79, 86–8, 91–5,
  104, 109–11, 158, 167, 199–200n;
  see also head ordering, head/affix
  correlation
word recognition 19, 31, 80–1, 85,
  101–2, 103, 107–8, 112–63, 166–
  75, 183–94, 205–6n; *see also*
  Cohort Model, Logogen Model,
  Search Model
word-monitoring 116–17
written modality *see* orthographic
  processing

X-bar syntax (*also* Theory,
  component) 5, 22–3, 51–5, 63–6,
  70, 73, 76, 79–80, 81, 172, 198n